Apple Training Series
# iLife '05

Michael Rubin

Apple Training Series: iLife '05
Michael Rubin
Copyright © 2005 by Michael Rubin

Published by Peachpit Press. For information on Peachpit Press books, contact:
Peachpit Press
1249 Eighth Street
Berkeley, CA 94710
(510) 524-2178
Fax: (510) 524-2221
http://www.peachpit.com
To report errors, please send a note to errata@peachpit.com
Peachpit Press is a division of Pearson Education

**Series Editor:** Serena Herr
**Managing Editor:** Kristin Kalning
**Production Coordinator:** Laurie Stewart, Happenstance Type-O-Rama
**Editor:** Nancy Peterson
**Technical Editors:** Fred Johnson and Tim Snell
**Copy Editor:** Emily K. Wolman
**Media Reviewer:** Eric Geoffroy
**Compositor:** Chris Gillespie, Happenstance Type-O-Rama
**Indexer:** Rebecca Plunkett
**Cover design:** Frances Baca Design and Tolleson Design
**Cover illustration:** Alicia Buelow; image © Michael A.Keller/CORBIS
**Cover production:** George Mattingly/GMD
**Interior design:** Frances Baca

ISBN 0-321-33020-X
9 8 7 6 5 4 3 2 1
Printed and bound in the United States of America

**Acknowledgments** This book represents a vortex of some of my favorite people whirling around many of my greatest passions. Foremost, I want to thank my friends at Apple—in particular Patricia Montesion, Steve Guttman, and Fred Johnson—for having a vision to enroll people in the digital lifestyle that meshes so well with my own, and for giving me the opportunity to speak directly to the people I want to reach with these media creation tools. Of course, the book was a collaboration with Peachpit Press—thanks to Nancy Ruenzel and Serena Herr for spearheading our efforts. Thank you, too, for pulling together such a sharp and supportive team: my editors, Kristin Kalning and Nancy Peterson; copy editor Emily Wolman; technical reviewers Eric Geoffroy and Tim Snell; compositor Chris Gillespie; and production coordinator Laurie Stewart. I get a chill even trying to imagine pulling off this book on our radical schedule without the team we had.

While this book reaches into the side of my brain engrossed with things digital and media, it magically embraces the other side of my brain—the Petroglyph side. Thanks to everyone at Petroglyph who tolerates my unusual projects: director of studios Richard Morse; Santa Cruz lounge manager Katy Pagni and her team, Rachel Hall and Heather Orr; our shareholders; and most importantly, all our staff and great customers whose ceramics grace these pages and whose passions I hope we captured.

A special thanks to our stars: Chris Hosmer, Fearon Hosmer, Alex Hodgson, Michelle DiBartolomeo, Tess Doud, Lihi Benisty, Steven Carrillo, and my production collaborator on so many of my videos, Lisa Strong-Aufhauser.

Finally, to my family, who encouraged me and supported the unprecedented pace of this book. Jonah and Alina, you were too young to end up in these pages, but you are the most important people in my life. And Jennifer. Do you need words here to acknowledge your contribution to this work? The cofounder of Petroglyph, the creative force of our company, the mother of our children, thank you for playing yourself in these pages and for finally accepting credit for the wonderful business we built together. This book is your book, too. You're in each line and every picture. I love you madly.

# Contents at a Glance

# Table of Contents

# Getting Started

Welcome to the official Apple training course for the iLife '05 suite of products—iTunes, iPhoto, iMovie, iDVD, and GarageBand. You don't need to have any special background to get started, other than having a Mac (and perhaps a healthy curiosity about what you can really do with it). Learning iLife really means learning to live digitally; you're not so much learning to use new software as learning how to comfortably integrate your Mac into the niches in your home, school, and work. The iLife tools are only part of the picture—and this book is not so much a training manual as it is a way to show you how to enrich your world by weaving digital audio, photos, and videos into many aspects of your life.

Even if you're a longtime Mac user, delving into these interesting and fun applications may be something you've put off, having chosen instead to focus on other, perhaps higher-level software tools. It's time to take a look at these (*deep breath*) life-altering products. Instead of teaching you all the geeky details of these hip tools, I'm going to concentrate on how real people really use them. I may even skip entire areas of functionality, all with an eye to having fun, achieving quick success, and forming a foundation of confidence from which you can build.

## What iLife Does for You

There was a time (probably last week) when your photographs were in one part of your house, your music collection somewhere else, VHS videotapes scattered around the television, and, if you have a camcorder, Hi-8 (or some such format) cassettes in a bag. Each medium is tricky to keep organized.

But when all your media is digital—in the form of digital snapshots, digital audio (CDs, MP3s, and so on), and digital video (DVDs and DV cassettes)—keeping them organized is pretty easy, sharing content is streamlined, and using the material interchangeably between formats is both simple and kind of fun.

A Macintosh is designed to sit at the epicenter of your digital home. It's just a computer, but now it's finely tuned to make the management and combining of all this content effortless. Better than that, Apple provides—free on all Macs—software that orchestrates the commingling of all this content. iLife is a family of products made up of programs designed to stand alone but also tuned to work together in remarkable ways.

What iLife teaches you is *media literacy:* the ability to communicate in a variety of powerful ways, different from speaking or writing or even doing page design. Making professional-quality videos and movies, and being able to combine picture and sound together effectively, is a skill that applies throughout your life. Once you have it, you'll be stunned how often you can use it—for personal pleasure or commercial advantage.

It's too simplistic to say that iTunes is the music software and iMovie is the video software. iTunes handles the organization of your music, true, but once your music is there, using it in slide shows and videos is very easy. There's music in iPhoto and iMovie too. You can't build a box around each component of iLife. So while you might want to learn all you can about each product, the truth is it may be more fun to learn a little bit about a bunch of products. Rather than focus on expertise in, say, iTunes, this book will aim to help you create real-world projects. Face it, learning software is no fun. But making movies or promoting your business or building a creative report for school can be. You'll end up learning the software along the way.

## The Methodology

This book moves through lessons by progressively increasing the complexity of the media you're using. You start by learning about audio alone, then move to managing still images, printing still images, turning still images into moving (*dynamic*) images, and exploring the possibilities of video. With digital content and the three core iLife applications (iTunes, iPhoto, and iMovie), you can create everything from scrapbook photos to T-shirts, books, DVDs, dynamic content for Web pages, and even a feature film ready for projection on the big screen.

### Course Structure

Beyond all, the lessons are meant to be practical—not esoteric projects to show off the software, but rather real-life projects from real-life people, with time constraints, well-worn equipment, and concerns about budget. The lessons cover three general areas: music and sound, still images, and movies.

▶   Lessons 1 and 2: Mostly music: use iTunes to make a custom CD, and play your music on both an iPod and through a regular stereo system.

▶   Lessons 3 through 6: Mostly still images: use images from your digital camera in iPhoto; print photos; make a slide show; and create a professional looking book of prints.

▶   Lessons 7 through 12: Mostly movies: combine still photos with music, special effects, and titles in iMovie; make a time-lapse video; learn to shoot video creatively and edit to maximum effect; add narration to your videos; mix sound with picture; and create original music that you add to videos.

▶   Lessons 13 and 14: All of the above (sharing your projects): upload slide shows and videos to the Web with an Apple .Mac account; email photographs; and burn DVDs of your projects using iDVD.

**Role Playing**

One of the most enjoyable aspects of this book is that you're going to assume the role of three different people, all using iLife, all using the same equipment. One is a parent, Christopher, overseeing his daughter's 12th birthday party. The second is a high school student, Charlie, putting together a report for school. And the third is a small-business owner, Jennifer, using her Mac for a variety of commercial media functions.

Your alter egos: Christopher, Charlie, and Jennifer

All three of them happen to be in the same place at the same time—a contemporary ceramics painting studio. You will see the one place and common event through iLife from three unique vantage points.

The setting: Petroglyph Ceramic Lounge, on a typical January day.

Therefore, you can progress through this book of lessons in a number of ways. You could start at the beginning and work systematically, Lesson 1 to Lesson 14. I recommend this.

I would not recommend the seemingly logical path where you skip from lesson to lesson, focusing on one product, say iPhoto. By the end you'd think you'd have a pretty good set of experiences in iPhoto, but you'll miss the intricate and powerful ways the different products intertwine and build on each other.

I would also encourage you to pass on trying to follow one personality—for instance, Jennifer, the business owner—through the iLife suite. Maybe you too own a business and are primarily interested in the ways your Mac and iLife can immediately impact your work. Again, this has its merits, but since all three people are using all the products, being too faithful about following the individual with your agenda will lead you to miss important points that may be the focus of one of the other characters.

## A Word About the Lesson Content

Often, training materials are professionally created—using actors, complicated production (with lights, microphones, tripods, and a crew), and so on. The resulting material is of high quality but bears little similarity to the kind of projects you will be working on. In order that this training be as real-world and practical as possible, it was made in precisely the way you would make your own videos—the quality of the shots (for better or worse) is comparable to what you can get with a typical consumer equipment; the sophistication of the projects is precisely what you can achieve using the iLife tools, with settings (and challenges) you will commonly find yourself in. The events depicted here were truly recorded in the way you are being taught to work. Hopefully, this will give you clear and realistic expectations about what you can do with your newfound skills.

## System Requirements

This book is written for iLife '05, which comes free with any new Macintosh computer. If you have an older version of iLife, you will need to upgrade to the current iLife version to follow along with every lesson. The upgrade can be purchased online at www.apple.com, and is available from any store that sells Apple software.

Before you begin the lessons in this book, you should have a working knowledge of your Mac and its operating system. You don't need to be an expert, but you do need to know how to use the mouse and standard menus and commands, and how to open, save, and close files. You should have a working understanding of how OS X helps organize files on your computer, and you should also be comfortable launching applications (from the Dock or at least the Applications folder). If you need to review any of these techniques, see the printed or online documentation that came with your computer.

The minimum system requirements for the iLife suite of products are:

▶ Macintosh computer with a PowerPC G3, G4, or G5 processor and built-in FireWire

▶ 600 MHz G3 for GarageBand, G4 for GarageBand software instruments

▶ 733 MHz G4 for iDVD

▶ 256 MB of physical RAM (512 MB is recommended)

▶ Mac OS X v.10.3.4 (Mac OS X v.10.3.6 is recommended)

▶ QuickTime 6.5.2 (included with iLife)

▶ 1024-by-768-pixel resolution

▶ 4.7 GB of free disk space to install iTunes, iPhoto, iMovie, iDVD, and GarageBand; 350 MB to install iTunes, iPhoto, and iMovie only; and an additional 4.2 GB to install all projects and media files on the accompanying training materials DVD

## Copying the iLife Lesson Files

The *Apple Training Series: iLife '05* DVD-ROM includes folders containing the lesson files used in this course. Each lesson has its own folder, and you should copy these folders to your hard drive to use the files for the lessons.

### To install the iLife Lesson files:

1    Insert the *ATS_iLife05* DVD into your DVD drive.

2    Drag the Lessons folder inside the iLife05_Book Files folder from the DVD onto your Desktop.

This will copy the folder to your hard drive. Inside this folder is the Lessons folder, which contains all of the files you'll use for this book.

## About the Apple Training Series

*Apple Training Series: iLife '05* is part of the official training series for Apple applications, developed by experts in the field and certified by Apple Computer. The lessons are designed to let you learn at your own pace. Although each lesson provides step-by-step instructions for creating specific projects, there's room for exploration and experimentation. You can progress through the book from beginning to end, or dive right into the lessons that interest you most. It's up to you.

For those who prefer to learn in an instructor-led setting, Apple also offers training courses at Apple Authorized Training Centers worldwide. These courses are taught by Apple Certified Trainers, and balance concepts and lectures with hands-on labs and exercises. Apple Authorized Training Centers have been carefully selected and have met Apple's highest standards in all areas, including facilities, instructors, course delivery, and infrastructure. The goal of the program is to offer Apple customers, from beginners to the most seasoned professionals, the highest quality training experience.

To find an Authorized Training Center near you, go to www.apple.com/training.

## Resources

*Apple Training Series: iLife '05* is not intended as a comprehensive reference manual, nor does it replace the documentation that comes with the applications. It's designed to be used in conjunction with other comprehensive guides that explain features, functions, and lots of interesting details. These resources include:

▶ Apple's Web site: www.apple.com.

▶ *The Macintosh iLife,* by Jim Heid (Peachpit Press), an accessible and popular reference to all the iLife products.

▶ *The Little Digital Video Book,* by Michael Rubin (Peachpit Press), a concise resource on how to make your videos have more impact and look professional. While the book is not about the iLife software specifically, it expands on many of the concepts touched on in the lessons on shooting and editing video.

# 1

| | |
|---|---|
| Lesson Files | A couple of CDs from your personal CD collection |
| Tools | iTunes, Internet connection (optional) |
| Time | Approximately 45 minutes |
| Goals | Play CDs in iTunes |
| | Import all or a portion of a CD into the iTunes Library |
| | Add or adjust CD information about albums or songs |
| | Browse and search efficiently through your music library |
| | Create and customize personal playlists of your favorite music |
| | Make custom CDs |

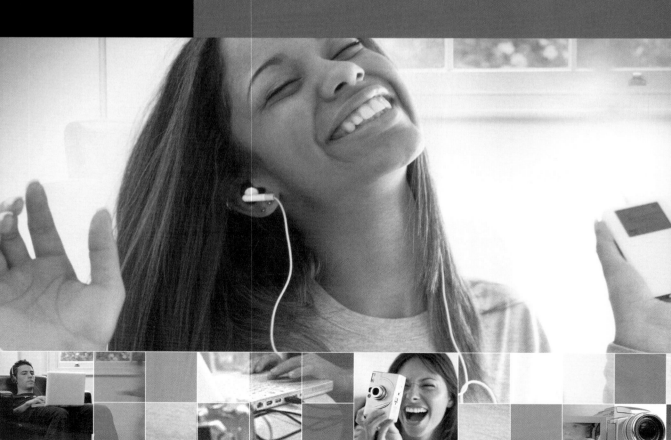

# Making a Custom CD from Your Music Collection

Imagine having instant access to songs you have always loved but haven't played in eons (because they were buried on albums you generally didn't like). Imagine setting up what amounts to your own private radio station—playing all your favorite tunes for hours on end (days, even). iTunes makes this possible. CDs, those silvery discs that have become the center of your musical world, are about to become archaic. It's time to start thinking of a CD as an *archive,* a safe backup. To really enjoy your media, you want it readily accessible and malleable as only a digital creation can be.

Although this lesson demonstrates a fundamental aspect of iTunes—that is, getting your CDs into your computer, organizing them, and burning a custom CD of your favorite songs—it has a broader goal. Somewhere near where you're sitting right now are probably dozens, perhaps hundreds of CDs that you've been purchasing for the last many years. The idea of this lesson is to initiate the ambitious project of moving that entire collection from discrete CDs into a single, massive jukebox—an enormous body of acoustic joy!

As discussed in the "Getting Ready" chapter, you're going to follow three characters through their adventures with iLife. In this lesson, let's begin by seeing what Christopher, the father of the birthday girl, is up to. He's working with his daughter to make a special birthday party CD as a gift to her guests. You'll start by working with just a few CDs to get into the groove.

## Starting iTunes

As with many Apple programs, you have multiple ways to launch iTunes. You might double-click the application file on your hard drive, located in the Applications folder. You could simply insert a music CD into your drive, which will automatically start iTunes. For the purposes of this lesson, single-click the iTunes icon that resides in the Dock.

### First-Time Use

Christopher uses iTunes all the time. But if this is the first time you've launched iTunes, the program's iTunes Setup Assistant will direct you through a series of windows.

1    Click the iTunes icon in the Dock.

2    Click Agree in the software license agreement window (but only if you mean it).

3    Click Next in each window to use iTunes' default settings. These settings, by the way, are pretty smartly selected. The only one you might want to skip is the one asking if you want to go to the Apple Music Store. You don't need to go there now, and can easily go later to download songs when you're ready.

4    Click Done. This concludes the set up and will take you right into iTunes—a clean, empty space where you can begin your lesson.

## Getting Songs from CDs into iTunes

There's a lot to look at in the iTunes interface—but perhaps the best way to get familiar with it is simply by putting a CD into your drive and seeing what happens. You can follow along with your own CD as you watch Christopher begin the process of making a CD for the birthday party.

When you insert an audio disc into your Mac's ComboDrive (or SuperDrive; it works for both CDs and DVDs), your CD will show up as a "source" in the left column, and details about it—a list of songs and their durations, among other things—will appear on the right if you're connected to the Internet. Christopher begins with a little Sheryl Crow.

### Playing Songs and CDs

Once your CD is onscreen, you can use iTunes as a simple CD player. You don't have to do anything fancy with iTunes in order to listen to it. The fast way to play a song is to double-click a line item in the song list. But if you want to see what you're doing, follow these steps.

1   Using your pointer, single-click a song title. A blue bar will highlight it.

2   Click the Play button.

The play and volume controls are together on the top left of the window. While a song is playing, the Play button turns into a Pause button (press it again to pause the song).

**NOTE ▶** The spacebar on your keyboard also acts as a Play/Pause button.

Also, while a song is playing, a speaker icon appears in the leftmost column of the list of songs.

As the song plays, look around at the iTunes window. At the top of the window is the album and song information, along with a bar representing the length of the song. A little black diamond shows what part of the song is playing. You can grab this diamond and scan backward or forward in the song.

There are also forward and reverse buttons alongside the Play/Pause button. Click either of these to skip to the next (or previous) track. Click and hold to scan through the track you're listening to.

When the song you initially selected is done playing, iTunes moves on to the CD's next track. Notice, however, that the blue selection bar stays where you started, although the speaker icon hops to the next song. This can be confusing at times.

**TIP** If you want to know what song you're listening to, look for the speaker icon and ignore the blue bar.

The checkmark next to each song title indicates that you want iTunes to play that song (if the opportunity arises) or import that song (in the event that you're pulling music into your Mac). Unselect a title, and iTunes will ignore the song—either skipping it when you import or, if it's already in your computer, skipping it when you're playing a list of tunes.

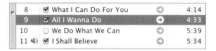

### Using Automatic CD Album Information

What if you insert a CD and it shows up on your Desktop merely as "Audio CD?" What if your CD shows up in iTunes but is clearly devoid of key information—namely, song and album titles? It surprises many people to learn that the song info you see in iTunes doesn't come from the CD. It comes from somewhere external to your Mac.

Here's the deal: Although your Mac can certainly tell that this is a music CD, and one that has, say, 11 songs of varying lengths, it doesn't know anything more specific about the album and its contents. And that is why you want to be connected to the Internet. Your Mac alone can't tell you this information, but a wonderful online database (called the Gracenote Compact Disc Database, or CDDB) is available to help. iTunes can gather this information automatically if you set it up to do so (which you did when you went through the Setup Assistant the first time you launched iTunes). If you loaded your favorite CD and the screen looked too blank for you, make sure you are connected to the Internet, and then do the following.

**1**   Go to iTunes > Preferences.

**2**   From the General panel that opens, make sure "Connect to Internet when needed" is checked.

That will allow iTunes to automatically go online and get disc data when you insert a CD into your Mac.

**3**   Click OK.

**4**   Select the Audio CD in the Source column.

**5**   Go to Advanced > Get CD Track Names.

This will access the Internet and find the information you seek from the CDDB.

Once the process is complete, the iTunes window should look similar to before, but with lots of useful data on the screen.

Now that you can play the CD in your Mac using iTunes, it's a good time to take a closer look at other sources in iTunes and how you work with them.

### Understanding iTunes Sources

When you open iTunes the first time, you'll see a big, empty table that you'll use to organize and ultimately play your music.

The organizational structure of iTunes is similar to that of iPhoto; you may even recognize it as similar to that of the Mac OS. On the left side of the window is a Source column. Your CD is a source. Choose a source, and details about its contents appear on the right side (although your other iTunes sources may not yet have any contents to reveal).

And just as the Mac OS offers a handful of different kinds of sources (hard disks, CDs and DVDs, connected servers, and so on), each with its own distinct icon, iTunes has a few of its own sources as well.

▶   CDs show up in the Source column only when you have a CD in your Mac. Eject a CD and it will disappear from this list.

▶   Library is the big container that will hold all of the audio files (songs, albums, downloads) you put on your Mac, including, of course, the songs you import from CDs. You'll make subsets of this potentially enormous collection to make it easy to find the songs you're looking for. When you move songs from CDs into iTunes, you're loading music into your Library.

▶   Music Store is the oft-mentioned Apple Music Store, where you can (legally!) download songs or albums directly into your iTunes collection—streamlining the process of building your Library.

▶   Playlists are malleable, expandable collections of songs that you build yourself. They are the heart and power of iTunes. Since you make them yourself, you won't see any playlists in the Source column when you start up, but soon you'll have many.

NOTE ▶ There are, of course, other sources, although you can ignore them for the time being. Radio uses your Internet connection to bring you online music channels for your listening pleasure. 60's Music, My Top Rated, Recently Played, Top 25 Most Played, and Party Shuffle (which selects songs from your Library or chosen playlist) are special sources that are built for you. These automatically generated playlists are signified by a small round gear in the Source icon. It's easy to explore them on your own, but you can disregard them for this book.

### Selecting and Importing Songs and Entire CDs

Getting music from a CD into your Mac is pretty simple. In the parlance of hipsters everywhere, the act of importing songs is called *ripping*.

The time it takes to import an album (or song) depends on a few factors—notably the speed of your Mac (a dual-gigahertz G5 will import an album faster than an 800 MHz G3, for instance). Import speed is measured by how much faster it is to import a song than to play it. A 10X import, for instance, will rip a five-minute song in 30 seconds, or a 60-minute album in six minutes.

> **NOTE** ▸ Casual observation indicates that a 300 MHz G3 rips at around four times faster than real time; a dual-gigahertz G4 rips at around 10X; and a dual-gigahertz G5 at 20X. For one or two songs, those differences are relatively small. But if you're moving 300 CDs into your music collection, the difference between ripping four albums per hour and ripping 20 per hour is significant and will radically impact your productivity—and probably your enjoyment of this experience.

**1** Select your CD as your source.

**2** Make sure there's a checkmark next to the titles of all of the songs you want to import into iTunes, and uncheck any songs that you don't want to import; those will remain on the CD, never to see the inside of your computer.

**3**   Click Import.

Notice that once a song begins to import, the information bar at the top of the iTunes window indicates the song being imported, the speed of the import, and the time remaining to complete the task.

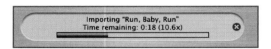

While importing, iTunes places a small orange import icon on the leftmost column of your track list, where the speaker is when you're playing a song.

| ▲ | Song Name | | Time |
|---|---|---|---|
| 1 🔄 ✓ | Run, Baby, Run | ● | 4:53 |
| 2 ✓ | Leaving Las Vegas | ● | 5:10 |
| 3 ✓ | Stong Enough | ● | 3:10 |
| 4 ✓ | Can't Cry Anymore | ● | 3:41 |

By default (as set in the preferences), when you start to import tracks, iTunes will also start to play them. (It can do both simultaneously.)

**NOTE ▶** Although playing while importing is generally an okay thing to do, it can be confusing too. The song that's playing is not necessarily the one being imported, and vice versa. Casual importers may find themselves waiting for the album to finish playing, not realizing it finished importing long before. If you want to stop songs from playing, click the Stop button (or the spacebar); this won't affect the importing. Keep an eye on the import icon and the track info at the top of the window to see your progress.

When a song has been completely imported, iTunes changes the import icon into a green checkmark. When the entire CD is done importing, it will "bing" politely.

Now that you've ripped your first CD, eject it and insert another. Rip a few more CDs, and then move on to the next section.

> **NOTE** ▶ By default, iTunes creates AAC audio files, which are considered an excellent audio format with good sound quality and small file size. Unfortunately, some MP3 players don't support it, and you might want to have MP3 audio files instead. You have control over the method and quality of compression that iTunes uses to copy a song. To adjust the settings, go to Preferences > Importing. From there, you can adjust the Import Using pop-up menu and select an audio format.

> AAC is also known as MP4 (the successor to the MP3 format). You might recognize it as the format of the songs that you purchase from the Apple Music Store as well as from streaming music providers such as XM and Sirius. Other formats include AIFF and WAV, which are standard audio formats that provide very high sound quality but generate large files. Commercial CDs tend to contain AIFF sound files.

## Change Info

Let's say you've finished ripping a handful of CDs and had no hitches. When iTunes automatically looked up information on the Internet about each CD you placed into your Mac, it loaded a bunch of data into a database it keeps in your iTunes Library. In most cases, you won't need to mess around here, but if the CD data doesn't come up the way you want it to—either because you don't have an Internet connection, because the data doesn't exist for your CD, or you simply don't agree with some of the characterizations the CDDB database offered—you'll need to add or adjust information. It's easy to do, and as you get more advanced with iTunes, you'll learn many interesting ways you can catalog and organize your collection.

> **NOTE** ▶ The Gracenote CDDB is compiled through user submissions and not from record companies. Consequently, there may be some errors or subjective opinions about data included.

### Adjusting Information Before Importing

Let's begin by adjusting information for a CD you haven't yet imported into your computer. Follow these steps if you have a CD with "problem" information.

**1**  Insert a new CD.

If the CDDB has info on this album, it will show up in the iTunes window.

In this example, the album is *Rock 'n' Roll Gumbo*—an album from New Orleans great Professor Longhair. The CDDB has information on the album but considers it to be in the blues genre. As far as I'm concerned, zydeco is a better genre classification. So let's change it.

**2**  Select the CD Source icon.

**3**    Choose File > Get Info.

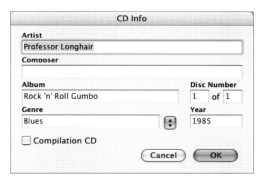

The CD Info window opens and gives you an opportunity to adjust basic info before you import. If you add info prior to importing, the data will follow the songs into iTunes automatically. If the CDDB did its job correctly, all this data should be filled in. In my example, I just want to change the genre.

**4**    Add or change information in the fields.

Christopher changed the "Blues" genre to "Zydeco."

**5**    Click OK when you're done.

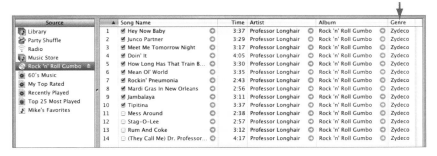

### Adjusting Information After Importing

Adjusting information prior to importing is good for data that's related to entire albums, but it's not the end of the process if you still need to add data about individual songs. In particular—say, for a custom CD that a friend has provided or for an arcane CD that isn't yet in the CDDB—you might need to add or change more info for the disc.

To do that, let's import our albums and check out the same Get Info function on albums and songs, this time using it in the Library. It looks similar to the way it did a moment ago, but now there are more fields and options.

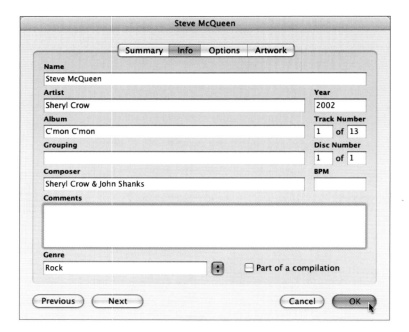

Here's the Library after a few albums have been imported. One of them was not recognized by the CDDB, and its tracks were sorted to the bottom of the list of songs.

See the five tracks at the bottom of the list with missing information? Since Christopher didn't input new info prior to importing, he'll have to do it now. First, he's going to add information that is common to all the songs—the album info.

**1** Select all five tracks. To do this, click Track 01, then hold down the Shift key and click Track 05.

All the tracks from 01 to 05 will be selected together.

**2**   Choose File > Get Info.

Since it's a little unusual to modify information for more than one track, iTunes will pop up a warning to make sure you intend to do this. If you're confident of your Mac skills, you could select "Do not ask me again"; however, it's a good rule to keep the safety on. Either way, click Yes in the warning window.

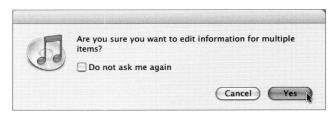

iTunes will now open the information window, in this case entitled Multiple Song Information. If the CDDB didn't recognize the CD, the window will start out blank. Fill in as much data as you can.

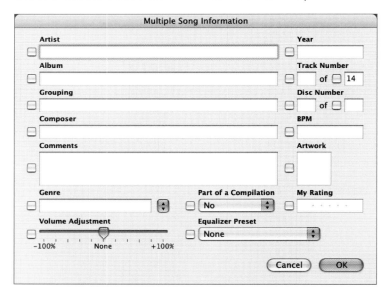

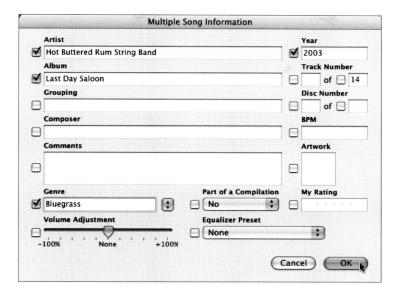

**3**  Click OK and check out your Library.

The songs have been updated, sorted by artist.

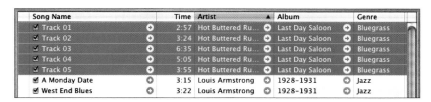

iTunes still doesn't know anything about the individual tracks. For that you'll need to go through song by song.

**4**    Select Track 01.

**5**    Choose File > Get Info.

Notice this is the third time we've chosen Get Info, and it has behaved slightly differently each time. First it was for a CD prior to importing, then it was for multiple tracks after importing, and now it's for a single track.

What you see initially is the Summary tab of information. Four tabs appear along the top of this window.

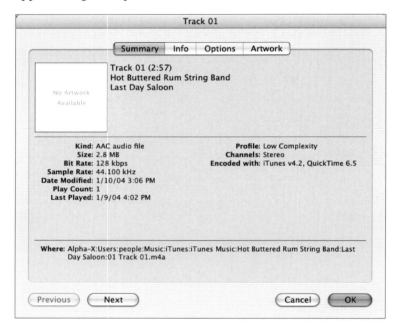

**6**    Select the Info tab, opening up an area in which you can enter a variety of important tidbits about your track.

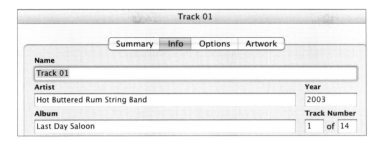

**7**   Change the name of Track 01 and click OK.

Track 1 is really called "Sweet Baby's Arms."

**8**   Repeat these steps for all unnamed tracks.

Before you know it, your Library is complete and looks something like this:

**TIP** ▶ If you can't see all the information about a track in the window, you can change the width of the column. When you move the pointer over the lines that separate columns, the cursor changes. You can drag the column border to the right or left to enlarge or narrow a column, respectively.

## Browsing and Viewing Your Tunes

Pouring all your CDs into iTunes isn't enough. Being able to find songs you're looking for is critical. Clicking any column in the iTunes Browser will sort that column alphabetically. Generally, an alphabetical arrangement by artist is pretty useful.

In the top of the window is a Search field; just start typing, and iTunes will do its best to find songs that you are describing—whether the letters you type are part of the name of a song, an artist, or an album. One particularly cool aspect of the search feature is that it starts looking as you type so you don't have to type an entire word, and you never need to press Return.

**TIP** ▶ By default, when you're searching for music, iTunes checks the Artist, Album, Composer, and Song Name fields. You can narrow your search by choosing just one of these fields. To do so, click the search icon (the magnifying glass) to the left of the Search field, choose the category you want to search, and then type your criteria in the Search field.

After Search, the most useful method of browsing a large collection is the built-in Browser. See that eye in the top corner of the window? Click it. The track info area will rearrange itself into some useful quadrants.

In this view, simply select one of the items in any of the three columns and you can quickly drill down any search through the collection. If you select All in any column, you get the full Library. Browsing by genre creates an experience that is akin to the way you might wander down aisles in a music store. If your tastes are more eclectic, you could skip genre and focus on artist.

**1**    Click an artist's name and only songs by that artist show in the window below.

**2**    Two albums from this artist are displayed together. Select one of the albums, on the right, and the search is narrowed even further:

**3**    To get back to the full Library, select All Artists (or All Genres) and you'll see all the songs again.

> **TIP**  If you don't want to browse with the Genre column visible—say you simply never use this very general criterion—you can make the column invisible in the Browser. Choose iTunes Menu > Preferences > General, unselect "Show genre when browsing," and then click OK.

Now that you've seen how to import and browse, you're ready for the key feature of iTunes: the capability to pull together songs from different albums and different artists based on whatever criteria you feel are important. It all comes down to playlists.

## Make Playlists

In the good ol' days, when you wanted to listen to music, you listened to a whole album. A CD was a nice, functional unit of music. Still, if you had the time, it was generally preferable to make a party tape or disc—a compilation of your favorites. New technologies produce new opportunities; introducing the *playlist*. It creates an experience akin to an instant, malleable, best-of CD.

A playlist is a set of songs that you build and sequence yourself. By making a playlist, you are not affecting your iTunes Library at all. The Library is where all the songs live; the playlist is just a convenient way to access some of them. It's also an essential building block if you want to burn a CD of some tracks (as Christopher wants to do for the birthday party), add a bunch of tunes to a slide show in iPhoto, or organize your music collection for your iPod.

**1**   Click the + button at the bottom of the Source column. This adds an untitled playlist to your Source list.

**2**   Type a name for the playlist. (Christopher calls his "Jessica's Birthday," which you may also want to do to make it easier to follow the lesson steps.) Click the new playlist in the Source column, and notice that there is nothing on the right side of the window. It's empty, since you haven't added any songs.

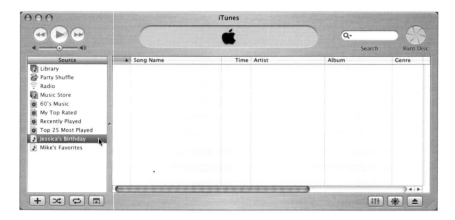

**3**    Click Library.

The main window shows the songs you've imported so far.

**4**    Drag a song from the list of tracks on the right and drop it on Jessica's Birthday.

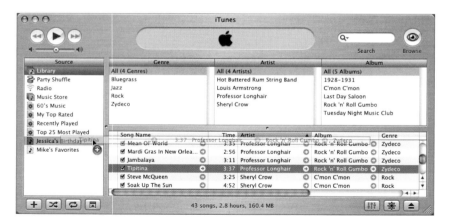

**5**    It may not look like anything happened at first, but if you select Jessica's Birthday you'll see your song in that playlist.

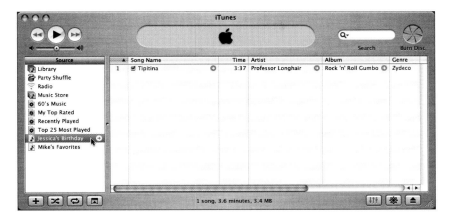

**6**    You can add more than one song at a time. Common to many Macintosh applications is Command-click—which lets you select a series of disconnected items at the same time. Go back to your Library, click one song, then hold down the Command key and click a second song from that list. Both songs will be selected. Drag the pair of songs to your playlist.

**NOTE** ▶ Shift-clicking works for selecting groups of contiguous songs.

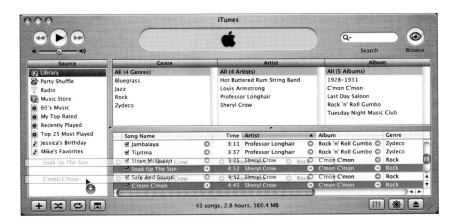

**7**   Click an album from the Album column and drag it to Jessica's Birthday.

All of the songs from that album are added at once.

You can add individual tracks or whole albums in many ways. This represents just the basics. No matter the method you use, before you know it the Jessica's Birthday playlist has a number of songs that you can play back-to-back.

> **TIP**  You can include a song in multiple playlists. You can even add songs to one playlist from another simply by dragging songs across the playlists.

> **TIP**  Deleting a song from a playlist will not delete it from your Library. Deleting from the Library, however, will remove it from your computer. You'll get a warning dialog, but be careful when you delete.

## Play a Playlist and Adjust Song Order

Whenever you select a playlist, iTunes will display some key information at the bottom of the screen: how many songs are in the list, how long it takes to play the entire list straight through, and (in case you care) how many bytes of data it represents. (This last bit of info is most useful when you want to burn the songs in a playlist to a CD.)

Playing the playlist is much like playing a CD. Choose a song and click Play (or just double-click the song), and the rest of the songs follow in the order they appear in the playlist.

### Random Play

Sometimes you want to be surprised by a song. Particularly with large playlists (or your Library), you just want iTunes to choose a song for you and play it. The Shuffle button at the bottom of the Source column handles this for you.

**1**   Select a playlist to play.

**2**   Click the Shuffle button.

  It will turn blue when it's shuffling your music.

  Clicking Shuffle will reorder the songs in your playlist (temporarily, and randomly). If you don't like the new order, click the Shuffle button again, and iTunes will restore the sequence of songs. You can always try again.

### Changing Order

But what if you don't like random playing, and you don't like the order in which you've dropped songs into your playlist? It's simple to change the order of your playlist in a more permanent way.

**1**   Click and drag a song within the playlist.

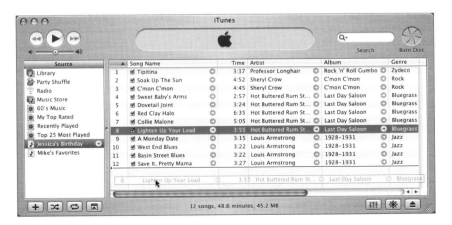

Notice the black line that indicates where the song will go if you release the mouse button.

**2** Release the mouse button when the song is where you want it.

## Burn a Custom CD

Once you have arranged a playlist, you might want to burn a CD for yourself. Once the Jessica's Birthday playlist is ready, all her father needs to do is alert iTunes he wants to burn a disc.

**1** Click Burn Disc icon at the top of the window.

The button will transform into a warning icon—alerting you it's ready to go, live and "hot." The information window will direct you to insert a blank CD into your Mac's combo drive.

**2**   Insert a blank CD.

iTunes will check to see if the disc is good and that the songs on the playlist will fit on it.

The size of the playlist (in megabytes; MB), noted at the bottom of the screen, is critical. A CD will hold only around 650 MB of music. iTunes is smart enough to coach you through splitting up your playlist over a couple CDs if it happens to be too big, or you could do it yourself.

**NOTE** ▶ iTunes measures sizes by the actual file size of the audio file. But when you burn a CD, iTunes converts all your files, regardless of their format to the CD standard format, which may be larger (or smaller) than what iTunes reports for your playlist. A 650 MB CD holds about 70 minutes of music regardless of how compressed your MP3 files are.

**3**   Click the Burn Disc icon.

iTunes will begin the process, spinning the Burn Disc icon as it works, and keeping you posted as to the burning status in the info window at the top of the screen. In a few minutes, the disc will be complete, and your Mac will eject it automatically.

### Custom CD Labels

The best complement to a custom CD is a custom label. Many software packages are available to streamline the label-making process. Some go so far as to insert photos (from iPhoto) and the list of songs (from your playlist in iTunes). They also provide cover art for your jewel case, as well as a label to affix to your CD.

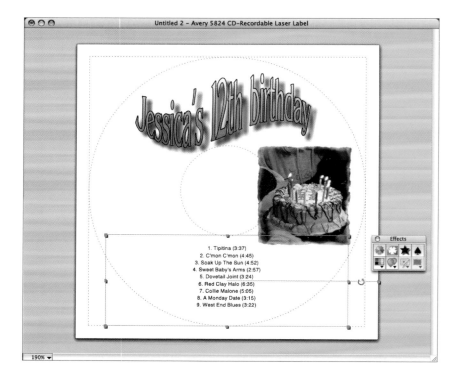

## What You've Learned

- ▶ Double-click the title of a song on a CD to play the song.

- ▶ Click Import to rip CDs to iTunes.

- ▶ Unselect the titles of songs you don't want to import.

- ▶ To adjust song and album information, use Get Info either before or after you import.

- ▶ Use iTunes' Browser and Search field to find songs.

- ▶ Create a new playlist with the + button.

- ▶ Drag one or multiple songs from the Library to a playlist to add them to that list.

- ▶ Drag tracks up or down in a playlist to change their order.

- ▶ Click the Burn Disc button visible in each playlist window to record all of those songs to a CD.

# 2

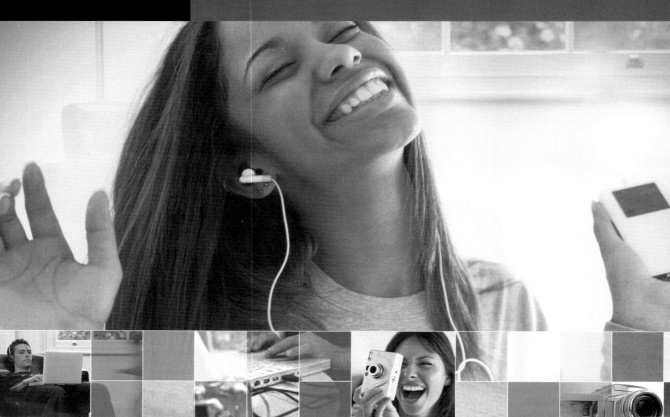

# DJ a Party with Your iPod

If you don't have an iPod, skip this lesson. Or go get one.

It's true, an iPod is just a glossy little hard drive that's well-suited for storing, accessing, and (of course) playing music. But if you talk to anyone who uses one, you'll quickly realize it's truly one of the best-designed portable tools you'll see these days. A book like this cannot describe the intense power and joy you will have when you can walk around—or drive, or fly—carrying (hang with me here) not just a few CDs, not just a Discman's worth of songs, but your *entire friggin' music collection* in your pocket.

Plugging in your headphones and enjoying your collection privately is great, but one day you'll want to take advantage of the fact that where ever you go you can hook up to a land-based stereo system and bring your music to a wider audience.

Christopher and the birthday party head out to a ceramics studio for the "big event," and he wants to bring along his iPod to hook into the studio's sound system for a private DJ experience. Since Jennifer, the studio owner, has an iPod, too (sometimes using it in the studio for special occasions), she's accustomed to this set up and is happy to help make the party as comfortable as possible.

## Moving Playlists to Your iPod

Your Mac and your iPod were made for each other, so moving your music to your iPod is an intuitive affair. When you connect your iPod to your Mac, the iPod automatically checks to make sure that the music on your Mac is also on your iPod. Consequently, if you've added new music to your iTunes Library, the iPod checks to make sure it is up to date.

> **NOTE** ▶ Be aware that an iPod is principally made for only one iTunes Music Library. If you have multiple computers with different music on each, your iPod can be a servant to only one of these masters. Moving an iPod around between different Macs can be less efficient than dedicating an iPod to a particular computer's Library.

1   Start by plugging your iPod into your Mac. If your iPod came with a dock, connect it to your Mac with the iPod Dock Connector to FireWire cable.

2   If you're using a Dock, place your iPod into it once it's hooked up to your Mac.

Notice that iTunes opens automatically when it sees your iPod.

iTunes also begins to transfer all the songs and playlists in your Library to your iPod. The icon representing your iPod in the Source list flashes red during the update. Do not disconnect your iPod while music is being transferred.

**NOTE** ▶ If this iPod has previously been synced with another Library, you'll get a warning when you hook it up. You'll have the option to override all the music on the iPod and sync it with the new Library, or to cancel the syncing process.

## Customizing iPod Playlists

You don't always have to copy every song from your Library to your iPod. If you have 20 GB of music on your Mac but only a 15 GB iPod, it won't even be possible. Consequently, you may want to be selective about which playlists you move to your iPod.

When an iPod is connected to your Mac, you'll see an iPod icon at the bottom of the iTunes screen.

**1**   Click the icon and you'll bring up the preferences associated with syncing your Mac and iPod.

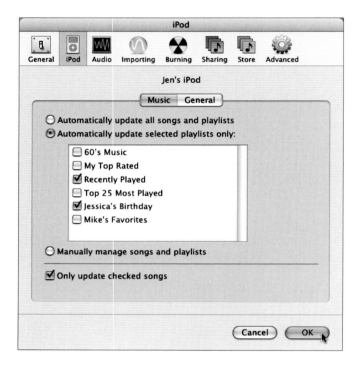

From the Preferences window, you can see all the iTunes playlists and can choose the ones you'd like on your iPod.

**2**   Check the playlists you want and click OK.

Now when you sync your iPod, only the selected playlists will be updated.

> **TIP** Name your playlists with your iPod in mind. This requires you to keep titles short (the iPod displays only 21 characters). Since the iPod alphabetizes titles, you can "trick" it into keeping your favorites at the top by inserting a hyphen (–) or a period (.) as the first character in the name.

## Playing Your iPod Music Through a Stereo

Because the iPod has such a compact and streamlined form, you might think of it as only an individual, private musical device. With headphones this is, of course, true. But it's very easy to hook an iPod into a more public music system. Whether you connect it to a mini FM broadcaster—so that you can hear your music on any nearby radio—or to speakers for direct playback, an iPod is definitely portable but not necessarily private.

With iPod in hand, and a single cable, Christopher can take his favorite music on the road, ready to hook into any available stereo system for a public music experience.

> **NOTE ▶** The law prohibits the public playing of copyrighted music—whether from CD or iPod or record album. Restaurants and retailers know this and tend not to put their private music collection over loudspeakers. They can be seriously fined. Instead, they often choose licensed collections (from services like Musak, AEI, DMX, and so on), for which they pay a small fee. The only way you can play your iPod over a stereo, legally, is if it's for a private group—yourself, your friends, your home. Christopher gets to play his iPod at the ceramics studio because it's a private party.

At the ceramics studio, Christopher checks with Jennifer, the studio owner, then plugs his iPod into the store's sound system. The cable required is different on each end: a ⅛-inch stereo miniplug to go into the iPod; a pair of RCA phone plugs on the other end, to go into a stereo.

**1**    Plug the ⅛-inch stereo miniplug into the top of the iPod.

**2**   Connect the pair of RCA plugs to the stereo.

Most stereo receivers have many audio input jacks for a variety of devices (CD players, turntables, and so on). If you find some empty jacks, you can use those, or choose the AUX input jacks usually provided for other assorted audio devices—like your iPod. The two jacks are color coded for stereo sound channels: red for right, white for left.

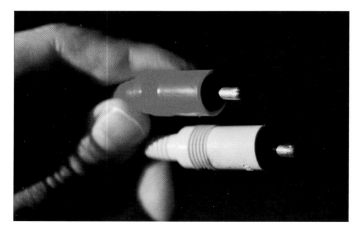

If your iPod is going to remain connected to the stereo for a while, you might want to use an adapter to plug it into a power source. If you have a Dock, you can set it up and hook the FireWire cable into a FireWire-AC adapter (which comes with your iPod). Then you won't have to worry about running out of juice.

**NOTE ▶**   If you're using an iPod with its Dock, the Dock sports its own plug for a "Line" connection to the stereo (it looks just like the little hole on the top of the iPod itself). You can select either plug to connect; they work in the same way.

With your iPod hooked up, set the stereo to play from the AUX source (or whichever source you hooked the iPod into) and start playing the music from your party playlist.

## Adding a Playlist to Your iPod Without iTunes

Christopher planned on using his Birthday Party playlist from iTunes on his iPod. But as the girls painted and talked, they wanted to hear other songs from the iPod that weren't on the Birthday Party playlist. The iPod makes it easy to add any song on the device to a playlist, even without a Mac or iTunes nearby.

With iPod in hand, scroll to the bottom of the Playlists screen and you'll find a playlist that you didn't create: the On-The-Go playlist.

**1**   Select a song. (You could also select every song by an artist, a whole playlist, or an album.)

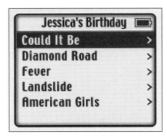

**2** Hold down the round Select button in the middle of the iPod dial until the selected item flashes for a moment.

Select button

When the flashing stops, the item has been added to your On-The-Go playlist.

**3** Repeat steps 1 and 2 for any other songs, artists, playlists, and albums you want to add.

**4** When you're ready to play your selections, select the On-The-Go playlist.

In the On-The-Go screen, you'll see a list of songs you've added to the list in the order in which you added them. (The songs—or items—you selected first will appear at the top of the list.)

**5**  Press Select to begin playing the playlist.

**6**  You get only one On-The-Go playlist. You can't remove a song, but you can clear the entire list and start again. To clear the On-The-Go playlist, scroll to the bottom of the playlist and select Clear Playlist.

In the resulting Clear screen, select Clear Playlist again, confirming that you really do want to wipe that playlist clean.

## What You've Learned

▸  For automatic syncing between your iPod and your Mac, plug your iPod Dock into your Mac, and then set your iPod on the Dock.

▸  iTunes lets you customize sync settings—such as syncing some playlists and not others—in the iPod Preferences window.

▸  To connect the iPod to any stereo receiver, use a ⅛-inch minijack-to-RCA stereo jack cable. This can plug into the jack on the top of the iPod or to a comparable jack in the iPod Dock.

# 3

| | |
|---|---|
| **Lesson Files** | Lessons > Lesson03 > L3.Student roll 1 |
| **Tools** | iPhoto |
| **Time** | Approximately 45 minutes |
| **Goals** | Learn how to use composition and lighting for better photographs |
| | Import pictures into iPhoto |
| | Rotate and delete images in iPhoto |

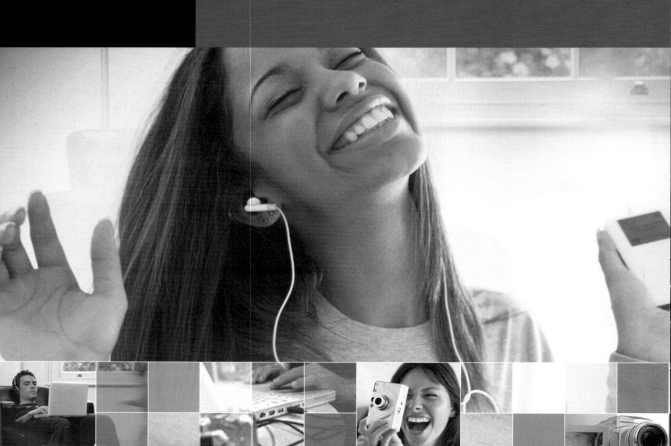

# Shooting Digital Snapshots and Putting Them in Your Mac

This lesson will demystify the way a computer can talk to (and control) a digital camera. It will give you some basic guidelines for handling your camera and creating impressive snapshots, as well as dealing with less-than-ideal lighting and subject orientation. It will also introduce you to iPhoto, the iLife tool for moving those photographs from camera to Mac, and ultimately organizing and sharing them.

You'll follow Jennifer, the studio owner, as she looks at her inventory. She might use a camera to help catalog and organize her ceramics, so that staff can identify pieces or vendors can fill a certain order. But as she gets more creative, she sees she can make beautiful photos of her ceramics that could inspire customers, creating not just "mug shots" but advertisements.

To see the process of getting shots into iPhoto, you'll also follow Charlie, the high school student, as he begins to prepare photos for his school project.

## Getting to Know Your Digital Camera

It can be daunting to buy a digital camera. The technology changes very quickly, as do the prices and features of the cameras. There are professional-quality cameras with interchangeable lenses, hefty weight, and high-end controls. There are compact consumer cameras with mostly automatic controls, a small zoom lens, and a flash. There are numerous features by which you can compare cameras, but perhaps the most significant is that of image quality. To make image-quality comparisons, all digital cameras are rated by a number of megapixels. Aside from how the camera feels in your hands, and, of course, its price, megapixels are a key measurement for digital cameras.

### Understanding Your Camera's Resolution

You can't talk about digital cameras without someone mentioning *megapixels*. Pixels are the smallest elements of a picture, like the dots on your TV screen if you look at it up close, or those of a newspaper photograph. Images are made up of these tiny dots of color and shade; the more of them, the higher the resolution; higher resolution means better-looking images. Of course, high-resolution images take up more space on your Mac's hard disk (and your camera's memory card) than low-resolution images do, so for any given memory card or storage device, there's a trade-off between more low-quality images and fewer high-quality images. A megapixel is a million pixels, and it's a pretty good place to start when comparing cameras. All digital cameras use between, say, 1 and 6 megapixels to capture an image. And in many ways, this defines how good the camera is.

But how many megapixels is enough? The answer depends on what you plan to do with your photographs. If you want to look at them on a TV set, the resolution can be pretty low, because a television is a very low-resolution display (equivalent to about 1/3 megapixel). Using images on the Internet allows even smaller files—and thus no matter how good your camera, you'll end up squeezing the image down to a radically lower pixel resolution (*well* below 1 megapixel). On the other hand, printing images demands the highest resolution—the larger the print, the higher the resolution you want.

High resolution

Low resolution

High resolution

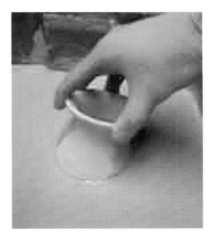

Low resolution

Prints this small make it hard to reveal the difference between resolutions. Still, the image on the left could be blown up to a poster and look pretty good. The one on the right is already suffering even though it's small.

**TIP** Images with lots of detail and color will look worse (revealing odd, digital-looking anomalies) with low-resolution cameras. However, images with large areas of solid color, good contrast, and few details—as you often find with close-up shots—tend to look okay with low-resolution cameras, at least better than wider shots.

So, if you have a low-megapixel camera, shoot more close-ups than scenic vistas. If you want more range, or plan to shoot wide, you may need a higher-megapixel camera.

A 2-megapixel image will print with excellent quality at typical snapshot sizes (3.5 × 5 and 4 × 6 inches). If you want to make enlargements at, say, 8 × 10, you may want to move up to 3 or 4 megapixels. And if you're a pro, or you plan to do really high-quality photography, 5 or 6 megapixels will likely do the trick. If you never plan to do anything more than display images on TV or on the Web, you can use the lowest-megapixel cameras available and save yourself some money.

**NOTE ▶** This, by the way, is why companies tend to demonstrate their DVDs, photos, and other compressed images using close-ups rather than wide shots. If you want to see how good an image really is, check the stadium crowd shots or the leaves turning on a million New England trees; these are far better indicators of potential problems than the model on the beach is. You really want a combination of both mottled details and solid colors to reveal different kinds of potential problems.

**TIP** Some companies offer combo camcorders and still cameras. In general, a camcorder image is of inferior image quality to a still camera; you might be better served by using separate devices, each well tuned for their task. Also keep in mind that you can grab a still frame from digital video any time you want (using iMovie, for instance) and don't have to have a special camcorder or specific feature to provide that function. It may be low resolution, but it's good for small snapshots or Web images.

## Shooting Great Photographs

### Take Lots of Photos

One of the best qualities of a digital camera is that it takes photos instantly—a 21st-century Polaroid Instamatic. You snap pictures pretty much the way you always have, but you can look immediately to see if the shot came out the way you hoped. And because no film or processing is needed, there's really no additional cost involved in shooting lots of pictures.

> **NOTE** ▶ There's no additional cost except for batteries, that is. Digital cameras chew up battery power, and that can get pricey. Some cameras can go through a custom battery pack in fewer than 100 shots. Keep this in mind as you compare your camera options.

Taking lots of shots gives you the opportunity to work the way professionals do. It used to be that you'd take one shot of something and hope it worked. But now you can shoot 1, 10, even 50 shots if it's important that you get that perfect snapshot. And like a professional, you can peruse all the pictures you took, throw out most of them, and keep the cream. Without changing anything about your photographic abilities, this technique alone will improve your photo collection.

### Read Your Camera Manual

It wouldn't be possible for this book to describe the specifics of how your model of digital camera works. Suffice it to say it has a shutter release button (the "snap button"), some automatic and preset exposure controls, and an LCD screen for viewing images. It also has a jack under a flap somewhere that lets you connect the camera to your Mac's USB port with a cable, which usually is included with the camera. Spend some time with the manual that came with your camera to familiarize yourself with the basics of shooting and exposure.

### Get the Exposure Right

As a rule of thumb, keep light behind *you* (not your subject) when you're shooting. Backlit subjects can be interesting once in a while (that hip silhouette look is very arty), but you'll probably miss the details you may want in your subject.

There's a fair amount of light in Jennifer's ceramics studio—it comes from skylights, from spot and task lighting pointing at the tables, and through the front window as ambient light. Shooting photos in the studio can be tricky because if you point the camera towards the front door, anyone you're shooting is going to have the bright daylight from the window behind them. If you can't get the light behind you, and you don't want a silhouette, your only option is to force your camera to flash even though it thinks there's enough light (after all, it sees plenty of light). Using a flash in this way is known as a *fill flash*. Any flash should be considered a last resort in photography—try instead to get a more naturalistic look through proper exposure.

Backlit subject                    Backlit subject with fill flash

Autofocus and autoexposure technologies are pretty advanced, and taking pictures in automatic mode will likely produce the best all-around images. As your skill and comfort expand, using more manual controls (like forcing the fill flash) will enhance your range and options as a photographer.

### Create Interesting Photographs Through Composition

Often the only difference between boring photos and stunning ones is the way you frame your subject—what photographers call *composition*. When composing your photos, consider not always centering your subject, a technique that can make your photos more appealing and dynamic. You also may want to move in closer than you normally would, cutting out space around your subject to keep attention from drifting. This technique often reveals more detail and emotion as well.

> **NOTE ▶** Cameras autofocus by looking at an object placed in the center of the frame. (Your camera may have a little box or marks in your view to indicate this center region.) Problem is this predisposes you to put the object you're shooting right in the middle. Some cameras allow you to off-set your frame once the camera has taken a focus reading. If your camera has this feature, you can push a button to lock in the focus, then move your view slightly before taking the picture. To create dynamic composition in your photos, this capability is important.

It can be tempting to photograph subjects in rigorous, rather clinical ways. If I say, "Take a photo of these three objects," many people will line them up and shoot them, from eye level, getting all three of the objects completely in frame.

Kinda dull composition

This kind of photo has its place and, once in a while, mixed in with other dynamic snapshots, is fun and important. Still, many people's scrapbook snapshots are always framed like this and are just about this interesting: everyone lined up, looking at the camera, pausing from whatever they were doing for a photo. Giving your subject the freedom to move naturally while you take candid snapshots is important. Composing scenes with some people close to you and others slightly obscured will allow for more naturalistic photos.

A little better composition

Once you're comfortable with a more relaxed style, try changing your vantage point. Taking shots from different angles, including from above and below, is another key to creating interesting photos. Too many pictures are shot from the photographer's point-of-view, just standing around with camera to her eye. Using a camera with a flip-out screen (which today's camcorders tend to have) allows a wider range of positions, from holding it over your head to setting it at ground level, without having to keep your head behind the camera.

Low angle (left), high angle (right)

Also, try moving closer to your subject, allowing the camera to see only a part of the object or person you're shooting. Letting the camera do some initial cropping like this is a great compositional tool. When you're photographing someone's face and want a very close shot, it doesn't look unusual even if you crop off the top of the head a little—the eyes are the important part.

Tight shot, cropped in the camera

**TIP** ▶ Every one of these guidelines applies both to still photography and video. As you get into video, keep these shooting rules handy to dramatically improve the photography in your videos.

Getting closer to subjects and cropping tightly as you frame a shot can be effective in giving your snapshots a professional look. An important rule of composition is called the "rule of thirds"—which says, in effect, don't put your subjects in the center of the frame, but rather a little off center (up/down or left/right). When you frame a snapshot, mentally create a grid of thirds across the screen, making sure your primary subject is located along one of the imaginary lines.

 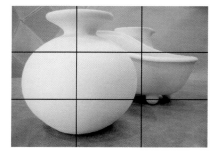

Similarly, feel free to leave objects in the foreground of your shots, probably out of focus, and use them to frame the rest of your image (while still using that rule of thirds). Foreground objects (window frames, door frames, people in profile, and so on) do not need to be immediately recognizable to add to the composition of the frame.

Finally, think about the background behind your subjects: You don't want it to compete with the subject too much. If it is visually "busy" or does not contrast with the subject enough, it can dilute the impact of your image.

Ideally, the background will be simple and will have some basic contrast with the foreground object.

**Summary Tips:**

▶   Get close to your subjects.

▶   Use foreground objects to frame your shot.

▶   Change your position to shift your point of view.

▶   Select the right background: less busy and more contrast with your subject. You don't want to have to hunt through a picture to find the subject.

## Getting Familiar with iPhoto

iPhoto is organized much like iTunes. On the left side of the screen are the sources—in this case, a Photo Library and a bunch of *albums*. An album is the equivalent of an iTunes playlist: a collection you create, a subset of your Library that organizes and simplifies viewing.

> **NOTE** ▶  Like iTunes, iPhoto has a few specialized collections—in this case *albums*—that are created automatically, including **Last Roll** and **Last 12 Months**.

iPhoto and iTunes are also similar in the way they work. You import content (from a CD in iTunes; from a camera in iPhoto), which is copied onto your hard disk and organized in your Library. Both programs have Smart Albums/Playlists; both let you make your own albums/playlists by dragging songs/photos from the Library. Both allow you to share songs/photos with other Mac users in your local network (around your office or home perhaps) with Apple's Rendezvous networks. (In short, if you can print to the same printer, you can probably share photos and music.) Both essentially organize your digital content; in addition to letting you easily burn CDs (from iTunes) and print photos (from iPhoto), both programs show up in other iLife applications. For instance, in iMovie and iDVD, you can select content from your Library or albums/playlists to make those applications more dynamic so that your movies are not just cut video, but video integrated with stills, moving stills, live sound, and recorded music.

If you understand the basics of iTunes, you already know much of what you need to know about iPhoto.

Here's the empty iPhoto window. If you weren't looking closely, you could easily mistake it for iTunes.

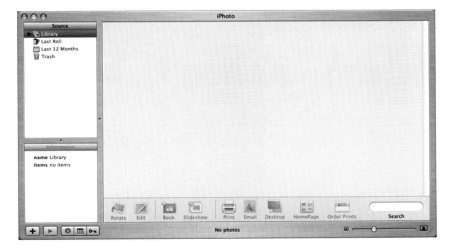

Your Mac is set up to open iPhoto, if it's not already open, and be prepared to import photos when you plug a digital camera into your computer.

## Importing from a Camera

For this lesson, we'll look at the importing process from the perspective of Charlie, the high school student, and imagine using his camera. This is how he manually imported his images into iPhoto.

Importing may seem challenging at first, but it really couldn't be easier.

**1**   Plug your camera into your Mac with the cable that came with your camera.

Two things will happen. Your camera will show up as a new source in the Source column, and the iPhoto window will display a large camera icon, letting you know it's ready to import the photos from your camera.

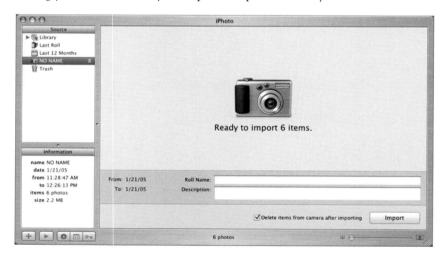

It's a good idea to erase photos from your camera after you import them, both to free up space on the memory card so you can take more pictures, and to keep from having to deal with duplicate photos later. You can do it yourself in your camera, but a really easy way is to have iPhoto erase photos automatically when it's done importing.

**2** If you want iPhoto to erase photos, check the box near the Import button.

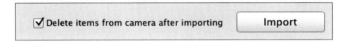

A pop-up window will appear asking you to confirm that you want to delete the originals.

**3** Select Delete Originals, and iPhoto will manage the rest.

The photos will appear as thumbnails in the iPhoto window, and you are done with your digital camera.

**4** Click the eject button to the right of the camera in the Source column, and your real camera can be safely disconnected from your Mac.

Of course, you don't have a camera loaded with Charlie's photographs, so to mimic his experience, you're going to add photos to your Library in the other way photos end up in iPhoto—copied from your hard disk.

**Preparing for the Lesson**
You will begin by dragging a folder full of photos to iPhoto.

**1** Launch iPhoto.

If you've never used the application before, the window will be empty. But even if it were not, iPhoto would be ready for your "roll" of film.

**2** Open the Lessons folder that you copied to your hard disk from the enclosed DVD.

**3**   Open the Lesson03 folder, and drag the entire folder called **L3.Student roll 1** into your open iPhoto window.

iPhoto will automatically start importing the folder of photographs as if it were a roll of film.

The iPhoto window is providing information about this import. If you had a camera attached, you would see it named here. At this point, iPhoto will indicate that no camera is connected, but will still show the photos importing. It runs through the images sequentially in the iPhoto window as they are copied into your Library, and it also shows how many images remain to be imported.

When all of the photos have been imported, the iPhoto window will reveal the pictures Charlie took in the studio as part of his report on the ceramic process.

Whenever you import new photos into iPhoto, they end up in the iPhoto Library.

The Library photos are organized in order of date and time imported. The default view of your photos is by *film roll,* which shows a film roll icon followed by the date of import and the name (if any) of the roll. The photos line up below the name of the role.

The small triangle next to the roll icon allows you to open and close the roll. When you have many rolls, this top line serves as the roll label even if the pictures aren't visible, and it makes browsing much easier.

### Change Roll Information

iPhoto automatically names each of your rolls of film, and dates it with the time and date of your import. Roll names come from the camera, and tend to be gibberish and pretty useless. If you dragged a folder in, as you just did, the roll name is the folder name, and the date is the date the folder was created, not when it was dragged into iPhoto. Now is a good time to see how to adjust this information.

**1**   Click the roll icon (or name).

iPhoto places blue squares around the roll's title line and individually on each photo in the roll. (If you do not see a roll icon in your Library viewer, click the View menu and choose Film Rolls.)

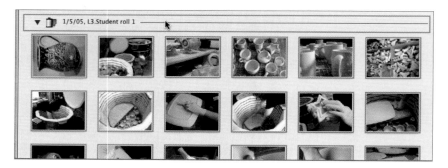

Notice the information fields on the left side of the window, beneath the sources.

**2**  Type new text in the data fields in the lower left. Remove the "L3" from
the title and change the date to today (the day you imported the roll).

The fields are not adjusted globally for every shot in the roll—only for the
roll itself. (This is similar to the Get Info work you did with iTunes in
Lesson 1.)

**NOTE ►**  In this digital age, the concept of film rolls may not really be
the best fundamental unit of picture organization. iPhoto 5 lets you
drag pictures from one roll to another and even create new rolls made up
of pictures previously in other rolls (Command-click a bunch of images
to select them, and then choose File > New Film Roll). This way your
"rolls" can be more like "events," regardless of how you originally shot
or input them.

## Delete Photos

If a picture didn't come out, waste little time leaving it around to clog the
pathways of productivity. Delete it. Select a photograph and press the Delete
key on your keyboard. If you delete a photo from your Library, it's removed
from your hard disk permanently. Make sure this is a move you want to make.

There are a few shots in Charlie's photo shoot that he wants to weed out immediately.

**1**    Scroll through the roll, looking at the photos. If the photos are hard to see, it's time to put the Size Slider to use. You can slide the knob (at the lower-right part of the iPhoto window) left and right, to grow and shrink the size of the images in your display.

You're not changing the photos, mind you, just zooming in to look around. Tiny pictures tend to be too small for all but the most general kind of visual searching; try a medium size where they are large enough to recognize— all the better for adjusting them a little. The good news is that you can change the size whenever you want, to best fit whatever kind of searching you are doing at the given moment.

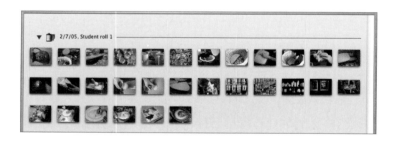

**2**   Find the photo of the painters that looks like this, and select it.

A blue box should outline the photo.

**3**   Press Delete on your keyboard.

The shot will disappear. It's gone from your hard disk.

**4**   Delete anything else you don't like or that is redundant.

**Rotate Photos**

Perhaps the most frequent adjustment you'll make to photographs, particularly right after you import them, is to reorient them so they are all right side up.

On the bottom of the iPhoto window, alongside a row of interesting-looking options (which, with great discipline, you are ignoring for the moment), is a button that rotates photographs counterclockwise (or, if you hold the Option key, clockwise). The first time you go through a roll of film, it's a good idea to delete bad pictures and rotate the remainder so they are oriented correctly. If no photos are selected, the button is greyed out.

**1**   The first photo in Charlie's roll is sideways. Select it.

**2**   Click the Rotate Photo button. The default is clockwise. (Hold down the Option key to toggle the rotation to a counterclockwise direction.)

If you want to change the default direction in which this button rotates photos, go to iPhoto Preferences and change the Rotate option. Most people tend to hold the camera in the vertical position one specific way all the time. You'll see in your own photos whether or not the default is right for you.

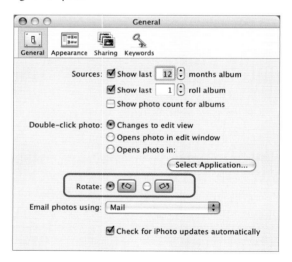

**3**  Continue through Charlie's roll of film until you have properly oriented all the images in the roll.

Once the images are rotated, iPhoto repositions them in the Library so each row accommodates the tallest image.

**TIP** ▶ To select multiple shots at once, click a photo, then hold down the Shift key before clicking another one; all of the photos from the first to the last you clicked will be selected. To select shots that aren't next to one another, use Command-click for the second (and subsequent) photos.

When you're done with this lesson, all the photos should be oriented properly and look like this in your iPhoto Library:

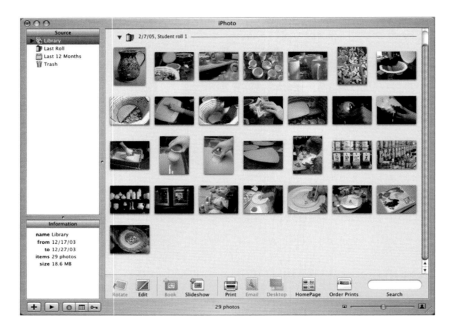

Now you're ready to do more subtle refinements on your rolls of film.

**NOTE ▶** Once you're more familiar with iPhoto, there is a more streamlined way to review and orient your photos. It involves using the Slideshow controls, which you'll work with in Lesson 5.

## What You've Learned

- ► Composition is important to good photography.

- ► When you're shooting, it's best to keep light behind *you,* not your subject.

- ► For more natural photos, try to avoid using the flash.

- ► Move closer to subjects, crop freely in the camera, and adjust your position to get a distinctive point of view.

- ► The rule of thirds says to keep subjects out of the center of the image; instead, move them to the sides or up and down a little in the frame.

- ► To import photos, you just plug your digital camera into your Mac, decide if you want iPhoto to delete original images from your camera, and let iPhoto do the rest.

- ► To move folders of photos into iPhoto from other locations on your hard disk, you just drag the folder into the iPhoto window.

- ► An important step right after you import photos is to do some quick adjustments, deleting bad images and rotating the remaining images to be oriented properly.

# 4

**Tools**   iPhoto

**Time**   Approximately 60 minutes

**Goals**   Learn how to make custom albums of photographs

Organize your photographs within albums and folders

Improve and adjust the look of your photographs

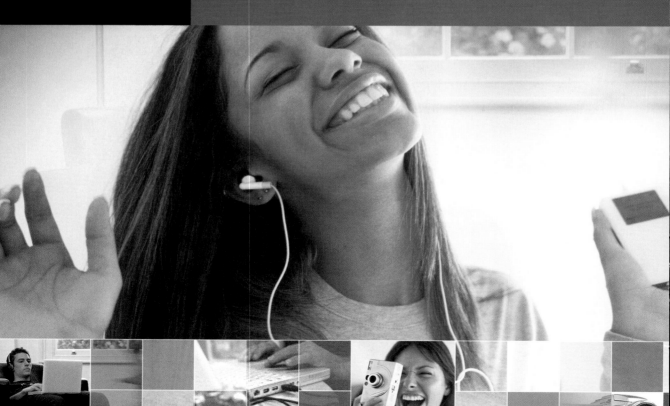

# Organizing and Refining Your Photos

When you start taking lots of digital photos of all the different events in your life, you'll want to keep them organized. Just like with traditional photography, you can create albums of digital photographs. One important difference is that digital albums are a lot more powerful. In this lesson, you'll learn the basics of organizing your collection into albums and making those photos look as good as can be, ultimately leading up to sharing them with friends and family.

As you move through this lesson, you'll become familiar with each of the photography projects going on at the studio. Charlie, for instance, was busy in the back room mostly, illustrating a report he wants to make for his class on the ceramic process. Consequently, he's shooting steps in the journey from a plain white object to a finished piece. Christopher, the father, is busy shooting his daughter's birthday party. Meanwhile, Jennifer, the studio owner, takes only a few shots, combining these images with those she's been collecting over the prior weeks and months. She's always looking to shoot images of inspiring customers' pieces and interesting events around her studio, and from time to time she illustrates a particular technique to help educate other customers.

Regardless of their individual agendas, all three characters will go through similar processes to organize their photographs.

## Preparing for the Lesson

Your first task will be to get the Lesson 4 media into iPhoto. Here's how to do it.

**1**  If it isn't already open, launch iPhoto.

You should see Lesson 3's Student roll 1 in the iPhoto window; if not, follow the steps in "Preparing for the Lesson" in Lesson 3 to bring in that material and prepare it. iPhoto is ready for your next rolls of film.

**2**  Open the Lessons folder that you copied to your hard disk from the enclosed DVD.

**3**  Open the Lesson04 folder and drag **L4.Biz roll 1**, **L4.Biz roll 2**, **L4.Biz roll 3**, and **L4.Dad roll 1** into your open iPhoto window.

When these four rolls are added to Student roll 1, your Library should look like this:

By default, iPhoto adds rolls to your Library and sorts them by roll date. To make viewing easier at this point, collapse each roll into a single line by clicking the black triangle on the left side of each roll icon. Before moving on, put your screen in this state:

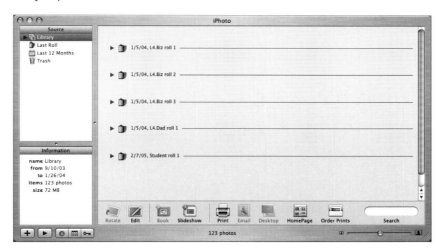

## Organizing Your Photos Into Albums

Regardless of whether you're playing the part of the parent, the student, or the studio owner, the primary method for organizing photos in iPhoto is to create albums. As I mentioned earlier, an album in iPhoto is virtually the same as a playlist in iTunes.

**1**  Click the + button at the bottom of the Source column to add a new album to the Source list.

**2**   Type the name *Birthday Party* for this album in the window, and click OK.

**3**   Drag the entire roll of film called **L4.Dad roll 1** from your Library onto the Birthday Party album icon in the Source list.

This will add all of the snapshots that Christopher shot at his daughter's birthday party.

**NOTE ▶** Adding images to an album does not remove them from the Library; it is as if they are in both places at once.

**4**   Click the album name to see the shots that you've moved into this subset
of your Library.

**NOTE** ▶ Notice that there are no film rolls in an album. All the images
now exist independently of the roll they came from. You can change the
order of images within the album, which is much easier than doing it
from the roll in the Library. You'll experiment with this in a moment.

**5**   Make three more albums. Jennifer, the studio owner, needs an album
called Company Press and one called Sgraffito. And for Charlie, create
one called Ceramic Process.

Albums are listed in the Source column in the order they were created.

**6** Go back to the Library and drag the entire roll called Student roll 1 to the Ceramic Process album.

**7** From the Library, click the black triangle to open **L4.Biz roll 1**. Make the images small enough that you can see the entire roll at once.

The business owner is looking through her recent shots and pulling together a bunch that illustrate the painting technique called "Sgraffito" (a process of scratching through one color to get to another). She also happens to have captured pictures of a few pieces that customers have done utilizing the technique. All of these will be aggregated in her Sgraffito album.

**8** Find the following shots and move them into the Sgraffito album.

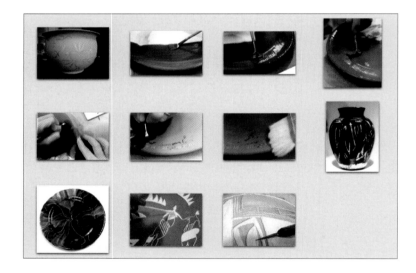

**TIP** You could select and move one photo at a time, or move the whole roll to the album and then toss out the extraneous images from the album (select them and press the Delete key)—whichever method feels more efficient.

**9**   Open the **L4.Biz roll 2** and **L4.Biz roll 3** albums, so all of Jennifer's snap-shots are visible in the Library.

For the Company Press album, the studio owner is pulling together partic-ularly interesting shots of her business—the look of her studios, a little bit about what happens there, some projects in the community, as well as some nice finished pieces by customers.

**10**   Find the following shots and move them into the Company Press album (some of the shots are included in **L4.Biz roll 1**):

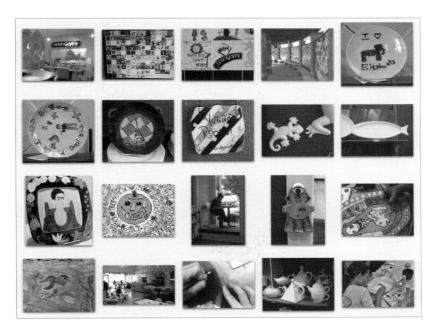

Remember, you don't always have to select and move one shot at a time. Just as in iTunes, if you want to select a group of contiguous shots, you can select the first, Shift-select the last, and then drag the entire batch to the appropriate album. Before you drop the shots on the album, notice that the number of images you're adding shows up in a red circle.

**TIP**▶   To select a noncontiguous set of shots, click the first shot and Command-click additional shots.

This is the essence of manual album creation. Christopher has an album of pictures from the birthday party, Charlie has an album of shots illustrating the ceramic process for school, and Jennifer has a few albums for various projects associated with her business.

Click each of the albums you now have in your Source list, and make sure they contain all of the right images. These four albums will play an important role in a number of upcoming lessons.

## Reordering Shots

The photos are placed in your album in the order you dragged them there, but odds are this isn't the order you ultimately want. You have the opportunity to rearrange them—maybe chronologically (Christopher's birthday party) or perhaps based on some theme (such as Jennifer's Sgraffito shots). Or you could group them by similar content with no concern for specific order. Whatever your strategy, it's easy to move photos to a new location within the album.

1   Open the Ceramic Process album by clicking it.

   Charlie is doing a report on ceramics for his class and has shot a number of excellent photos for the purpose. Part of the preparation of his report, however, is getting the shots into some kind of logical sequence. The order in which he shot them (and the order in which they appear in the album) does not correspond with a logical narration of the process.

2   Move the shot of the finished ceramic piece from the beginning of the album to the end. To do so, just click and drag it to the new position.

A black bar pops up within the sequence of thumbnail images to indicate where the photo will be placed when you release the mouse button.

**3**   Organize the rest of the shots so they tell a story.

For instance, the shots of raw bisque (clay that has been fired until it's hard and white) should come toward the beginning of the album. When you're done moving the shots around, they should look like this:

**4**   Before you're done with this album, go through it and delete any shots that are too similar.

Remember, Charlie is going to make a presentation and he wants it to be as concise as possible. It's pretty easy to whittle the 29 shots on his roll down to a respectable 17, which should illustrate what he has learned about ceramics.

## Adding Comments, Keywords, and Ratings to Images

Including information such as comments and keywords with your photographs is not only useful in keeping organized, but a great memory jogger when years have passed and you're not quite sure where a picture was taken or who the guy was standing on your left. iPhoto provides a number of methods to help you catalog pictures.

Adding a comment to a photo is the most basic approach and can be the most detailed. It's also perhaps the least useful, because iPhoto can show you this information—but can't do much with it. Selecting one or a few keywords to attach to an image is exceptionally powerful, even though it provides less information than a comment. Selecting a rating is also easy, and can be used by iPhoto in interesting ways, especially when combined with keywords.

Going through your rolls of film and adding information for each picture may be beyond your commitment to your photo collection. Regardless of whether you add notes, keywords, or ratings to one photo or all of them, iPhoto does its best to simplify the work involved, and it offers powerful organizational features if you're willing to do the work.

### Adding Comments

You can add comments to individual images, whole albums, or entire rolls by adding notes to the Information windows of these items.

**The Information Window**  You used the Information window at the lower-left corner of the iPhoto display back when you changed the name of one of your rolls in Lesson 3. Now let's explore the tool in more detail. The Information box gives you a running commentary about items that you select. If you click a roll, it will not only report on the title and date, but also how many photos are in it, and the total size (in MB) of the set. Click an individual image and you'll see additional information about the format (for instance, JPEG or TIFF), its dimensions (in pixels), and a rating (which you'll explore in a moment). Whether you select one image or a roll, in the Library or an album, it's easy to add or update the information.

> **TIP**  If you don't see this box, click the Info button at the bottom of the iPhoto window.

Notice how the data changes depending on what you select. Compare the data in the Information windows for different items by first selecting the Library, then an album, and finally a photo.

Library info                    Album info                    Image info

**The Comments Field**  When you select any item—an image, an album, or a roll—a comments field becomes available at the bottom of the Information window. You can add a comment by clicking that field to make it active and then entering new information.

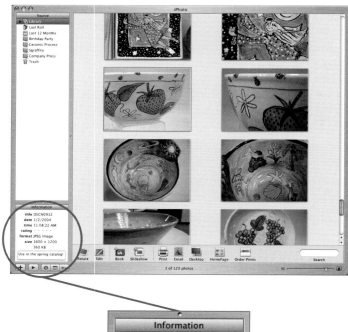

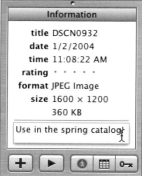

Adding notes to the comments field is a good way to include a detailed description that might be useful down the road (like who is in a picture or where a shot was taken).

If your comments are going to be elaborate, you can easily make the Information box taller, extending the visible comments field, by clicking the dot centered above the box and dragging up.

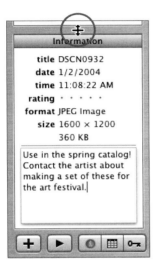

### Adding Keywords

For general organization, iPhoto offers a keywords feature.

A *keyword* is a preset word or phrase that you can assign to any image. Assigning keywords makes it easy to find specific kinds of photos in your collection. You can select a keyword from a preset list, which forces you to catalog shots and helps avoid that age-old organizational problem of having different labels—as in Dog, Dogs, Pets, Our Dog—for the same type of photo. Each variation on a label would only make it a little more difficult to keep all the dog shots together.

You can also create your own keywords if the ones provided with the program aren't enough.

Helping one of our characters use keywords will make the process even clearer:

**1**   Go to iPhoto > Preferences, and select Keywords.

iPhoto will present the short list of built-in keywords. These options are a good start, but studio-owner Jennifer needs some specific keywords related to the way she plans to organize her photos.

**2**   Add a new keyword: *Customer Pieces*. (As you can see, a keyword can be either a word or short phrase.)

Now you've created a new keyword that you can assign to one or more photos.

**3**  From the Library of photos from Jennifer (**L4.Biz roll 3**), find an image of a finished customer piece and select it.

Go to Photos > Get Info. Once you've selected a shot, select the appropriate keyword—in this case, Customer Pieces.

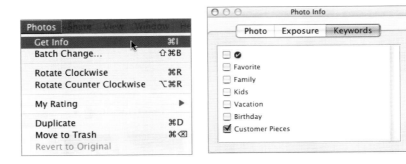

This adds the keyword to the stored data about this photo.

4   Select a group of shots of finished pieces.

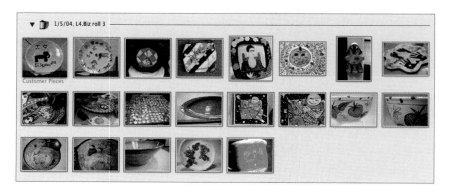

5   Go back to the Keywords window (which should be open) and assign
    Customer Pieces to those shots as well.

Notice that assigning works just as well with one photo as with a group.

If you're unsure of the keywords you have used, or you simply want to see
what you've done, turn on the View > Keywords option. The photo will
carry the assigned word in the Library and in every folder that contains
the photo.

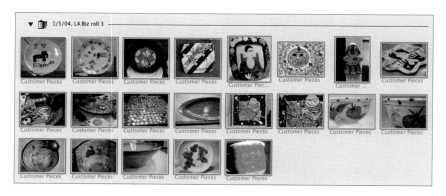

**NOTE** ▶ You can assign more than one keyword to a photo.

**6**    Go through all the business owner's photographs in the Library and assign the keyword Customer Pieces to all images of finished, glazed ceramic objects.

**7**    To find all the photos with a given keyword, select the keyword button (it looks like a key) at the bottom of the Source column.

**Adding Ratings**

In addition to assigning keywords to your photos, you can categorize your shots even further by using ratings. iPhoto provides a scale of one to five stars (five stars being the best) that you can assign to any image. It can be too much work to rate everything, but sometimes rating—or rating selectively— is useful.

Take Jennifer's shots of customer pieces, for instance. By definition, everything labeled with the keyword Customer Pieces is a customer's finished piece. But Jennifer is more interested in the really good photos of customers' pieces—and the keyword alone doesn't communicate this information. By going through the pieces and rating each one, she can store a little more valuable information with each photo.

**1**    Select one of the customer piece shots.

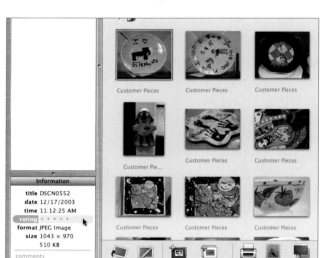

**2**    Choose View > My Rating.

This reveals any ratings you give. Otherwise, you can see your ratings only on individually selected shots in the Information window.

**3**    Using your cursor, in the Information box, click and drag across the rating line.

This will add stars to a photo's rating.

**4**    Rate a number of images, based on your own preferences.

The rating stars will show up beneath the photos, along with the keywords.

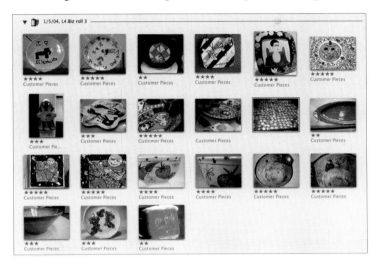

Once you have rated a number of the customer pieces, you're ready to use one of the most powerful organizational tools in iPhoto: Smart Albums.

> **TIP** ▶ You can also rate images and make a few other useful adjustments while watching the images in a slide show (discussed in Lesson 5).

## Creating Smart Albums

While it's easy to add a regular album to iPhoto, a Smart Album is a great tool for creatively organizing your collection. You can set up this type of album to automatically pull certain shots into it without you having to manually put them there. It's the fastest way to make albums and keep them current.

For instance, you could let iPhoto aggregate all images taken between November 27 and December 31 of every year. This would create a holiday album that would continue to fill up with holiday photos for years. Or you might choose to collect only your favorite images of your kids in a single album. Assign the Kids keyword to those new photos and rate the images; iPhoto adds to the Smart Album indefinitely.

Jennifer wants an album that stores only the best photos of the top customers' pieces—she wants to use them to inspire other customers and also show the incredible range of creativity that flows through her studio.

**1**    Choose File > New Smart Album.

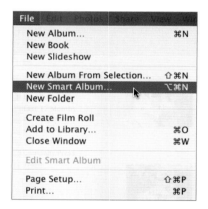

A window pops up, prompting you to name the Smart Album and set the criteria by which it will automatically gather images.

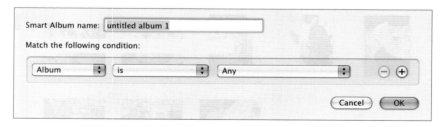

**2**   Type *Cool Pieces* as the name of the Smart Album.

**3**   Click each of the window's three pull-down menus to set up the conditions. You can create many permutations from these options, allowing for a large quantity of creative assortments of your photographs. For Jennifer, set the condition to select photos whose keyword is Customer Pieces.

When you're done, the window should look like this. The condition will pull together all the photos marked with the keyword Customer Pieces.

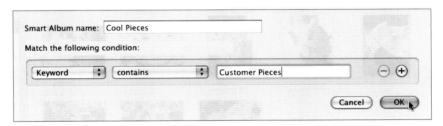

**TIP** ► If you haven't yet rated all your Customer Pieces, you could make this Smart Album with only one condition. Then, working from inside the Smart Album, you can rate the photos, which would be easier than working from the disparate rolls in the Library. Whether you're rating images during a slide show or doing so from the main iPhoto window, working from the Smart Album is a good first step to streamlining your rating process.

**4** Click the + button to add a new condition. Because the photos are already rated, you can set this one to look for ratings of four stars or better (this means you need to select "is greater than" three stars; the search will not include three-star ratings).

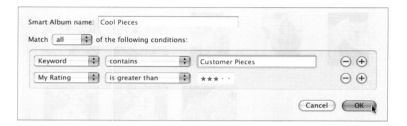

**5** Click OK.

iPhoto creates a new Smart Album in your Source list. This album has a little gear icon by its title, denoting that the contents are generated automatically.

**6** Select your new Cool Pieces Smart Album, which should show you the best pieces that customers have painted.

**TIP** ▶ While it's not necessarily faster, there is an alternative to selecting File > New Smart Album. Simply press the + button, which you used to add a new album to your Source list. Instead of adding a new album, use the pull-down menu to select a new Smart Album. Then follow the rest of the process as outlined in the previous steps.

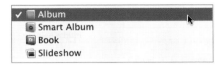

## Cropping Photos

Perhaps the most important control you have as a photographer is selecting the composition and framing of your photos. And while you do your best when shooting the camera, you may want to cut out parts of an image that are distracting, or reshape the frame to highlight some aspect of the photo. Since it's all too easy to shoot from a little too far away, tightly cropping a photograph is a way to increase the impact and sophistication of many shots.

**1** Double-click the photo that looks like this in the Company Press album:

Double-clicking opens up the shot in the Edit window, which will look like this:

Running along the top of the window are the other photos in this album. From this window, you can select an individual shot and edit it in a number of powerful ways (many of which will be covered in the following lesson).

2   Click the cursor anywhere in the image, and drag a rectangle across your image.

When you let go, the rectangle remains visible. If you missed the framing you were looking for, you can drag each side of the rectangle in or out to refine your frame.

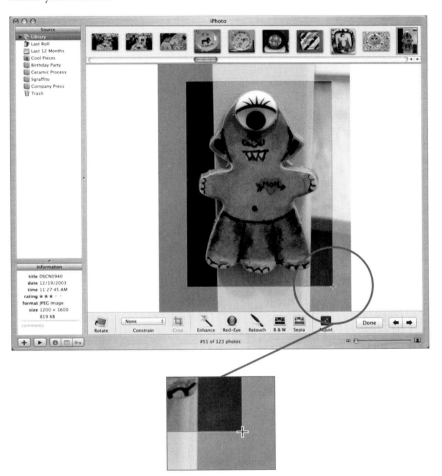

**3**    Once you have the photograph set up with the frame and shape you prefer, click the Crop button.

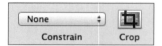

This disposes of the edges you don't want and redraws the new image in your window.

**Cropping to Fit a Frame**

Sometimes you crop not only to cut out bad stuff, but also to guarantee your photograph will fit in a picture frame (or CD case, or TV set). In these cases, you want to force the shape of your cropping to match the length and width ratios of your frame—known as the *aspect ratio*.

The following technique gives you prints whose proportions fit perfectly in a picture frame or a CD jewel case. It's worth noting that cropping a photo in an album, like changing a name or date, affects the original photo in the Library.

**1**    Find and click this photo from the photos along the top bar of the window:

**2**    Next to the Crop button is the Constrain pop-up menu. Click the menu and choose 3 × 5.

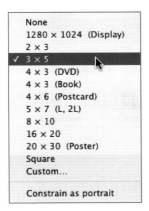

This preselects a cropping frame that is in the ratio of 3:5—effectively allowing your image to fit into a 3-by-5-inch frame. By clicking within the cropping frame and dragging to a new position, you are able to move this 3:5 rectangle around over your photo prior to cropping. Remember that you can also click and drag the edges of your rectangle if you want to resize it.

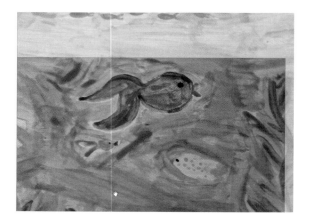

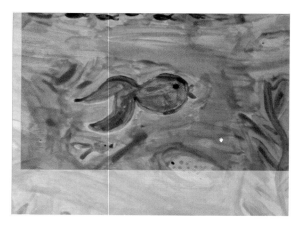

**TIP** ▶ Even if you centered your subject when you shot your photograph, cropping gives you another chance to offset your subject and create an aesthetically pleasing composition (using the rule of thirds).

**3**  Click the Crop button when you have positioned the frame aesthetically.

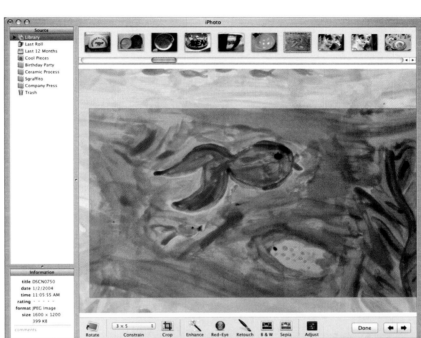

**TIP** If you don't want to alter your original photo, make a copy of it first and then crop the copy. Select the image and then choose Photos > Duplicate, and a copy will be placed in your Library.

**TIP** Don't forget that you can always undo a bad crop as well as virtually anything else you accidentally apply to a photo. To undo, press the keyboard shortcut Command-Z or go to the Edit menu and select Undo.

## Adjusting the Look of Images

iPhoto comes with some powerful tools for tweaking the images you took with your camera. In the Edit window, below the image, is a set of tools for automatically and manually adjusting images. On the right side is Adjust: manual controls for adjusting an array of image "exposure" settings (brightness, contrast, tint, and so on). In the middle are buttons for one-click "magic" image controls.

The most impressive of these tools is the simple power of Enhance.

### Making Changes with Enhance

Let's go back to the fish image we just cropped. It's a little dark, and not quite as crisp as it could be.

1    If it is not there, click the image to bring it to the center of the Edit window.

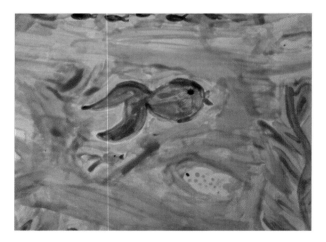

2    Click Enhance.

iPhoto does a quick analysis of your image and determines the best way to adjust brightness, contrast, color balance, and white balance in order to improve your image.

It doesn't always work perfectly, but it's pretty good, and most images benefit. If you don't like the results of Enhance, press Command-Z to undo it.

**TIP** ▶ If Enhance didn't help, you can try your hand at using the manual image-adjustment tools which you can access by pressing the Adjust button. The adjust tools offer a range of functions comparable to those in dedicated image-manipulation software, but can be confusing for novices. If the automatic Enhance looks inappropriate to your photo, experiment with the sliders in Adjust. For power users, if Adjust isn't enough, you can tweak the image with more-professional tools.

Go through all of the images in all four albums, and crop or enhance until you are satisfied with them.

## Removing Red-Eye

If you're using a flash, it's not uncommon to end up with that satanic-looking red-eye—the bane of photographers everywhere. It's caused when the flash reflects off the subject's retina and creates that characteristic glow. Some cameras minimize red-eye by shining a light for a moment before the actual photo is taken; this causes the pupil to constrict before the flash goes off and therefore reduces the retina reflection. Not all cameras have this feature, and even if they do, they don't catch every incident.

If you don't get rid of red-eye when you shoot, you can do it on your Mac. iPhoto simply does a little color correction on your subject's eyes—taking that which was red and making it black.

**1**    Open Christopher's Birthday Party album.

There's one shot of a party guest with that eerie red-eye.

**2**    Double-click the photo.

**3**    Click the Red-Eye tool.

A message appears on the screen instructing you to click the center of each eye.

**4**    Click in the red areas you want made black; it could take a few clicks if the red is uneven.

And, like magic, the devil eyes are gone.

When you're done working in the Edit window, click Done to save your work and return to the main iPhoto window.

### Straightening Crooked Photos

When you're holding your camera taking pictures, it is very easy to snap a shot that's crooked. With many images it might not be a problem; maybe it's not distracting. But in images with distinct horizontal or vertical elements (flag-poles, the ocean horizon, and so on), an important adjustment is the ability to even up those awkward angles. iPhoto makes this simple.

**1**    Open Charlie's album of the Ceramic Process.

Most of these shots are pretty good, but Charlie doesn't like the angle in one of the photographs of dipping a piece in glaze.

**2**    Double-click the image to return to the Edit pane.

**3** Click Adjust.

A floating transparent window of sophisticated image-adjustment tools appears.

**4** Click and drag the slider for Straighten.

This superimposes a grid over the image and rotates the image gradually until you feel it is better aligned with the grid.

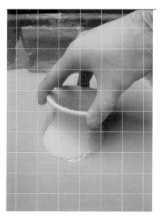

**5**    Using the back edge of the glaze bucket as a guide, rotate the image until it is squarer.

**6**    Click Done to save your changes and return to the main window.

## Organizing Your Sources Into Folders

In no time at all, the sources in iPhoto start filling up the Source column and become increasingly difficult to sort through. It only gets worse as you create slide shows and books, as you'll begin to do in the next lesson. Now is the time to learn how to organize your sources.

The way iLife is structured is, in many ways, like the Mac OS itself, with sources in the left column and details of the content in the large window to the right. Conveniently, iPhoto gives you the opportunity to arrange your sources into folders for easy organization.

For now, create three folders, one for each of our personas.

**1**    Choose File > New Folder.

This adds an untitled folder to your sources.

**2** Double-click the folder name and change it to Biz Owner.

**3** In the Source list, drag all the source material that belongs to Jennifer into her folder.

This includes the Sgraffito and Company Press albums as well as the Smart Album Cool Pieces.

**4** Go ahead and make folders for the student and the dad, as well. Add the appropriate albums to appropriate folders.

You'll use these folders for organizing new work in upcoming lessons.

## What You've Learned

▶  Press the + button to add new albums.

▶  Put photos in a specific album by dragging and dropping an image (or groups of them) from the Library to the chosen album.

▶  Rearrange the sequence of images within an album by dragging and dropping them.

▶  Use the Crop tool to reframe an image to fit in a frame or to improve composition.

▶  Constrain the Crop tool to perfectly reframe an image in a proportion you specify, for use in a variety of output formats, such as picture frames or CD cases.

▶  Automatically improve image problems in some photos with the Enhance feature.

▶  Correct that eerie red glow that your flash sometimes creates using the Red-Eye feature.

▶  Adjust crooked images and frame them with precision using the Straighten feature.

▶  Use folders to organize and neaten the many kinds of source materials you create in iPhoto.

# 5

| | |
|---|---|
| Lesson Files | No files for this lesson |
| Tools | iPhoto, color printer (optional), .Mac account (optional) |
| Time | Approximately 45 minutes |
| Goals | Print photos from iPhoto |
| | Make a book using iPhoto's connection to high-quality publication services |
| | Create a quick and easy slide show of photos with music |

# Printing and Sharing Your Photos

Importing and organizing collections are important, but the value of a good collection is being able to share it with other people. Thanks to all of the resources at hand today, you have many ways you can do that. Back in the old days, you'd hand a visitor a thick stack of pictures to flip through. Or you'd reproduce a few special shots from negatives and mail them to family. Or an unsuspecting guest sat down on a sofa and was handed a tome of family adventures to view and examine mindfully, page after page. Moving photos into the digital domain still allows for each of these methods, but it also adds considerable flexibility for creativity and ingenuity.

In this lesson, you'll examine three methods our subjects chose to share the fruits of their digital labor. Because Charlie is in a relatively low-tech environment at school (no projectors, no DVD players, few computers), he will print glossy-paper copies for cutting and pasting on posterboard. Jennifer's project is part of her business operations and will be printed as a high-quality book for her discerning audience. And Christopher, to have some fun himself while entertaining his daughter and her pals, will make a quick slide show to display on his Mac during the birthday party.

## Preparation for Sharing

No matter what your intended output for your photos, the creation of an album in iPhoto is an important first step. While it's certainly not required, it makes all the effort that follows far simpler and the process more enjoyable. In each part of this lesson, you'll use a different album from among the albums you created in Lesson 4.

No matter what project you're creating—whether following along with the lessons in this book or working independently on your own projects—take the time to go through your albums several times: Check that the order of images is appropriate; make sure you don't want to add or delete any; and do last-minute tweaks to orientation, framing, image quality, and so on.

## Printing Paper Images

Charlie, the high school student, is creating a class presentation about the ceramic process. Since his school's hardware is limited, he has chosen to make a poster for a short lecture he will give in the classroom. As with all projects, it starts with albums of photos—in this case, the album called Ceramic Process.

Once Charlie has opened the album, he's going to print 4-by-6-inch copies of each image using the Print Photos option at the bottom of the screen.

**1**   Select an album.

If you don't select any photos, iPhoto will print all the images in the album by default. If you select one or more photos from within an album, it's those photos that will be prepared for printing.

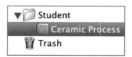

**2** Click Print.

The Print button is located in the bar of output options along the bottom of the iPhoto window.

Clicking Print brings up a printing window that allows you to choose a printer, set the margins, and choose the number of copies you want. There are also advanced options you can access from this window, if you have specific printing requirements.

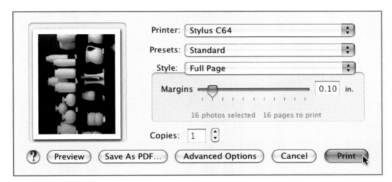

**NOTE ▶** Advanced options include print settings (picking a type of paper, printing with draft quality or photo quality) and iPhoto settings (printing smaller than 8½-by-11 paper, printing multiple copies of a single print on each page, printing contact sheets).

**3** Print a copy of the first photo.

Charlie printed all the photos in the album. High-quality prints tend to take longer to come out of the printer than those of lower quality. Using the advanced options, Charlie set the print quality to correspond to the type (and quality) of paper he's printing on—plain white paper. For a high school report, the image quality doesn't need to be professional caliber.

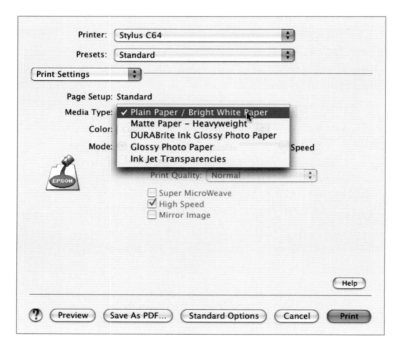

Charlie's advanced options are specific to his printer.

**4**  Use scissors or a paper cutter to cleanly chop up the print (if required) or trim borders for a clean, report-ready style.

Charlie added captions to his photographs, using information he researched about the ceramic process. He used a word-processing program to type up the captions, set the width of the columns to that of the photos, and used a font that looked legible and academic. Probably the most challenging part of his process was manually assembling the poster.

## Making a Bound Book

Jennifer, the studio owner, is interested in investing in a number of glossy, soft-cover portfolio books of ideas and examples of customers' pieces to distribute to her studios. She also wants to create a special linen-cover hardbound version of the album that includes her homemade publicity photos of the ceramic process, projects the studio has contributed to the community, and nice shots of each of her studio locations. These special books will be holiday presents for key staff members and some of her best customers.

In general, Jennifer shoots video in her studio, using the footage to make training tapes and also to generate still images for her Web site. Occasionally she takes digital still images, which she loads into iPhoto. Over the years she has taken hundreds of photos, and she has aggregated the best pictures in albums based on some basic themes: images of bisque (the inventory of her studios), shots of her studios in action, shots of finished customer pieces that might inspire other customers, and shots of techniques that illustrate and demystify the process.

iPhoto is designed to make, among other things, a good-quality hardback book of images. In addition to an 8½-by-11-inch hardcover book, iPhoto '05 allows you to make softcover books in small, medium, and large formats. The software helps you put photos on pages, and then lets you automatically access a Web site where you can order the book (or books) you designed.

Large hardbound books are impressive but not inexpensive. A double-sided 20-page book of, say, 30 photos might cost around $35; single-sided pages are slightly more expensive. On the other hand, a medium-sized softcover book is only around $10. Hardback books make excellent keepsakes, specialty photo albums, and business gifts; the softcover books can be a viable alternative for scrapbooking.

In addition to letting you create hardcover and softcover books, iPhoto '05 offers you more than a dozen different book styles—predesigned formats that let you vary the size of images, the arrangement of photos on each page, and the position and font of notes and captions.

The quality of Jennifer's photos varies greatly: sometimes 3 megapixels from the still cameras in the studios, sometimes 1 megapixel from a digital camera she used many years ago, and sometimes ⅓ megapixel as frame grabs from a videotape (which you will do in Lesson 13). Keep in mind the image differences when you print photos—if you try making an image larger than its resolution will support, it will look lousy, perhaps compromising the overall impact of the book.

The first step is deciding what the book will be for, what photos to include, and in what general order they should appear in the book (and, therefore, in the iPhoto album). You can modify the order later, but it is most efficient to try to organize them before you start building your book.

**Choosing a Theme**

Once you've decided the purpose of the book and what photos to include, it's time to choose the right look for your book.

**1**    Open the Cool Pieces album.

This album was generated automatically based on keyword and rating selections (from Lesson 4). This reveals images that Jennifer wants to put in her picture book of ideas.

In most albums, the photos appear in the order in which they were dragged in and can be reordered. In Smart Albums, the order is fixed.

**2**   Click the Book button.

Book, like Slideshow, does more than give you a new way to view your photos; it creates a new object (a book, in this case, or a slide show), which is added to your sources (hence the plus sign).

When you click the Book button, a theme window pops up from which you select the book format (hardcover or softcover) and size (small, medium, or large), and then choose from a series of themes appropriate for that format.

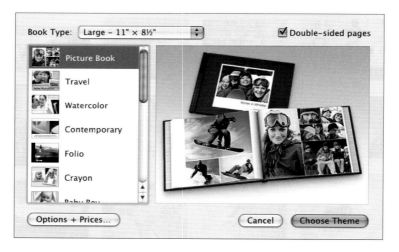

**3**   Click the Book Type pull-down menu to review your options.

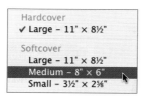

Jennifer would choose the large hardcover book, which is the default selection, for her formal high-end gift, but not for her studio idea books. Better than a scrapbook, she can inexpensively print in duplicate a softcover compendium of customer artwork and distribute it to all of her studios.

Click the various theme options to preview roughly how they will look. There are no wrong answers here. And even after you select one theme, you can easily change your mind later if it doesn't seem to be working for your book.

Jennifer settled on the Contemporary theme.

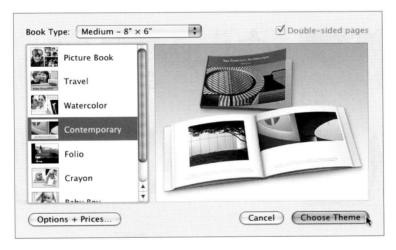

**NOTE** ▶ For many themes, you have the option of printing single-sided or double-sided pages. Since the minimum number of pieces of paper in a book is 10, the minimum number of pages is either 10 (single-sided) or 20 (double-sided).

**4**  Once you have selected the book type and theme, click Choose Theme at the bottom of the theme window.

Before the window switches to the Book view, iPhoto wants to know if you'd like to place the images on the pages yourself or if it should take a stab at the layout automatically.

The automatic option is very nice for anyone under time pressure (business deadlines or screaming kids)—it eliminates most of the work. But in some cases, it can be just as much work revising the computer's choices as making them the way you want from the start.

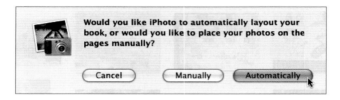

**5** Click the Manually button.

iPhoto reveals the workspace where you can organize and lay out your book.

### Creating a Cover

Let's start by designing the first pages presented in your book—the cover, front and back.

A preview of how the page looks     Page layout or photo workspace

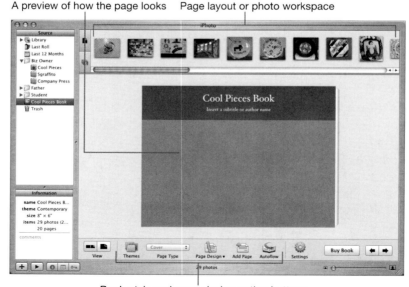

Book-style and page-design option buttons

By default, iPhoto gives your book the album's name. It also takes a guess as to the design of your book pages, although it's very easy to change them while you work, using the Themes button at the bottom of the window.

Displayed in the Book view is the template for the book's cover. The light gray regions on book pages are placeholders where you can drop the photos. On the cover, there is one gray space for a photo.

Running across the top of the window are the photos in the album.

**1** Click and drag the first photo in the album down into the placeholder.

**2** Change this book's title to *Petroglyph Idea Book* (Petroglyph is the name of Jennifer's company) and add the subtitle *Spring 2005—Volume 1.*

As Jennifer reviews the book, she doesn't think the painted skull is the right image for the cover. So try a few others.

**3** Click and drag a second, then a third photo of your choosing over the skull photo on the cover, and drop them on top.

As each photo replaces the one before it on the cover, the old image returns to the album bar.

But none of the photos is right for Jennifer. It may be a book to give her customers painting ideas, but not all the images she wants were in the Smart Album of Cool Pieces.

**4** Click the Biz Owner folder from among the sources.

Selecting a folder opens all the images in all the albums in that folder at one time.

Scan through the other images for something that might be appropriate for the cover. Maybe a wide shot of the studio interior?

**5**   Drag another photo from the Library onto the Cool Piece Book icon in the sources.

This adds a new photo to the book, even though it doesn't change anything about the Smart Album that was the original source for the book. A book is an independent object; you can add more photos to it just as you would an album.

**6**   Click the Cool Pieces Book from the sources.

Notice that the new photo is now in the bar along the top.

**7**   Drag and drop the new photo on top of the photo you want to replace on the cover.

The bar at the top of the window has two views; the bottom tab is a storage space for all the photos in the book not yet placed on a specific page. When you opt to manually create your book, this space is full of photos; when you opt for automatic book layout, this space starts out empty.

The top tab reveals thumbnails for the pages (or two-page spreads) that comprise the book. Even in thumbnails, the gray placeholders for the photos are clearly visible. The page or pages highlighted in blue are presently displayed in the larger window below.

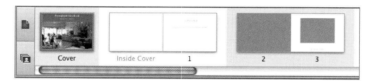

To move to the next (or any) layout, click the corresponding thumbnails in the bar.

8    Move to page 1.

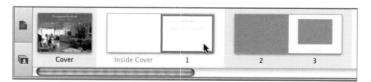

On all books, the back of the inside cover is blank, and the book begins on the right-hand page.

**9**   Click the text blocks to add some appropriate text to the page.

While the first line could easily be the same as the title on the cover, Jennifer made it one of her company slogans, "Personalize Your Presents®".

If the pages are too small for you to work with, use the size slider bar at the bottom of the window for appropriate enlargements.

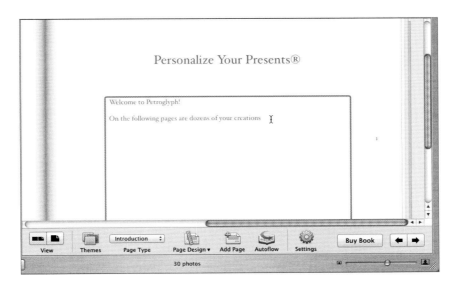

## Designing Interior Pages

Following the first two pages of the book (the cover and inside front cover) is a blank page. After that are the "real" pages of your book. Let's add photos to the existing layouts on the following few pages.

**1**   Click the next page in the book.

**2** Change the viewer at the top of the window to present the clipboard of
photos, and find some images to place in the book.

In this theme, some pages have text placeholders at the bottom of the pages.

3   You can add text to these placeholders or, for now, delete the text to simplify the design of the page.

4   Go to the next pair of pages and add a few more images to the layout so that it looks like this:

Jennifer wants the page on the right to be similar to the page on the left: both with two images side by side, one a close-up and one a wider shot of the same object. The page on the right needs to have a different layout.

To change the design of a selected page, use the tools beneath the main window, which let you adjust the number of photos on a page.

**5** Select Two from the Page Type pop-up menu.

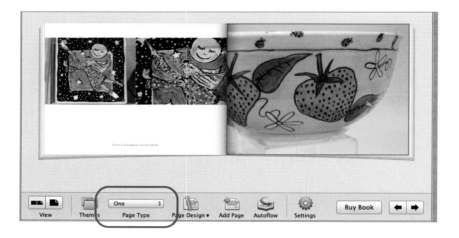

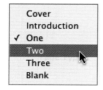

The page immediately rearranges to the new layout. If there are available photos still unplaced in the book, iPhoto will add one to the page.

Now two photos are on the page…but they are the wrong photos.

6   Drag two new images—two photos of the same bowl—from the unplaced photos (at the top of the window) over those currently placed on the page so that the layout looks like this:

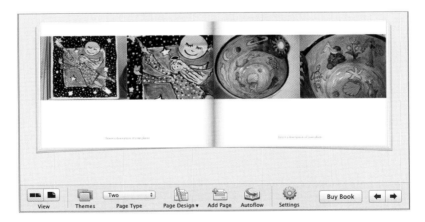

In this manner, you can adjust every page for the number of photos you want, and place the photos of your choice on each page.

Some page types (only in some book themes) give you more than one option for how to position the photos on the page.

**7**   Find the next page with a single image on a page (that is, the page type value is One).

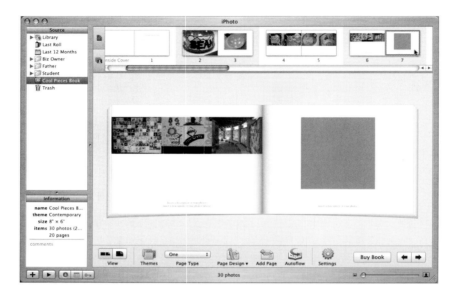

**8**   Drag a photo from the choices at the top of the window down into the blank space.

Before                                      After

This photo layout is elegant, but not your only option.

**9**   Click the Page Design button.

This reveals a pull-down menu of different ways a single image can be displayed on a page.

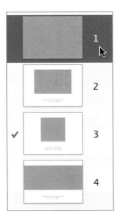 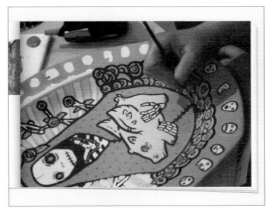

This photo looks fine large, running from edge to edge of the page (called "bleeding" to the edge). But not all of Jennifer's photos will look good this large.

**10**   Locate the photo of a red mug and drag it over this full-page photo.

iPhoto is always looking at the resolution of your images and determining if photos of a given quality will reproduce well at the size they are specified in the book. If it finds a quality problem, it will insert a small yellow caution sign (with an exclamation point in it) over the problem picture, alerting you that the image will not look good when printed. In the case of the red mug, the problem is displaying a low-resolution image at a large size in the book.

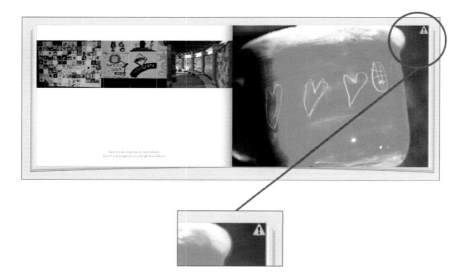

Depending on the scope of the problem, making the photo smaller often helps.

**11** Change the page design to a layout that makes the image smaller.

The warning sign should be gone, which means reducing the size solved the low-resolution problem. If the warning icon persists, change the page design to include more images (which reduces the sizes of each photo). If that still doesn't solve the problem, it may be necessary to leave a poorer-looking image in the book (with jaggies, or jagged edges, probably), or remove the photo altogether.

**12** Go through the remaining photos and design a book to your liking, trying to use all the photos in the album. If at some point you want to let the computer do the work for you, select the Autoflow button, which will finish the project automatically.

Whatever you do, keep this book to 20 pages. Thus, if a picture is spilling over to page 21, change the design of prior pages to shorten the book. You can make these books any length you want, but the price increases by number of pages (not number of photos). So you need to have control over the length of your product.

**NOTE ▶** The book-printing service requires that books be a minimum of 10 double-sided pages; if your book is shorter, it will add blank pages to fill out the number.

## Printing the Book

When you've finished the book and reviewed the text to your liking, the book is ready to print. You can choose from a couple of methods. To make a print-out of your custom book on your own printer, use the File > Print command. From there, you can select your printer, the number of copies, and, if you are so inclined, the option to generate a PDF file of your book.

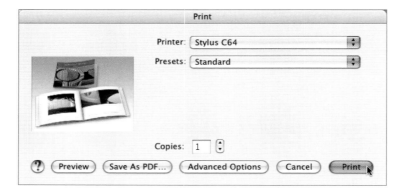

**NOTE ▶** The PDF file will be an exceptionally large one, but for some kinds of paperless distribution, like posting on the Web or emailing, it might be desirable.

The most interesting option is to use iPhoto's built-in high-quality book production. iPhoto contacts an outside service to create linen-bound hardback books or softcover books, which are printed and shipped to you in a few days. This is the process Jennifer uses for her idea book.

**1**  Once you're sure the book looks the way you want, click Buy Book on the bottom right of the iPhoto window.

iPhoto takes a few moments to assemble the book and prepare a file of information, and then it connects to the bookmaking service.

**2**   Select a color for the cover and the quantity of books.

The book service will give you a price, at which point you can choose whether to place your order. Jennifer ordered four books.

**3**   To finish up, drag the Cool Pieces Book from where it resides in your sources, and drop it in your Biz Owner folder.

## Making a Quick Slide Show

One of the things iPhoto does best is generate an automatic slide show from all or some of the photos in your collection. A slide show is a good way to review a new roll of film. Similar to tools in the main iPhoto window, the slide show tools in iPhoto let you instantly rate images and adjust their orientation.

Christopher, the father, takes snapshots during his daughter's birthday party; while she and her friends are working, he decides to make a slide show of images from the party—a little instant nostalgia.

Christopher's first step is to hook up his still camera to the computer (as described in Lesson 3).

Then he imports the images into iPhoto. He makes a Birthday Party album and drags the whole roll to it. Finally, he does some quick weeding out, reorienting, and enhancing of photos. In all, it takes about five minutes.

**1**   Click the Birthday Party album; you'll see what Christopher sees.

Before making any album into a slide show, verify that you like the order of images. Christopher doesn't like the order of the photos and wants to change it. This is how the images are presently arranged:

**2**   Rearrange the photos as Christopher does by moving all of the painting photos to the beginning.

The finished pieces should show up right after those, and the cake scene should be at the end.

**3**   This is also a good time to adjust the exposure of any images that are too dark or have red-eye (see Lesson 4).

**4** As a rule of thumb with slides, less is more, so delete any shots that are either redundant or of distractingly poor quality.

The final order and quantity should be something closer to this:

When the order of images is appropriate, you're ready to turn this collection of photographs into a slide-show presentation.

**5** Click the Slideshow button on the bottom of the iPhoto window.

This adds a new slide show source, composed of the images in the Birthday Party Album, to iPhoto.

In some respects, the Slideshow window looks like the Book window. The images from the original album are lined up across the top of the window, in the order they are placed in the album.

While it's easiest to get the slides in the right order when they're spread out in the album window, you can tweak slide order from within the slide show window just by clicking and dragging images around in the lineup at the top of the window.

For every slide show, there are two key considerations:

▶   How long you want each slide to be displayed

▶   What music will play during the show, if any

Use the Settings and Music buttons along the bottom of the window to set the duration and add music.

**6**   Click the Settings button.

This reveals a window of options for your slide show. Look through the options.

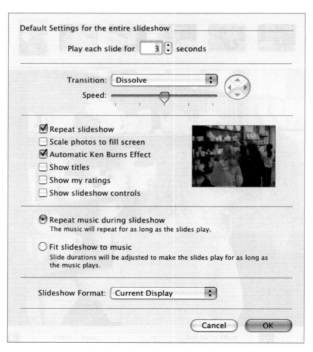

**7**   Play each slide for three seconds.

It's a little on the long side, but for kids who might be distracted—maybe laughing at each other or turning away in embarrassment—it's appropriate. Anyway, it's the default.

**8**   Leave the Transition setting set to Dissolve.

A *transition* is the way one slide changes into the next. If you want, experiment with various options, changing how fast or slowly the transition occurs (with the slider beneath the setting). When you're done, return the setting to Dissolve. A *dissolve* is a classic transition that isn't distracting and suits almost any situation.

**NOTE** ▶ Direction is an attribute of some kinds of transitions—such as Cube and Wipe—which lets you determine whether slides should replace each other from left to right or right to left. You can set direction with the group of four arrow buttons to the right of the transition effect, but it doesn't apply to Dissolve.

**9**   Clear (deselect) all of the check boxes in the middle of the window, including "Repeat slideshow."

In most cases, you won't want to restart a slide show once it has run through all the images—it will go on forever if you let it. A business owner might have an in-store display kiosk that circulated endlessly through a slide show, but most situations don't call for an endlessly repeating slide show (and your viewers probably won't appreciate it).

**10**   While you will become a master of the Ken Burns effect in the next lesson, turn it off for now.

With these settings, Christopher is creating a quick and simple slide show, made as efficiently as possible.

**11** Select OK to save your slide-show settings.

This returns you to the main Slideshow window.

**12** Click the Music button to select the soundtrack for your show. If you don't want music with your slide show, clear the "Play music during slideshow" option and you're ready to play.

But Christopher wants music to accompany the show.

**13** Click the iTunes playlists that may be more appropriate than the default (Sample Music).

Christopher has iTunes set up, so he selects his iTunes playlist called Jessica's Birthday (which he made in Lesson 1). You can select any of your available playlists or go right to your music Library and select a song.

You can select one song (which will repeat endlessly if given the chance) or a single playlist. To use an entire playlist, make sure you do *not* select a song, or just that song will play. Once you click a playlist, its contents become visible, as shown here.

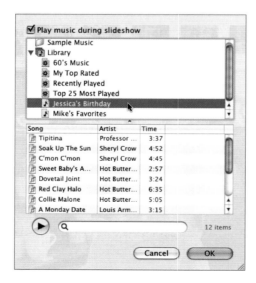

**14** Click OK.

This returns you to the Slideshow window.

**15** Click the Play button at the bottom left of the window.

Immediately, iPhoto will fade out your Mac's display, start the music, and begin the slide show. To stop the show at any point, press the spacebar to pause on a given slide; click your mouse to exit the slide show entirely.

**16** To finish up, drag the Birthday Party slide show from where it resides in your sources, and drop it in the Father folder.

## Other Sharing Options

When you're browsing through an album, look along the bottom of iPhoto's window; you'll notice other options besides Print, Slideshow, and Book.

▶   **Email**  This option gives you a simple way to attach photos to an email. Select the photos you want and click Email in the toolbar at the bottom of the window. iPhoto will ask you to select a compression size. (Do your friends want photos as large as you can make them? Do you have a dial-up connection, which necessitates small, highly compressed images?) Then, when you click Compose, iPhoto will attach the images to a blank email in your default email program.

▶   **Order Prints**  Much like Buy Book (in the Book window), this option connects you to an online printing service where you can select sizes and quantities of individual prints, and have them billed and shipped to you.

▶   **HomePage**  This option, which is related to your .Mac account, will be discussed in some detail in Lesson 13.

▶   **Desktop**  With this option, you can instantly change the Desktop picture on your Mac to the selected photo (usually controlled via your Mac's Preferences > Desktop pictures). This is a cool feature, but it's not easy to undo.

## What You've Learned

▶   Once you've organized albums from your photos, a number of output options are available.

▶   Printing one photo or an album of shots is easy using the Print command.

▶   You can create hardcover or softcover books for professional printing using various predesigned themes.

▶   Setting up a book requires going through the Book window page by page and selecting a design for each page. By balancing the order of images and the number of images on a page, you can customize a book quickly.

▶ Assembling a slide show is a very fast project with minimal effort and great payback.

▶ A slide show can display images from an album (or the Library). You can set the duration of each image; two to three seconds is probably ideal.

▶ Selecting music to accompany a slide show in iPhoto is easy, since the program connects automatically to your playlists in iTunes. iPhoto can play one song or an entire iTunes playlist to accompany a slide show.

**6**

Lesson Files

Tools     iPhoto, iMovie

Time     Approximately 90 minutes

Goals     Customize slide shows in iPhoto

Learn the Ken Burns Effect

Control slide durations

Get familiar with iMovie

Bring still photos into iMovie

Add photos to a movie as either still or moving images

Adjust durations of shots in the slide show

Add dissolves and other transition effects between shots

Add music to your dynamic slide show

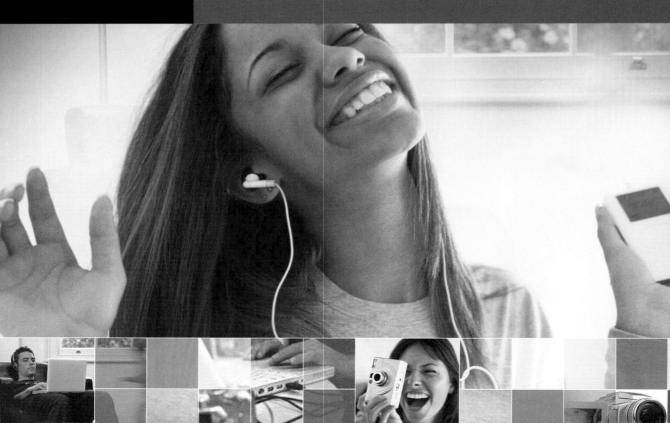

## Lesson 6
# Building a Dynamic Slide Show

As you've seen, in virtually no time you can make a slide show in iPhoto—it's quick and clean. But what do you get if you're willing to spend a few more minutes messing with your slides?

If you've got a little more time, you can take control of when and how each image appears on screen, producing a nuanced and professional presentation. One of the newest—and significant—features of iPhoto is that it lets you make a dynamic slide show that, until now, was possible only with video-editing software like iMovie.

Christopher made a quick slide show for his daughter Jessica and her friends at the birthday party, which was fun and easy. But now that he's home and has a little free time over the weekend, he wants to make a more interesting slide show for Jessica's grandparents to watch. iPhoto can help him do this. In the first part of this lesson, we'll go through the advanced features of iPhoto—manipulating not only collections of images, but also image timing (duration) and motion (pans and zooms).

iPhoto is so advanced that it overlaps in interesting ways with iMovie—which starts with still images and moves into moving video. iMovie isn't just for editing video from a camcorder—it can also make real videos from your iPhoto still images. So in this lesson, we'll also work with

Jennifer, the business owner.Her marketing and training needs often go just beyond what iPhoto can do, so she delves into iMovie territory. This lesson will show why and when one application is more appropriate than the other.

## Customizing Your Slide Show

In Lesson 5, Christopher created a slide show at his daughter's party in just a few minutes. It's the most traditional kind of slide show, the kind that families have enjoyed for generations, huddled around a projector, maybe with a carousel of slides and a screen Dad pulled out of the closet.

In a conventional, manual slide show, the person holding the clicker decides when to take you to the next slide—effectively deciding on the duration of each slide. By contrast, a quick iPhoto slide show automatically moves you through slides, held rigid on the screen like photographs, each for a preset amount of time. For you traditionalists, there are tools you can use to take the car out of automatic, and get hold of the stick shift, so to speak. In this lesson, we'll explore how to do that with iPhoto.

Before you learn to control how long images get displayed, let's look at a way to make them dynamic. The key is to make the images move on screen, which is exactly what you can do with the Ken Burns Effect.

### The Automatic Ken Burns Effect

Imagine that you have an enormous photograph, and that you also have a video camera. You can use your camera to look around at the photograph (panning side to side or tilting up and down as you take it in); you can also zoom in or out. Well, the Mac is your camcorder, and the Ken Burns Effect— an iPhoto feature that moves your photos around on the screen—creates the video you'd make with your camcorder.

Depending on the duration of your slide on the screen, you can move around quickly or slowly. Slowly is almost always better. And even if you have no patience for creating this sort of effect, one click can revolutionize your presentations.

**1**   Click Christopher's Birthday Party Slideshow.

With luck, you placed it in the Father folder at the end of Lesson 5.

**2**   Click the Settings button in the bar of buttons at the lower side of the window.

**3**   Select the Automatic Ken Burns Effect check box from the setting selections in the middle of the window.

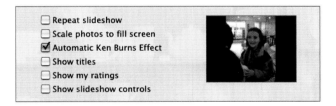

**4**   Click OK.

iPhoto returns you to the main window.

**5**   Without changing anything else, go ahead and play the slide show.

Like magic, the photos are moving dynamically, zooming, panning, radically shifting the nature of a slide show.

What you should notice is that now that the slides move, they seem to go by a little too quickly. While 3-second shots were plenty for an automatic and static slide show, once the camera starts moving around, shots need to be longer. About 5 seconds would be better.

**6**   Click Settings again and change the slide duration.

Experiment with different settings, but in the end, choose 5 seconds.

**7**   Click Okay and play the slide show again.

> **TIP** ▶ As a rule of thumb, moving shots must be longer than their static counterparts.

Adding the Ken Burns Effect, even when you have absolutely no control over the zooming and panning process, produces a remarkably dynamic and interesting slide show. It's almost always worth the few extra moments of your time.

> **NOTE** ▶ Ken Burns is an innovative documentary filmmaker who has created a number of popular movies *(The Civil War, Baseball, Jazz)*. He often uses the visual effect of moving the camera slowly across still images to tell stories. He didn't invent it, but he sure is good at it. Burns has excited many young filmmakers about movies in general and, in particular, documentaries.

## The Real Ken Burns Effect

You've used iPhoto to set the duration of every slide to the same number of seconds, and used the Ken Burns Effect to gaze around at your photos without regard to what was in the photo. But using the controls at the bottom of the slide show window, you can manually override these functions on a slide-by-slide basis if the Mac doesn't display a slide the way you think it should.

**1**   Start by selecting Preview.

The preview window shows you the selected slide in your show and the slide after it, just as the images will play in your slide show.

**2**   Select the Ken Burns Effect check box in the button bar.

You can now override the automatic effect. None of the other images in your slide show will be affected by this; it is a slide-by-slide adjustment. Here's how it works: You use the Start/End switch and adjust the framing of the image to set where the camera starts and finishes on your photo.

Christopher wants to adjust the effect on the first shot.

**3**   Click the first shot in the slide show.

At the bottom-right corner is the Zoom slider. When you make the image larger or smaller with this, iPhoto remembers the scale for the start position of the Ken Burns Effect.

**4**   Zoom in slightly on the photo.

Once you zoom in, you can reposition the image on the screen, to reframe it. Since it's larger than the window, you can move left or right, up and down. Simply by clicking and holding (which makes the cursor a hand), the image itself can be dragged around.

**5**   Click and drag the image around the screen until the framing looks good to you.

Framing an image is a subtle process. And it's one of the reasons this might be considered slow and meticulous work. There is no right answer as to how much to zoom in, and how to reframe the image. It's a creative decision based on personal taste, a sense of composition, and storytelling. What do you want to see first? What would be interesting to reveal as this shot remains on the screen? Should it reveal something surprising?

**6**   Once you have chosen a starting position, switch the Ken Burns Effect position to End.

The screen will reframe to show the whole photograph, giving you the opportunity to choose how you'd like this shot to look at the end of the camera move.

**7**    Using the Zoom slider and dragging the frame to reposition it, find where you want the move to end.

You could leave the framing at the iPhoto default, which is what you see when you click End, if you want the image to zoom all the way out. But it looks a little better if you zoom in just until the image fills the screen.

It can't be overstated: If you're using this effect correctly, it is going to feel like you're barely moving the photo. The natural tendency is to zoom too much, move too much—in other words, you'll tend to make the difference between the start and end frame gigantic. Much more impressive camerawork usually involves very slight, subtle shifts of the image—pulling back just a bit, or panning a little from side to side. You'll be amazed: Using tiny-but-smart Ken Burns Effects will make you look like a professional.

**8**   Click Preview to see what you have done.

Since the move should always been slow and steady, the more you move the camera (the farther the start and end points are), the longer the shot needs to be to compensate. But wait. You established the duration of this shot, like all the slides, in the Settings window. You will need to override that and adjust this slide's duration individually.

**9**   Click Adjust.

A dark, transparent window pops up over the slide. In a slide show, the Adjust button does not allow you to adjust the image exposure or photographic qualities, just its duration. (You can also adjust the kind of transition that ends the shot and begins the next shot, but we'll get into transitions later.)

**10** Adjust the slide duration by setting the "Play this slide for" value to 8 (seconds).

**11** Go through the slide show slide by slide, using the Preview button, and decide whether you like the automatic Ken Burns Effect, or whether you want to tweak the shot for better-looking results.

## Making Slide Shows with iMovie

iPhoto '05 makes it easy to adjust the duration of your slides, and it couldn't be simpler to make impressive shows with judicious use of the Ken Burns Effect. But even the most advanced presentations from iPhoto are just a jumping-off place for iMovie slide shows. Where iPhoto is image-centric, iMovie lets you take a broader stance, and look at elements and their durations in a different way.

### Where iMovie Kicks In

The first thing you probably noticed when you clicked the Preview button in iPhoto was that the slides preview without any sound. While this allows you to focus on the image and its motion, it does not make for easy synchronization with the music track. iMovie always shows images and sound together. This is one reason why you might use iMovie instead of iPhoto for a dynamic slide show.

The next thing you may have noticed when you selected any frame in your slide show and clicked Play (instead of Preview) was that the selected music started at the beginning even though you may have wanted the music to play from the middle of the slide show. Unfortunately, there is simply no good way to efficiently link certain sounds to individual images in iPhoto. Adding music is ancillary to the slide-show process. Music is integral in iMovie, and it always maintains the proper relationship of images to sound and music.

Third, while you can control the duration of each slide in iPhoto, you are limited to whole-second increments: A given image might be onscreen for 1 second or 3 seconds, but never 2½. In many cases this would hardly seem to matter, but for precise synchronization of images to sound, a finer degree of control is important. iMovie works in units that are fractions of a second (1/30th of a second, to be precise).

Finally, there are no title or text capabilities in iPhoto, but there are in iMovie.

For Christopher's final version of his dynamic iPhoto slide show (which is in the Lesson06 folder), he didn't need any text on the screen, and he didn't really care where images transitioned from one to the next with regard to the music. But Jennifer does.

## Making Movies Without a Camcorder

It would be natural to assume that, since iMovie is designed for making movies, you would need a camcorder to explore its power or to create interesting projects. This is not the case. Even with only a still camera (and iPhoto), you can use iMovie to build sophisticated and dynamic slide shows, which is another word for videos.

In Lesson 4, Jennifer used an iPhoto slide show as a way to generate automatic in-store presentations of customers' pieces, but she also wants to use her photos to educate customers about interesting painting techniques. Some images need to be onscreen just as something is happening in the music; she might want to add narration at some point. She wants to add text to the screen, and she needs text and titles integrated with the images and music. So she is going to make a slide show in iMovie.

## Exploring iMovie

Although iTunes and iPhoto have a consistent interface—similar, in fact, to the Mac OS itself—iMovie is unique. The nature of creating motion pictures dictates some different tools in the interface and a few pretty interesting capabilities.

**1**   Launch iMovie.

**2**   Click Create a New Project.

This will prepare a workspace for your movies.

**3**   Name the project.

Since you'll be working on a customer training video (following along with Jennifer, the studio owner), name this project *Sgraffito Technique.*

**4**   Click Create.

This lets iMovie keep your work files in the Movies folder, which is the default in the Where pull-down menu. Use this default unless you really want to put the files somewhere else (like on the Desktop).

**TIP** There are reasons other than organizational ones to keep your movies in the Movies folder—the most important involves easy connectivity with iDVD.

Workspace          Viewer                              Clip pane

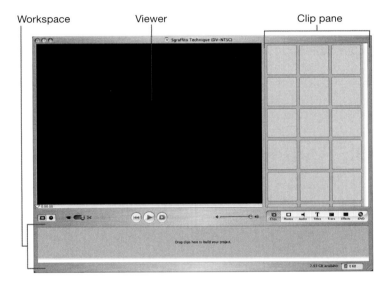

Take a look at the iMovie interface. Over the next few lessons, you'll explore this tool in more detail, but for the moment let's focus on a few key regions.

▶   **Viewer**  The big, black empty space is your Viewer, a television set of sorts, where you will watch all the video you are manipulating—either raw material still in your camera, or the pieces of video you're editing.

▶   **Clip pane**  The grid of small squares to the right of the Viewer is your Clip pane, a storage area that holds bits of video that you import into iMovie from your camera (or other sources, as you'll see). But this area isn't only for video clips. The buttons underneath these squares can change the region into a toolbox with an array of other specific functions.

Raw material starts in this upper-right hand part of the screen (whether from the Clip pane or other menu), and then moves to the bottom of the screen as you work with it.

▶ **Workspace** The long, horizontal area under the Clip pane is your video workspace. In this area, you'll assemble a video clip by clip. The view of what you're building in this workspace is adjustable: You might want to see your video as a series of representative slides (Clip view) or see the video tracks in lengths relative to their duration (Timeline view). Each viewing option will be useful at some point. In truth, while you're working, you'll find yourself toggling back and forth between views.

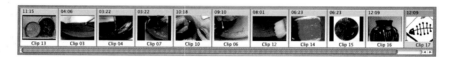

The Clip View button (above) and the workspace presented in the Clip view (below). This view gives you a good way to visualize the pieces of your project as you assemble them. It also notes the name and duration of each clip.

The Timeline View button (above) and the same workspace shown in the Timeline view (below). You can still see the clips, but the duration of each is represented by the size of the box. In this graphical view, it's easy to see how long a shot will play, or where you are watching within a given shot—both key aspects of moving images versus still ones.

In the Timeline view is a vertical line called the *playhead,* which shows the frame in your sequence that you are seeing in the Viewer.

A good way to play your sequence is to drag the playhead to the beginning of your project and click the Play button under the Viewer.

For many projects, the video camera is your primary source for material. In this lesson, however, since you're not working with video, you'll access all your raw material via the row of buttons beneath the Clip pane. These are particularly important for accessing raw material from the other iLife applications as well as for providing key tools in the construction of your video.

## Accessing and Using Photographs from iPhoto

Jennifer's project is a quick one—turning some still photos of a painting technique (called sgraffito) into an easy lesson for customers. The video will run on a large display in the studio.

She wants to build the video mainly from six photographs. Beyond that, she'll add some shots of finished pieces made with this technique to the beginning and end. She has also dashed off a simple script that she wants to use in the slide show for a little clearer explanation.

The script is included in the folder for Lesson 6, called **Sgraffito Script.txt**.

While there are more advanced ways to integrate the script—using voiceover narration, for instance—she wants to do a video with no dialogue, so the movie could play in a busy, noisy studio with sound off and still make sense.

### Adding Images from iPhoto

iMovie connects to iPhoto so effortlessly, it's impressive even to someone used to more professional video software. From inside iMovie, you have direct access to your iPhoto Library and (better still) all of your albums.

**1**    Click the Photos button.

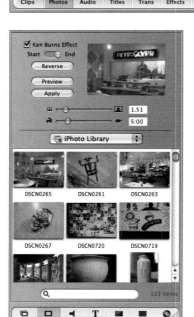

The Clip pane disappears and the photo tools take its place. At the top of the region are tools for adding motion to still photos (just as in iPhoto, you add motion by using the Ken Burns Effect), and at the bottom is a window into your iPhoto Library.

**2**    Click the Photo Library pull-down menu above the photos and select the Sgraffito album, rather than browsing through the entire Library (which, if you have hundreds or thousands of images, could be somewhat inefficient).

Recognize the other items here? That's right: It's the source lineup from iPhoto.

When you select an album, it will immediately appear in the scrollable window below, with the first image selected and shown in the window above, ready for modification (if you so choose) and, ultimately, introduction into your growing video project.

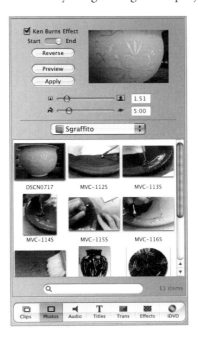

By default, iMovie turns a still image from iPhoto into a dynamic moving image using the Ken Burns Effect tools. Notice the Ken Burns Effect check box is selected, and the image in the window is moving slightly. You'll experiment with this in a moment, but at this point, don't use the Ken Burns Effect.

**3**    Clear the Ken Burns Effect check box at the top of the photo tools area.

The picture in the adjacent window will stop moving. Notice that the Start, Finish, Reverse, and Preview options are grayed out. When you place a static photo into a video project, you have only a couple of options: size and position (framing).

**4**    Click and drag the photo. Drag left. Drag right. Have fun.

Moving the photo around isn't very interesting unless the photo is much larger than the TV screen. Beneath the photo is a Zoom slider—from normal size (the actual image size, represented by 1.00) on the left to enormous (five times the actual image size, or 5.00) on the right. It works precisely as it did in iPhoto.

**5**    Slide the Zoom slider around to experiment with the image size.

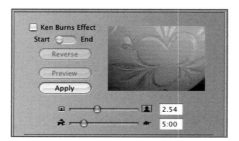

Once you've got the still photo looking the way you want, use the Duration slider (the one beneath the first, with the rabbit and turtle) to control the duration of a shot (how long it will remain on the screen).

This is a process that you began exploring in the iPhoto slide show, but iMovie builds on this power, where duration and timing are the name of the game. The box to the right of the Duration slider displays the actual seconds and frames of the shot, which you control. No decision, by the way, is permanent. If you make a shot too short, it's simple to adjust it later.

**NOTE** ▶ Units of video are called frames. Video plays at 30 frames per second, which means that one frame is ¹⁄₃₀ of a second long. It doesn't seem like a long time (and it's not), but for filmmakers it's enough to make a difference.

**6**  Set the duration of the shot to 8 seconds. If you can't get exactly 8 seconds by moving the slider, you can also click the box to the right, type in *8:00*, and press Return.

Remember, this is a still image—it has no intrinsic duration. Show someone your real-world scrapbook and they may glance at an image for a moment or sit with it for 20 seconds or more. But slide shows and movies take this power away from viewers and give it to you, the media creator. You have the challenge of making sure that your audience gets to see the image long enough without getting bored.

How long should a photo be on screen? There's no simple answer; trust your instincts. Good filmmakers understand that different images may require different amounts of time to be "read." Close-up shots may be easily read and enjoyed in a second or two. Wide shots and images with lots of interesting detail may need longer, 4 or 5 seconds perhaps, for the audience to feel satisfied and not rushed.

Now you're ready to put the shot into your movie.

**7**  Click Apply.

iMovie converts the still image into a video snippet of the duration you specified and places it in the timeline.

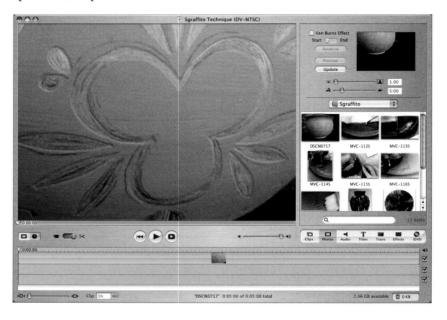

Now you see how to take a still image from iPhoto and put it into iMovie. It's not quite as simple as it was in iPhoto, but it is through this process that you can add images from an iPhoto album and build them into a static slide show in iMovie. Durations of each shot can be any length you choose, and not just in whole-second increments. This will be important in a moment.

### Using the Ken Burns Effect

Static images can be beautiful, and when presented on the screen give the audience the opportunity to scan around the image with their eyes freely, focusing on whatever aspect is interesting. But in filmmaking, the filmmaker has the opportunity to take control and direct the audience's attention. Skillful use of the Ken Burns Effect does just this.

**1**    Select the Ken Burns Effect check box.

Notice that the Start and End buttons are now available.

The Ken Burns Effect works exactly as it did in iPhoto: You decide how you want your shot to look at the beginning and at the end, and choose how long it should take to move from beginning to end.

**2**    Select one of the detailed images of the sgraffito technique (**MVC-110S**) from the scrollable photos in the album presented in the Library.

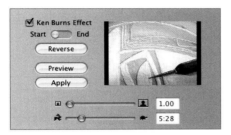

**3**    Click the Start button.

Now you're ready to set up the starting position for your shot.

**4**    Use the Zoom slider to enlarge the shot slightly, to around two times the image size (2.00).

**5**    Using the hand cursor, click and drag the image around until you like its position.

This is where Jennifer started her shot.

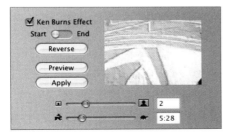

**TIP** ▶ As mentioned earlier, if you want to zoom in by a precise amount rather than just sliding the slider and eyeballing it, you can type a number into the box to the right of the Duration slider for an exact enlargement multiple.

6    Click the End toggle once you've found the starting point. Do what you did before: Using the size and drag functions, position the frame the way you want it to end.

Jennifer wants the shot to pull back until it's zoomed out to "normal" size. In this case, normal size is around 1.15 times enlargement, which fills the screen with the image and doesn't leave any black bars on the sides.

**NOTE** ▶ Shots don't have to zoom. You could just move the frame slowly from left to right (called a *pan*) or up and down (called a *tilt*). Or you could choose to zoom in rather than out—a shot could start wide (a multiple of 1.00) and zoom in. Different shots lend themselves to different methods. It all depends on what you want the audience to see and when.

7    Click Preview to see how your move will look once you've set it up.

Jennifer finds the move interesting, but it's too fast. This is a common problem with the Ken Burns Effect—people want to move their shots too quickly. A nice, slow, steady move is easier and far more interesting to watch.

8    To slow down the move, slide the Duration slider to the right, toward the turtle, setting it to approximately 10 seconds.

The length of the shot will be displayed in the box on the right (in seconds and frames).

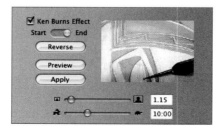

You can go back and forth, adjusting the start and end points as well as the duration until you're satisfied with the preview.

**TIP** ▶ Zooms and moves do not need to be very large to be effective. Small shifts left and right or subtle pushes in or out are plenty. If the move is going to be more substantial, the duration of the shot must be increased so that the move takes place over a longer time span. Remember: slow moves.

**9**   Click Apply.

This moves your shot down into your workspace.

It may take a moment or two before you can play the shot, however, because your Mac has to prepare a piece of video from the still image; the longer the shot, the longer it will take.

Now this shot will be appended to the first shot you placed in your project. In the Clip view, the sequence of shots looks like this.

Using the Ken Burns Effect, you can go step by step through a project, selecting shots in the order you want them (or at least the order you think you want them—you might rearrange shots later), applying this camera move, and placing them into your timeline.

**TIP** ▶ Not every shot needs to move! Smart juxtapositions of moving shots and nonmoving stills can be very effective (and a little faster to work with).

**10** Play your video and see what you've got so far.

There are a few ways to do this, and it can be a little confusing. If you just click the Play button under the Viewer, only the selected shot plays, which probably is less than your entire sequence. For the greatest clarity, deselect the clips in the Clip view by clicking a blank area of the workspace, then change to Timeline view by clicking the little clock button on the top left of the workspace. Click in the timescale along the top of the timeline to pop the playhead to your pointer, drag the playhead back to where you want to play from (the beginning, if that's what you want), and click Play.

**TIP** You should practice changing the view of your workspace from Timeline view to Clip view and back until you get comfortable with it. Some functions are more suited to one view and some to another, but in any event, it's important to be able to move back and forth easily.

**11** Add the next six album shots that show the progression of painting and then scratching the design into the plate. On each one, use the Ken Burns Effect and try a different method of moving the image—from close up to zoomed out, from left to right, from zoomed out to pushing in close, and so on.

**TIP** After using the Ken Burns Effect, when you select the next image to work on, the window retains the same setting it just used. This makes applying the same effect to a number of shots quick. There is also a Reverse button that switches the settings so that it does the opposite (a zoom in becomes a zoom out). An easy and interesting effect is to zoom in on one shot and then pull back on the next. Reverse makes this easy.

When you add a shot that contains a special effect (like the Ken Burns Effect), your Mac must *render* the shot—build it frame by frame—before you can see it play. The process of rendering is dependent on your Mac's CPU—faster processors take less time to render. You can see a red bar in a shot denoting the rendering process and how far along it is. When the bar disappears, the shot is rendered and can be played.

**NOTE** ▶ While your shots are being rendered, the playback of your sequence will be hindered.

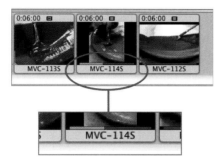

The red bar shows shots that are being rendered.

iMovie makes it easy to add a series of shots to your sequence, all with the same settings for zoom and duration. Once you've got one set up, iMovie will default to those settings for the next shot you bring up. Assuming you want shots to move similarly, this is great.

Unfortunately, decisions about how to move and position the shot are often particular to the individual shot. The good news: Once you've added a shot to your sequence, you can always select it in your timeline and revise any aspect of it—zoom, position, and speed (as discussed a little later in the lesson). You can even select multiple shots and revise them together, the same way.

When you're done, the backbone of the video is done. It should look something like this in Clip view:

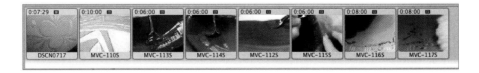

It's only the backbone because the addition of the narrative—using titles and effects—may necessitate lengthening, shortening, or shifting bits.

## Creating Titles

One of the important distinguishing features of iMovie as compared to iPhoto is the ability to add text and titles. Titles are elements that can be made to play over a black (or single-colored) screen, or over the moving video of your project.

### Adding Titles over Video

**1**    Open the text document **Sgraffito Script.txt**.

This is the narrative that Jennifer needs to incorporate into the dynamic slide show. You're going to start with the title.

**2**    Click the Titles button.

This opens a window in which you can build and preview text and titles you want to add to your sequence.

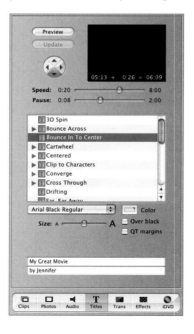

**3**  Click the first shot in the sequence (always on the far left of the workspace)— the still shot of the pink sgraffito vase.

A still shot is a good choice for an opening title. By selecting a shot in the timeline, you are indicating to iMovie that this image is the one to which you want to add a title.

**TIP**  Any time you have text onscreen for viewers to read, it's important to make it as legible as possible. This means keeping the text from competing with the background. There are many techniques to keep titles legible, from making the letters as large as possible to putting white titles over a neutral or dark background. Moving video tends to compete with titles for attention and can make reading titles a little harder.

**4**  Select a style of title.

Fancy can be fun, but simple and clear is often the fastest and easiest choice. Clicking a title style from the list will start a preview of the style in the small video window at the top of the column.

Check out a few styles, then select Centered > Centered Title. Many title styles have two variations: the basic kind, usually with fields for one or two lines of text, and the "multiple," which provides for additional fields that appear sequentially. You can create fields for additional lines in the multiple title by pressing the plus button (+), which is visible when the option is available.

**5**  Change the title text from the default ("My Great Movie") to Jennifer's actual title—"The Sgraffito Technique"—by typing it into the field at the bottom of the Titles window.

There's the option for a subtitle also.

**6**  Add the subtitle "Scratching Your Designs".

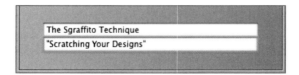

**7**  Use the Size slider to adjust the size of the text on the screen.

You should make titles as large as possible without reaching the edges of the screen. You can also change the font and color here, but for now, leave them as is.

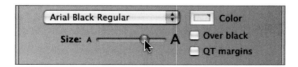

With each adjustment, click the Preview button. You will see your title in the large display, where it is easier to judge its size and timing.

**8** Use the Speed and Pause sliders to adjust the timing of your titles and effects.

The Speed slider controls how long a title takes to generate—to move in and perform its little dance, as it were. It's best to think of speed as the duration of the title effect. More important, in many cases, is how long you let the title remain onscreen after it appears. You control this with the Pause slider. For guaranteed readability, leave the title onscreen for as long as the slider will allow—at least 3 or 4 seconds.

iMovie will present the total duration of your title as the sum of two values: the length of the title generation (the speed) and how long it sits onscreen (the pause).

**9** When you're satisfied with the preview, drag the title effect to the beginning of the shot where you want it.

Once you've dropped the title onto the shot, iMovie begins to render the effect.

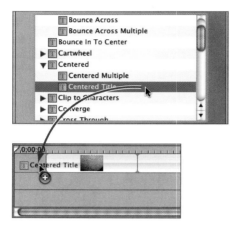

**NOTE** ▶ iMovie will effectively break your clip into two parts: the part with the title over it (with the duration you specified) and the remaining part, without the title.

 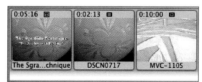

The title, as seen in Timeline view (left) and Clip view (right).

### Adding Titles over Black

Adding titles over still images or moving video produces exciting results, but for maximum clarity it's often best simply to insert title "cards" (as they did in silent movies). In iMovie, this means adding titles over black, and it's as easy as selecting a check box.

For the next title, Jennifer wants a simple card explaining briefly what sgraffito means. Using the same techniques you just learned, she adds text from her script over a black background.

**1**   Select a different title style: Scrolling Block.

**2**   Select the "Over black" check box.

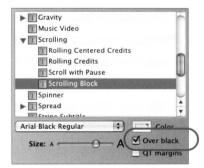

> **TIP**   Checking QT Margins adjusts your title for better visibility if you plan to export your movie to QuickTime for emailing to friends or publishing to the Web. Clear this box if you plan to show your movie full size on a television set or if you are going to burn to a DVD for TV viewing.

**3**   In the empty text field below the font-selection tools, type in the first section of text from the script.

You might need to experiment with where to place line breaks (returns) to cause the text to read smoothly onscreen.

The text block should read: *Sgraffito is an ancient art form. The word literally means "to scratch."*

**4** Adjust the generation of the title by moving the Speed slider and previewing the results.

You want a long block of scrolling text to move slowly and be easily readable. About 15 seconds is good.

**5** Drag the scrolling block of text to the timeline, and drop it between the title shot and the first shot of the blue and white piece.

**6** Now, without changing any of the settings, change the text block to include the next section of text: *You probably tried something like this when you were a kid. With crayons. It's easy.*

**NOTE ▶** If you wanted the first title card to say this instead of what you wrote in step 3, you could now click the Update button, which would revise the existing title.

**7** Preview the new block of text. Adjust the duration to fit.

**8** When you like this new scrolling block title, drag it down to the timeline and drop it after the blue and white sgraffito piece.

Through this method, Jennifer can continue to add title cards or rolling text blocks throughout her training video. But titles are not enough. To build a truly sophisticated video, particularly a dynamic presentation from still images, some basic transition effects are required. Fades and dissolves are the key.

## Applying Transition Effects

A *transition effect* is a special effect that alters the way you move from one shot to the next. The classic transition effect is the *cross dissolve*—where one shot disappears and is replaced by the next shot. But just as important is the *fade-out* (where one shot disappears to black) and the *fade-in* (where the next shot changes from black into an image). Slightly more hokey, but no less important, are *wipes*: geometric patterns that mediate the transition from one shot to the next. iMovie provides a series of different kinds of wipes as well.

Those who are new to making videos tend to overuse effects. Because iMovie makes it so easy to add effects and provides so many interesting options (as, in fact, all professional video tools do), it's tempting to play with them and cobble together a visual oddity for your video projects. But go easy: Less is more.

In truth, transition effects are used very sparingly in Hollywood movies and television programming. Almost all shows begin with a quick fade-in, and they end (at commercial breaks, for instance) with a quick fade-out. Dissolves are relatively rare, occurring only to show the passage of time or perhaps a change of location. You hardly ever see wipes. Oddly enough, almost all transitions from one shot to another are just plain cuts—exactly what you now have in your sequence.

But in this particular kind of sequence—a video invented from still images—transition effects would help. You're going to add a series of them, one after another, and then preview the results.

As with adding shots from iPhoto or the Titles window, you begin by selecting the menu button for Transition effects.

**1**   Click the Trans (short for transition effects) button.

**2**   Click Fade Out.

**3**   Using the Speed slider, set the speed of the fade-out to 00:14.

This is 14 frames, which is just about ½ second. It wouldn't be a problem if your fade-out were 1 second. But whether it's ½ second or 1 second, it should be fast. And for visual consistency, all the fades you use within a project should be the same speed.

**4**   Drag the fade-out to the end of the shot before the first scrolling title.

This means the first image will fade to black, and then the titles will start to scroll.

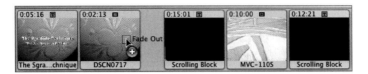

If you were using this transition between two video clips, you would fade in on the other side, but since it's transitioning to a title over black, it's not necessary.

**5**   Fade in on the head of the blue and white sgraffito clip (**MVC-110S**), then fade out on the end.

**6**   Drop a fade-in on the very beginning of the first shot for good measure.

Every video project should begin with a nice little fade-in. In this way, titles and video clips can transition back and forth smoothly.

**7**   Finish adding titles to the video, either over black or over the clips (as you feel appropriate).

Instructions and steps are effective as subtitles (or subtitle multiples, depending on how much you have to add).

**TIP** ▶ If you don't want a title to start at the beginning of the shot, "fake" a beginning by breaking a clip a moment after the start, then apply the effect to the second part of the clip. Lesson 7 will explore this and other ways to break up your clips.

**8**   Add some "beauty" shots of finished pieces that exhibit the sgraffito technique.

These are in the photo album you accessed through the Photos tab—in the Sgraffito album or perhaps in other Biz Owner rolls.

And that's it. Because this video will be shown in a busy studio, Jennifer doesn't want narration or music to accompany the images—it would compete with the store ambience. A QuickTime movie of Jennifer's finished video project, **Sgraffito Technique.mov**, is in your Lesson 6 lessons folder.

## Making Simple Adjustments to a Dynamic Slide Show

Christopher's dynamic video is much simpler than Jennifer's. His objective is only to create a fun home video from the stills he shot at the party, so he's happy to use the automatic Ken Burns Effect in iPhoto. But with a little additional focus, he found that he could make a pretty remarkable slide show with iMovie.

He started by dragging shots from his Birthday Party album into iMovie and used pretty much the same Ken Burns Effect move in each, with some slight variations. He wants only a basic title at the start; after that, simple dissolves between some of the shots are more than adequate. All of this is already in place in the iMovie project you'll work with in this part of the lesson. But Christopher wants to do a couple of quick tweaks, such as adjusting slide duration, which will give you a chance to see how to reedit a project. You'll also add music to Christopher's slide show.

**1**   Open the file **Birthday Party**, which is in the Start_Birthday_Project6 folder (in the Lesson6 folder).

As you can see, most of the still shots have been converted to video clips and are already assembled in the workspace. Notice that the opening title is in place at the start. The Clip view is handy for reviewing and arranging still images and slide shows (which is why it's very clear and similar, in fact, to the way shots are represented in iPhoto).

Kind of like in iPhoto, if you don't like the order of any shots, you can move them around by clicking and dragging them to a new location in the workspace.

For this project, however, change to the Timeline view of the workspace.

**2**   Click the little clock on the top left of the workspace.

Timeline view is good for dealing with issues typical of moving video— the length of shots, the positions of moments relative to running time, relative durations, and, of course, music.

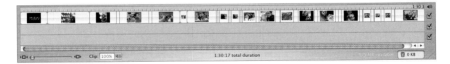

Additional controls are available when you're in this view. In particular, the Zoom Timeline slider appears, which controls how much of the sequence you can see at one time in the workspace. Push the Zoom slider all the way to the left, and all your shots are reduced so they fit in the window.

**3**   Adjust the Zoom slider as needed to see your shots.

**4**    Christopher doesn't like the second shot (the first one after the title), so select it and press Delete.

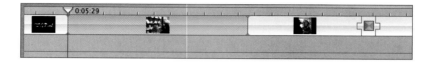

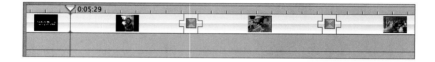

**5**    Christopher thinks the Ken Burns move is too fast on shot 4, so select the shot.

**6**    Click the Photos button.

The shot will reappear in the small window in the upper part of the Photo pane, ready for adjustments.

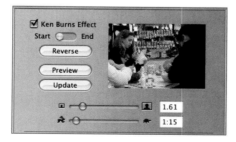

**7**    Change the duration of the Ken Burns Effect.

It should be much longer for such a long pan—try 6 or 7 seconds.

**8**   Click Update.

iMovie will rerender the new duration.

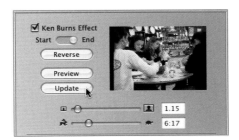

Except for this updated shot, every transition has a transition effect across it—mostly cross dissolves, but a few fade-out/fade-in pairs.

**9**   Add 20-frame cross dissolves to the beginning and end of this updated shot.

Adding a cross dissolve is the same as adding a fade, except it affects both the end of one shot and the beginning of the next. Drag the effect into the space between two shots.

iMovie always tells you the total length of your video (called the total running time). At this point in your reedit, the running time of the sequence should be around 1:25, give or take. It's displayed below the timeline or clip workspace, at the bottom center of the iMovie window.

## Adding Music from iTunes

For Jennifer, it's no problem that her still photos have no intrinsic sounds. They're just photographs, after all. But Christopher wants to add music to his dynamic slide show.

To add music to your video, you never need to leave iMovie. Just as you accessed your iTunes library and playlists from iPhoto, you can do the same from iMovie.

**1**   Click the Audio button.

This opens the Audio window—a view into iTunes (as well as a few other tools, which you'll use later).

**2**   From here, select the playlist you wish to access, or just leave it pointing at the Library, and find the song you want to add to your movie.

**NOTE** ▶ You can also use the Search field to find what you are looking for.

**3**   Click and drag the song to your timeline.

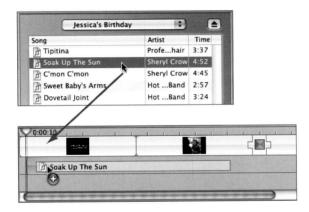

iMovie will import the song to your file and place it wherever your play-head is parked. (Or you could place the song at the start of your movie by dragging it there.)

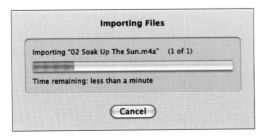

TIP ▶ You could also precisely move the playhead to the spot where you want the music to begin, and click the Place at Playhead button, which will automatically insert the music at the right location.

And that's it! You'll see the long purple track of audio underneath all your video clips, likely extending long past the end of your video if the video is shorter than the music. You can slide the song around to begin at any point you choose (although starting at the beginning is always a good idea).

And most important, now that the music is in place, you can make adjustments to the durations of your clips to better fit with musical cues in the song.

## What You've Learned

▶ With the Ken Burns Effect and adjustments to slide durations, a slide show in iPhoto can be an exceptionally dynamic presentation.

▶ You'll get the most impressive effects with the Ken Burns Effect if you use shifts that are small (either zooming in or out just a little, or panning left or right just a little).

▶ You can access your iPhoto albums from within iMovie.

▶ Add motion to still photos using the Ken Burns Effect in iMovie just as in iPhoto: Set the start and end points of the move, select a duration, and apply them to each photo.

▶ Change the arrangement of your workspace using Clip view and Timeline view.

▶ Drag shots around the workspace in either Clip or Timeline view to reorder them.

▶   To delete a shot, select it and press Delete.

▶   You can change an existing shot through the Photo window by making adjustments and selecting Update.

▶   You can access iTunes and drag songs to your timeline from within iMovie.

# 7

**Lesson Files**  Lessons > Lesson07 > Start_Timelapse_Project7

Lessons > Lesson07 > Finished_Timelapse_Project7

**Tools**  iMovie, camcorder (optional), iSight (optional)

**Time**  Approximately 90 minutes

**Goals**  Learn how to set up and shoot a time-lapse video

Edit the video in iMovie

Learn how to use an iSight camera to get video you can use in iMovie

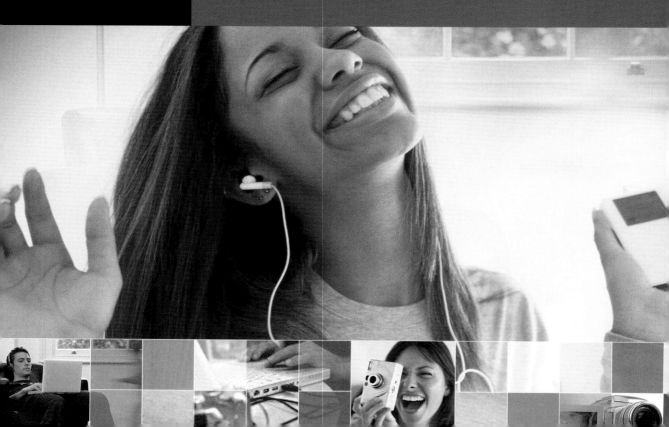

## Lesson 7
# Making a Time-Lapse Video

While it sounds like a film you'd see in a seventh-grade science class, a time-lapse video is just a small variation on what you do anyway with a video camera: that is, to compress real time into something more convenient and interesting. Officially, a time-lapse video is one shot of a slowly changing event, such as a flower blooming, that you speed up through photographic or editing tricks. This lesson will show you the elements involved in making a cool-looking time-lapse video, which can be applied to the most unscientific kinds of personal projects.

Studio owner Jennifer uses the time-lapse video technique all the time. There's nothing more satisfying than seeing a blank canvas (a ceramic piece) evolve over an hour or so into a finished product. Whenever a familiar customer pops into the store—one who she happens to know paints in an interesting style—Jennifer makes a time-lapse video for the in-store display, for the fun and education of other customers.

Charlie creates another variation on the time-lapse theme. He uses an iSight camera to keep a daily video journal for a class project. Because the iSight is attached to the Mac, it works nicely for doing time-lapse photography as well as other projects, as you'll see in the second part of this lesson.

## Preparation

The key to a successful time-lapse project is simple: Set up the camera someplace interesting, and then don't move it. Not a smidgen. Not a breath. While this sounds easy, you might be surprised at just how much you bump into your camcorder in the rigors of using the thing. Even if you set the camera on a table or use a tripod, just touching the Record button to turn it on and off is too much contact. So part of preparing for a time-lapse shoot is finding the remote control that (hopefully) came with your digital camcorder. You may have thought the remote control was only for playing back tapes, but the control also has a red Record button, and this is what you should use to start and stop your camera when you create a time-lapse project.

With camera and remote control, you're ready to find a subject and get set up.

**NOTE ▶** Your tripod needn't be a fancy, pricey model designed for video; it can be an inexpensive, old still-photography tripod. The difference is in the "head"—the top part of the tripod that holds the camera and swivels around. For video, the swiveling must be slow and smooth, and the mechanics to execute this (usually involving what is known as a fluid head) are expensive. A still-photography tripod just needs to lock the camera down and hold it stationary—much more affordable. Jennifer uses a tripod that's about 25 years old but works like a charm.

## Finding a Project

Anything that moves or evolves slowly, over a long period of time, is an appropriate potential subject for time-lapse video. The span of time needs to be long enough, though, that you might otherwise miss the event because of the sheer boredom or impracticality involved in watching for it. On the other end of the spectrum, the time span can't be too long, or you increase the chances of bumping (or needing to move) the camera while you create your video. Needless to say, a multiple-day project can be challenging to execute. For now, let's focus on the kinds of events whose time span is 30 minutes to 3 hours.

For Charlie, and other students interested in science projects, this may be limiting. The really good scientific stuff—like plants growing or butterflies emerging from cocoons—tends to happen over days or weeks. But social science—watching people—can be a good project, too. Parents like Christopher can capture whole meals with their young kids (I've seen videos of a dirtying floor beneath an infant having dinner; when cut to 30 seconds it can be reasonably amusing) or the slow, delightful process of their child waking up on a Saturday morning. A time-lapse of a teen's room, going from clean to messy, is similarly amusing. Around the house, it's a fun and memorable way to document building a model, making a quilt, or remodeling a room. As long as the camera doesn't move, these video projects work. Business owners can demystify many parts of their company's workings. (Jennifer has made time-lapse videos of kiln loading, the glazing process, and painting methods.) Time-lapse is an interesting technique for training tapes and can be attractive for customers. Customer education can be provided in many ways—pamphlets and instructional booklets are two—but little can replace watching the process over an expert's shoulder.

**TIP** Integrating a short time-lapse sequence into a longer project of still or moving video creates an interesting element.

## Setting Up the Camera

Find a camera position with a good vantage point of what you want to shoot. In some cases, it works to set the camera on a table or chair and zoom out wide. In all cases, a tripod will help. Using a tripod increases the kinds of positions in which you can hold the camera: It can be at eye level or higher; it can be up in a corner somewhere; it can be right in the middle of things, zoomed in tight on the activity you've chosen.

Before you start, set up the tripod; load a new, clean digital tape into your camera; lock it into the tripod; and check the focus and exposure. (And, if the project is long or important, maybe do a little test or rehearsal.) Then, turn on your camera and get hold of the remote. Using the remote only—never touching the camera—start recording.

Depending on the event's actual length, you may try one of two options. For shorter events (say, under an hour), you will let the tape roll, undisturbed, until it runs out. Later you can carefully select the best parts. For longer events, turn on the camcorder for shorter periods of time—say, a few minutes— then off again. And then, a little bit later (how much later depends on how long the event is), do it again. For a two-hour event, you might try shooting five minutes, then stopping for five minutes, repeatedly. Or you could just improvise. Jennifer's plan is to shoot Richard painting a plate in the Italian brushstroke style, something she's seen him do in about 30 minutes.

## Shaping the Raw Material

When you're done, you have a long, probably pretty boring clip of video. Congrats! The key to improving it is removing most of it and building a short (say, 60-second) version of the events of the day. To do this, you need to use video-editing software like iMovie.

**1**    Open the iMovie project **Start_Timelapse_Project7** in the Lesson07 folder.

Start_Timelapse_Project7

Inside all iMovie project folders lie three important items. Ignore the Media folder, the .mov file, and any other folders here, and focus on the iMovie project file (a document with a little star on it).

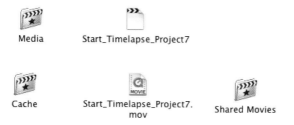

| Media | Start_Timelapse_Project7 |

| Cache | Start_Timelapse_Project7.mov | Shared Movies |

**2**    Double-click the project file **Start_Timelapse_Project7**.

The iMovie project included with this book will open. Unlike in the earlier iMovie lessons that used iPhoto for source material, your Clip pane will have a clip of video.

**3**    Click the clip in the Clip pane.

It will appear in the Viewer.

You can play the clip by clicking the Play button, or you can scan over the entire clip by dragging the playhead around in the Scrubber bar—the blue, horizontal segment beneath the Viewer window. You will explore this important region of the iMovie display in Lesson 8, but for now, just check it out from time to time.

**4**  Drag the clip to the workspace at the bottom of the screen.

The clip should pop into view.

**NOTE ►** As discussed in Lesson 6, the way shots are currently presented in your workspace is called Timeline view, represented by the clock icon. The alternative view is the Clip view, which presents each shot as a single frame, like a photograph. While Clip view is quite useful for some projects, it is less useful for this time-lapse project.

Timeline View button

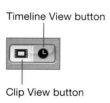

Clip View button

**5**  To scan through the clip, grab the playhead and drag it around in the timeline.

Notice that this also moves a playhead in the Scrubber bar under the Viewer. If you don't see a playhead, click in the ruler area to make it appear.

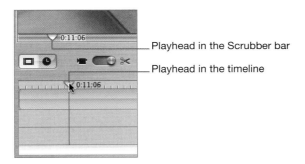

Playhead in the Scrubber bar

Playhead in the timeline

This gives you a relatively interesting vantage point from which to observe your time-lapse event: As you drag the playhead, the event zooms by before your eyes, the painting being created and erased as you move to the right and left.

**NOTE** ▶ One way to simulate a time-lapse experience is to take a long long video and speed it up. In iMovie 5, you can find this special effect under the Effect button. Speeding up video produces a rather comical, Keystone Kops look. Yet this effect isn't appropriate in every situation— in particular, it's not right for Jennifer's customers.

6   Turn off the sound by unchecking the sound check box to the right of the timeline.

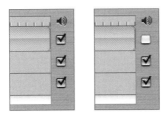

sound on (left); sound muted (right)

The audio is still part of the video, but it doesn't play. For most time-lapse videos, sound is not useful. Sound increases the reality of video, but this project is more surreal.

## Making Your First Cut

You're now going to experience the most fundamental way to edit video: chopping up a clip of video and tossing out the parts you don't want.

As a business owner, Jennifer doesn't have a lot of time for editing video. *Editing* is the art of cutting up video and making something interesting out of the pieces. Far simpler, and better suited to Jennifer's schedule, is simply cutting up video and throwing out the bits that aren't good. Actually, this isn't really editing; it's called *culling*. Jennifer culls all her video material. It's fast and easy. Making a time-lapse video is really just a specific method of culling videotape and looking for good bits.

Before you begin to cull Jennifer's video, here's a quick editing lesson: Whenever you chop up a piece of video, you should think of each cut you make as actually two cuts—the first indicates where a segment of the video will begin, and the second indicates where it will end. When you do this, you will have cut the original clip into three pieces (in order, left to right in the timeline): the material ahead of the section you liked, the section you liked, and the material after the section you liked.

But you don't always want to throw out the bits you don't use. There's plenty of good video in those "trimmings." Keep that in mind over the next few steps.

1   Start playing the time-lapse clip from the very beginning.

Don't think of this as watching your video, but rather as looking for where you want your video to start. If you want your video to start at the beginning of this clip (which makes sense with this video), then pretend you already made a chop right at the beginning and threw away the material you didn't need.

2   Look for a nice frame on which to end the first "shot."

You can stop anywhere in the clip by pressing the spacebar. You can advance forward or backward with the precision of one frame at a time by using the arrow keys on your keyboard.

NOTE ► When you make the transition from video consumer to video producer, one of the first skills you develop is the ability to separate yourself from your material. It may be video of your family, your company, or your vacation, but when you sit down to edit, you need to stop "watching" your video and start "looking at" it. You're looking for things in it, and observing how subjects on the screen move around. It's very different from watching (and enjoying) a video.

3 When you have the playhead at the spot where you want the shot to end, choose Edit > Split Video Clip at Playhead.

You can see the frame in the Viewer.

When you chop your video into pieces, you'll see that although none of them moves, the timeline shows that what had been one clip is now two.

And while this book doesn't delve into most keyboard shortcuts, the Split Video Clip at Playhead command is such an elemental part of cutting your video that its shortcut is critical to learn: Command-T. It's an important tool—perhaps the most important you will learn in this lesson. With this excellent chopper, you can cut, delete, and rearrange video with the power of a professional. You are going to see more sophisticated tools for editing—in iMovie as well as in professional-level software like Final Cut Express and Pro—but not much beats a good digital razor blade to simplify editing down to the basics.

**TIP** ▶ Command-T has many powerful uses in iMovie. In the Lesson 6 Sgraffito video, for instance, Jennifer used it to force a break in clips when she wanted a title to begin at someplace other than the start of a shot. By breaking any clip, a title could be added in the middle.

Each time Jennifer clicked Record (which creates the material between the jumps), she recorded for 10 or 20 seconds. As you roll through each segment she recorded, look for one 3- to 6-second clip.

Let's recap: Your video starts at the beginning of the big clip. You rolled a few seconds in and found a good place for the first shot to end, and you chopped it there. That defines the first shot.

**NOTE** ▶ In time-lapse video projects, you will find a rhythm between how long a shot is and how much time you cut out before the next shot. For this video, each shot seems to work when it is 3 to 6 seconds long. If shots are much longer, you start to lose the momentum in the time-lapse effect.

4   Keep rolling through your video from this point and look for the spot where you want the second shot to begin.

You will pass a *jump*—a place where Jennifer stopped the camera and then started it a little bit later. You don't want to see any of Jennifer's jumps in your finished project.

**5** When you find a good starting place for the next shot, make another chop (Command-T).

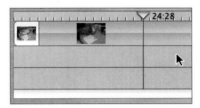

Now you have created three pieces of video: The first is the first shot; the middle one is basically garbage that you've decided you don't need; and the third is the remainder of the video.

**6** Select the middle piece (the one you don't want) and delete it.

It's a little hard to see in an illustration, but you just created a good jump. You threw out a snippet of video and have begun the process to reduce the 2½ minutes of video into something shorter and more interesting.

**7** Continue this process: From here, keep rolling through and find a good frame with which to end the second shot.

Again, keep it between 3 and 6 seconds long.

**NOTE** ▶ About two-thirds of the way through the video, Jennifer reposi-
tioned the camera—she zoomed in tighter. During a shoot, it's generally
never a good idea to move or zoom the camera in, but on long projects it
can sometimes work if you do it once (and only once).

Snip, snip, delete. Snip, snip, delete. Work through the whole source clip
until you reach the end. Your sequence should be about 60 seconds long,
with 13 individual shots.

One addition that makes the time-lapse video effect particularly striking is
to drop cross dissolves over every transition.

**8**   Add one-second cross dissolves between every pair of shots.

As described in Lesson 6, open the Trans window, select Cross Dissolve,
set the duration to :30, and then drag the Cross Dissolve icon onto each
transition in the timeline.

You'll have to zoom out to see the transitions.

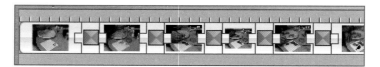

**NOTE** ▶ Once you've set the duration of the cross dissolve (or any transition effect), iMovie will default to this setting next time you select this
effect. Since in general you want to have consistent durations for these
kinds of transitions, it's a great feature.

**9**   Add a title card.

To do this, as you learned in Lesson 6, click the Titles button. From the Title
workspace make a simple, centered title card over black as the first shot in
the sequence. Jennifer's title reads *The Italian Brushstroke Technique.* (If you

really want to have fun, you can try some of the other title methods now
and see what each one does. But remember, particularly for Jennifer—who
uses her video in her business—simple is usually better.)

And now you (and Jennifer) have created a time-lapse video. If you'd like to
see Jennifer's finished project, check out **Finished_Timelapse_Project7** in the
Lesson07 folder. The setup and editing method you just practiced works for any
topic, not just painting ceramics. With a digital video camera and without any
complicated tricks in iMovie, you now know enough to cull any video as well
as a professional. In addition, you understand the fundamentals of iMovie and
editing well enough that expanding your skills will be easy.

## Using Your iSight Camera Instead of a Tripod

A time-lapse video is really nothing more than a video created from a single
camera shot, coming from a camcorder that is completely unmoving. If you
don't have a camcorder and a tripod, but do have an iSight camera on your
Mac, technically speaking, you have the same setup. If the iSight camera is
affixed to a laptop, you can shoot anywhere your Mac can go. Point it out a
window, at a construction site, whatever and wherever.

But even sitting at a desk, you can use an iSight camera combined with iMovie
and the techniques you learned to build a time-lapse video to create other
kinds of projects.

When Jennifer started her company a decade ago, she often set up a tripod
and camcorder and recorded her thoughts, her process, the setbacks and
accomplishments. If she had an iSight camera and iMovie, the process would
have been considerably easier (not scattered among dozens of old VHS tapes).
Charlie has decided to use his parents' setup to make a video journal for a
class project.

Because iMovie works with Apple's iSight camera as easily as it does with
iPhoto and iTunes, you can use this videoconferencing camera as a typical
video camera, and record the video and edit the results into a compelling
document.

**NOTE** ▶ A growing body of funsters are using iMovie and the iSight camera to shoot movies. Unlike recording to tape, the material you shoot with the camera goes right into the editing software in one step.

Charlie uses his parents' iSight setup on the family computer to keep a private series of thoughts on school and life.

**1**    Make sure your iSight camera is set up and working.

If you don't know how to use the iSight camera, use the Set-Up Assistant in iChat AV to establish the connections and make sure the camera is communicating properly. This isn't a required step for working with iMovie, but iChat is nicely equipped to walk you through the iSight connection.

**TIP** ▶ If you use iChat to make the connection, make sure you turn off iChat before you launch iMovie. You may have to quit iMovie and relaunch it, if you're already in that program. iMovie may not see the camera if you have iChat turned on.

iMovie has a switch that toggles between the input and editing of video. Whichever source is selected, the Viewer in iMovie displays video of that source.

The video-editing setting is the scissors, which has been the setting for the past few lessons.

**2**   Drag the switch to the left side—the camera—for inputting video.

If only the iSight camera is connected to your Mac, your one option with this mode will be to enable the camera—and you'll see just one option in the camera pull-down menu. You can access the option from the triangle on the left of the little camera icon.

**NOTE ▸** If, in addition to your iSight camera, a camcorder is connected to your Mac with a FireWire cable (and the camera is turned on and set to play back video), there will be a pair of options in the pull-down menu. Regardless, choose iSight.

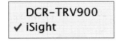

Once you've selected iSight, iMovie gets its raw material feed from a new source—and the video from the camera shows up in the Viewer.

**3**   To record the image you see, click the Record With iSight button above the grayed-out video shuttle controls.

Immediately, iMovie will go into recording mode, placing a new clip in the Clip pane and displaying the running time in seconds along the bottom of the clip while it records.

No need to panic that you're being recorded: The great thing about the mastering of editing techniques is that you now can get rid of video you don't like (particularly if you find it unflattering).

**4** When you're done recording, click Record With iSight again.

This ends the recording. Now you have a clip in iMovie that is ready to edit like any video clip.

Charlie kept a daily journal about the events in his home; he also used stills and video he shot around his house and neighborhood to intercut with this journal material. After a few weeks of recording and a day of editing, he presented a short documentary to his class.

## What You've Learned

▶  To set up a camera for a time-lapse video, you need a tripod and a remote control.

▶  Use Command-T to chop up a clip in iMovie.

▶  When you chop up a piece of video, always think of it as creating three pieces with two cuts—the piece ahead of the clip you like, the clip you like, and the piece that trails the clip you like.

▶  To create the time-lapse effect, simply delete the pieces you don't like.

▶  The time-lapse effect works best with 1-second cross dissolves between clips.

▶  Use your iSight camera as a source for making videos; if the camera is attached to your Mac, then the video is comparable to the time-lapse video in terms of how you might edit it.

# 8

**Lesson Files**    Lessons > Lesson08 > Start_QuickVideo_Project8

Lessons > Lesson08 > Example_BizOwnerVideo.alias

**Tools**    iMovie

**Time**    Approximately 60 minutes

**Goals**    Learn how shooting video and editing video are part of a single process

Learn basic camera functions and how to shoot properly

Learn to recognize video material that's suited for editing

Understand how to get video from a camcorder into iMovie

Trim and arrange shots in iMovie

See how to make a very basic video

# Shooting and Assembling a Very Simple Movie

You started working with still images in the early lessons of this book, moved on to dynamic still images, and then explored culling video. Now you'll make an important transition to *editing* video.

Up to this point, you used the editing tools in iMovie to cut up raw material and throw out parts you didn't want, but you maintained shots in the timeline according to the order in which you shot them. You also treated the segments you liked as if they were slides—discrete elements to be shortened or lengthened, but ultimately almost like still images. Now you will see how an editor uses different portions of a single video shot to build structure. To tell a story, you will rearrange the order of video clips, which will likely have no relationship to the order in which they were shot. This is the essence of editing, and it's important to understand before digging deeper into Hollywood-style shooting (as you'll do in Lesson 10) and editing (Lesson 11).

Having built a slide show from a series of static shots with Christopher, and then following along with Jennifer as she turned her still images into a more dynamic presentation using iMovie, you might start to wonder if it's worth the extra effort to use video. But video has properties you just can't get from a dynamic slide show. Partly because of the power of sound, a video is more "real" and possibly more personal. Also, video allows you to see the way people behave and interact with more subtlety. Finally, by using cinematic techniques to gather elements and put them together, you have more power to convey emotion and direct the viewer's experience.

Once you have command over both stills and video, using iPhoto *and* iMovie, you'll become a far more sophisticated media creator—with a range of options for any given project.

This lesson is a quick introduction by Christopher to the language of Hollywood filmmaking. By seeing how shooting and editing work together, and how you can impart emotion to the viewer through your work as a director and editor, a world of high-quality personal videos opens up. Then, in subsequent lessons, you'll be ready to acquire skills that can be applied to everything from your first school project to a feature film debuting at a prestigious festival.

## A New Way to Think About Video

There's an important distinction between the video that you *shoot* and a video that you *make*. You probably don't need a lesson to shoot with your camcorder. But making videos is an entirely different beast. Jennifer tends to shoot with her camcorder as if it were a still camera. Her video looks good, but she'd be hard-pressed to *make* something out of it. Christopher understands that shooting is his opportunity to get some raw materials with which to build. And like building a house, it's not enough to have lots of materials; rather, you need the right pieces to fit together.

Think of making a video as the union of two distinct tasks: shooting and editing. Camera plus computer. Professionals call this duo *production* and *postproduction.* Any way you slice it, a video is both of these in tandem.

Everything you do—before, during, and after shooting—needs to all fit together. For instance, a video recording of 30 minutes will require 6 GB of free hard disk space on your Mac. It's hard to think of the video you shoot without considering the consequences on your computer. And if you have only a few hours to dedicate to a project, small increases in how much you record explode into considerably more work when you edit. Labeling tapes properly and keeping records of what's on each one is work you do long before you get to your computer, but ultimately it will save hours when you're ready to make a video.

Consequently, "video" is a process—a series of interlocking activities. Until you have some perspective on the entire arc, it's hard to focus on any one part.

## Organizing Your Video

Following the most basic rules of organization will make everything else you do in video streamlined and manageable. Nothing is worse than knowing you shot something important but being utterly stumped when you try to find it. Not remembering what tape has that perfect sunrise shot, for instance, or shuttling aimlessly back and forth between tapes trying to guess, is enough to keep anyone from enjoying the process.

Label your tapes. Period. There is no substitute for this rule. Label them and, after they are shot, sit down for an enjoyable romp watching them. While watching, make notes about what's on the tape using a paper *log sheet,* one for each videocassette. Labeling your cassettes and keeping log sheets is important if you ever hope to find material you shoot.

Right after you buy a digital videocassette, take it out of the wrapper, put the enclosed blank label on the cassette, and number it—starting with 1 and counting from there. You can add other info if you'd like, but the unique tape number is critical. You don't want three cassettes labeled *24*.

**TIP** ▶ You could use just a number (1, 2, 3…), but if you plan on doing lots of video editing, you may want to differentiate between the tapes you shoot in your camera and the tapes onto which you record finished video from your Mac. In that case, use a letter before the number: S for a tape you shoot and F for a tape containing final video. (Alternately, you could pick any logical letters; professionals use M for the master tape that final videos go onto.)

Then print out a blank tape log sheet (a version is online at www.nonlinear. info/dv/log.pdf) and write the tape number at the top and information about what's on the tape below. If you keep all your tape log sheets together in a folder or binder, you'll never lose track of a great shot—and even if you never edit your tapes, you'll be able to grab one on a whim and watch something you know you'll enjoy.

Without this organization strategy, in no time you'll have a dusty box of unlabeled or poorly identified cassettes with nary a clue as to what's on most of them.

Good tape-logging style

**TIP** ▸ The numbers that keep track of the frames on a videotape are called timecode and are important in keeping accurate log sheets. If no number is already on the tape when you start recording, the camera starts at 00 and adds numbers while you shoot. Then the number increases incrementally, 30 frames every second, ultimately counting seconds, minutes, and hours.

Timecode is almost always presented in the top-right corner of your videotape. Camcorders can turn the display of the timecode on or off, but even if you can't see it, every frame has a number. As you get more comfortable with video and your camcorder, you will learn how to keep that number from ever jumping back to 00 in the middle of a tape. If you can keep this timecode continuous, ascending, and unbroken for an entire tape, a world of easy organization opens up to you. You can work without timecode, but if you do lots of video, it's a valuable reference, allowing you to jot down the number on your log sheet along with a description of the shot. It will greatly help you find shots quickly. For more information on video organization, check out *The Little Digital Video Book* (Peachpit Press, 2001).

## Getting to Know Your Digital Camcorder

For this section of the lesson, break out your camcorder. Get a cassette, label it, and load it. Now you're ready to shoot. Put the camcorder in your hand and notice where your fingers naturally fall on the body of the device. There are three primary controls on the camcorder that you'll rely on almost exclusively while shooting video: the shooting/playback switch, the Record button, and Zoom. Follow along to get familiar with these controls.

1   Turn on your camcorder.

This may not be as straightforward as it sounds. There generally isn't going to be an on/off button, but rather a swivel switch that powers up the camera and engages one of a number of selected settings. There's probably not a single name for this thing, but we'll call it the shooting/playback switch. This toggles the camcorder from video recording to video playback. (It may do a few other things, but ignore those for now.) The switch is usually very near the red Record button.

**2**   Find the Record button.

It's almost always a little red button under your thumb. When you press it once, it starts recording. Press it again and it stops.

**TIP** ▶ The camera may beep when it starts and stops recording. There may also be a small red light near the lens that flashes while recording. Both of these features are great when you're starting out but may be distracting later on. Most camcorders let you turn off these features, but the method is usually buried in the onscreen menus. Check your manual if you want to adjust them.

**3**   Find the zoom control.

On smaller camcorders, it's sometimes a little knobby thing on the side or top edge; on larger camcorders, it might be a rocker switch. Either way, the control is (or should be) under your index finger.

**4** Adjust the straps on your camera to put your fingers in as natural a position as possible for recording and zooming.

You don't want to have to look for either of these functions. Finding the shooting/playback switch does not need to be as quick, although you do want to be able to turn your camera on (by switching to shooting) with little trouble.

In addition to these three controls, there's always an LCD screen, hinged to the left side of the camcorder and ranging from tiny (1.5" diagonally) to *grande* (3.5" diagonally). Larger is more useful, perhaps, but it makes for a larger and heavier camera, and tends to demand more battery power to use—so find the trade-off that works for you.

Using a camcorder is usually a two-handed affair. One hand, your right, goes through the strap and is poised over the Record button and the zoom control. Your left hand is purely for stabilization. This is not a minor task. Use your left hand to steady the camera, either by lightly holding the extended LCD or gripping the camera body. Keep your elbows pulled in tight, and for heaven's sake, don't move.

## Shooting Video

Now you have a camcorder in your hands and under control. You need to shoot something. At this stage it doesn't matter what you shoot; you just need to get some footage on tape.

A good starting point that will illustrate some shooting basics is a simple personal portrait.

**1**   Record 5 seconds of black.

Before you start any project, it is good form to record a few seconds of black—of nothing (the floor, the lens cap, your hand). With a new video-cassette, this gets the tape to roll away from the head; for a variety of technical reasons, material at the very beginning of a tape is hard to use. This trick has the added benefit of providing a very clear demarcation of where a particular scene begins. When you're watching the videotape on fast-forward, the black gap gives you a cue that something new is about to start.

**2**   Record three unique shots of where you are right now.

Each should be about five seconds long. The first shot should show the audience where you are located. In a classroom? At home at a desk? Lying in bed? The second shot should tell us something about who you are. What personal items are with you? What sets you apart from the next person? And the third shot should represent what you're doing at the moment. Reading a book? Snacking?

Make the shots very different from each other. Each should be unique. Practice holding still while you shoot. Practice using the composition rules you learned from still photography.

**3**   When you're done with your shots, record another few seconds of black.

**4**   Switch your camcorder from camera mode to playback mode (sometimes labeled VCR or VTR).

Shuttle controls—those familiar play, fast-forward, and rewind buttons—should appear on your camera somewhere (maybe on the LCD, maybe on the body).

**5**    Rewind the tape to the beginning.

**6**    Play the tape and watch it on the LCD screen.

Notice the counting number on the top right of the LCD. That is your timecode number. It starts at 00:00 and counts seconds and frames. Timecode is really useful for locating shots on your tape.

**7**    Stop the camera when your last shot concludes and the black rolls into view.

You always want to stop your camera on the black and never let it roll into the "blue" area. If you do this consistently, the timecode counter on the tape will never reset to zero, and every shot on the tape will have a unique (and thus useful) number.

Now that you've got some video recorded, it's time to put it into iMovie. You can follow along with your video, but I'll use Christopher's video to demonstrate.

### Keep Video Short

The example you're about to see from Christopher, and probably the video you just shot, is quite short. When you create your own videos independently of this book, keep in mind that digital video consumes a lot of hard disk space even though the image quality is actually inferior to that of the poorest digital still-camera image. The reason video requires so much space is that it comprises many quickly moving still frames (just like film). A second of video is made of 30 discrete frames; even at low quality, that's an awful lot of images to be stored. A video clip of 5 minutes takes up a gigabyte on your hard disk. In other words, that 60-minute tape you shot at the party, if copied into your Mac, is going to fill up 12 GB of space.

Because of this (and other factors), start by keeping your video projects limited: Shoot fewer than 20 minutes of video for anything you intend to edit. This not only will save precious hard disk space, but also will keep the project relatively short and manageable.

## Getting Video into iMovie

Unlike iPhoto, iMovie doesn't automatically import your video when you plug in your camcorder. Still, it's pretty easy. In Lesson 7, you saw how iMovie can get video from the iSight camera; it's just as easy to get video from your digital camcorder.

**1**  Plug your camcorder into your Mac with a FireWire cable.

 FireWire is the standard type of computer connection for digital video (and other high-bandwidth computer connections). Its technical name is IEEE 1394, but it's also referred to as i.Link, Sony's brand name.

 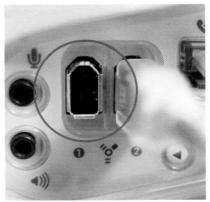

FireWire jacks: A 4-pin jack on a digital camcorder (left); and a 6-pin jack on the back of a Mac (right)

At each end of your FireWire cable is a different type of connector. The tiny one, which tends to plug into a camcorder, is a *4-pin connector*. The big one is shaped like a D and is called a *6-pin connector*. A 4-pin-to-6-pin FireWire cable, then, is the essential link between camcorder and Mac.

FireWire connectors: The smaller 4-pin side (left) and the D-shaped 6-pin side (right)

**NOTE** ▶ The common connector between a Mac and an external hard drive is a 6-pin-to-6-pin FireWire cable.

2   Make sure your camcorder is turned on and set to play back your tape.

That setting is probably labeled something like VCR; it's often a switch located near the red Record button on the back of the camera.

**3**  In iMovie, change the mode from editing (the scissors) to capturing video
(the camera).

If you have an iSight camera plugged in, you'll need to select your camcorder from the pull-down menu under the camera icon. If not, just
switch it to the left.

Now iMovie is looking at, and controlling, your camcorder.

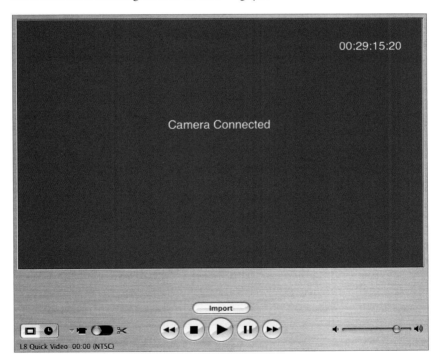

4   If you click the big Play arrow under the display, your tape will start rolling, and you can watch it on your Mac.

5   Click Stop (the square).

The tape stops and the screen goes blue.

6   Click the Rewind button onscreen.

The camera goes into a fast rewind. (If you click Play and then hold down the Rewind button, it will go into slow rewind, and you can watch the video onscreen.)

You'll also see a number on the top of the display in iMovie—this matches the timecode number on the videotape and should help you locate where you want to be, provided you're using timecode to keep yourself organized.

Christopher got home after the party and rewound his tape just to the point where he started recording that morning. Then he clicked Play to watch it. Of course, if you're going to take the time to watch a tape, you've got the time to import it.

**7**   When the tape is rolling and you find the beginning of the material you want to put in your Mac, click Import.

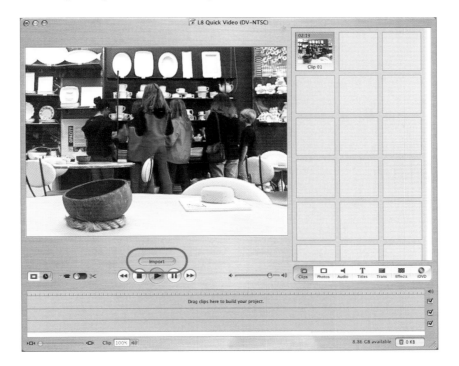

**TIP**   For most video you shoot, import the entire bunch of material you will use for editing, and avoid starting and stopping the import process to find small bits you think you want to edit. By grabbing all the video in one big chunk (or at one time), you save a great deal of wear and tear on rather fragile consumer camcorders. Getting everything in the computer has the additional benefit of sometimes revealing small gems of video that you might have missed if you imported discrete moments from your tapes.

Again, as you saw in Lesson 7, the video you import immediately shows up in the Clip pane. iMovie is pretty smart about video playing from a tape. Whenever it "sees" that you stopped the camera and started recording again—even though there is no discernible break in the picture on the tape—it ends one clip and starts making another. (This works only if you have already set the date and time on your camcorder.) This is usually very useful (although in Lesson 11, you'll learn when it's not as useful). For Christopher's video—just like yours—he started and stopped his camcorder three times, and so there are three clips in the Clip pane.

NOTE ▶ Funny thing: Getting digital content into a given application is generally known as *importing*. Still, tradition tends to confer other names to this process. Getting songs into a computer is sometimes called *ripping*. Getting video into a computer is often called *capturing*. Truth is, the words all mean the same thing.

## Getting the Right Shots

For this part of the lesson, close the iMovie project you created to import your clips. You're going to use material Christopher and Jennifer have shot to explore principles of shooting and editing.

The bits of video you need for movie editing are called *coverage*. You need a certain minimum of coverage to have video elements you can edit. There is also such a thing as too much coverage—dozens of shots from dozens of angles. It can be too much to manage and makes for hard-to-watch videos. Simple shooting not only makes sense, but it's also pretty much the most professional approach to a video project. In this lesson, you'll witness the minimum of necessary coverage and see how potent it is for editing.

**1**   Open Lesson08 > **Example_BizOwnerVideo.alias.**

(The alias is linked to the project in Lesson13 > Start_BizVideo_Lesson13 > **BizOwnerVideo.**)

Some still images from Jennifer's studio videotape

**2**   Click the shot in the Clip pane and watch the few minutes of video that Jennifer shot in her studio.

She used her camcorder with good technique. She framed shots with nice composition in mind. She followed good videography rules—she held the camera steady and didn't use the zoom (much). But the shots are little more than moving stills. Each is nice, but few have any relationship to each other. And while they might be assembled in some clever way to give you the feeling of being in the studio (with the sound adding an important element), they're not the right pieces for editing.

The problem with Jennifer's video is that she had no agenda when she shot it. She just pointed the camera at whatever interested her. So, what she ended up with is a slide show of moving pictures. You'll need to go further and gather specific *kinds* of shots, shots that will go together neatly when you edit the video.

The secret, then, of making videos good and creating them easily does not lie in knowing how to edit, and it doesn't lie in good videography. The secret is in shooting *holistically,* which means always keeping the eventual editing in mind.

In Hollywood, a scene is set up, and the director shoots it a number of times from a number of angles. By having different shots of the same subjects doing the same things, an editor can assemble that material in ways that have great impact. It doesn't take too many shots to get the material you need to do this. And you don't need to have actors with scripts. Almost any event in the real world has a natural kind of repetitiveness to it, and you can leverage this by moving decisively into specific positions, gathering up the bits of video you need to make the video.

## Getting Shots with Relationships

Instead of shooting a series of interesting shots with your camcorder, think of every shot as having some kind of relationship to at least one other shot. If you shoot someone from far off, your next shot should be the same person from closer. If you shoot someone from the front, think about also shooting them from the back. If you show someone reading a book, show the audience what they are reading. Whatever you do, get a minimum of two shots that relate; you will use these when you go to edit.

Having relationships between shots highlights one of the most significant differences between video projects and still-image projects. With a still camera, you pick it up and shoot once in a while. You might shoot bits and pieces throughout an event. With video, you want to pick up the camcorder and shoot one scene, getting proper coverage from multiple angles, and then be done with it. You're not going to try to shoot many bits of lots of different scenes, but lots of shots of one scene.

Have a look at the video for this lesson, Start_QuickVideo_Project8 > **L8 Quick Video**, in the Lesson08 folder. This is an iMovie project that Christopher is working on. He shot a couple of minutes of the girls trying to find the ceramics they wanted to paint.

If he were using a still camera, this moment might have been condensed to a single shot, probably not even an interesting shot. But in video, he can expand the moment and begin to show their interactions, moods, and dynamics. For the audience, he can also make it compelling by creating bits of interest, maybe even suspense. Video makes this possible.

Notice there are three shots in iMovie, three distinct vantage points of the same event. More than anything else, this is the key to making videos.

## What Editing Does to Video

Even though you have only three clips in your Clip pane, you have ample coverage to make a short movie. (Actually, it will be less a movie and more what is called a sketch.) The traditional way to approach iMovie is largely clip-based, meaning the program is designed for you to drop clips of video into your workspace, drag them around until they are in the right order, and trim their length so they don't bore people. While this is a perfectly legitimate way to approach your video, it misses both the power and fun of editing, so you won't do that here. You will take three shots and cut them up into lots of smaller pieces. By arranging the pieces, you can control the viewer's experience.

As you look at Christopher's video, instead of seeing three clips in the Clip pane that need shortening and organizing, recognize his video as 2 minutes of raw footage taken from three vantage points.

### Trimming and Arranging Your Footage

The methods Christopher uses to edit his short video are precisely the same ones Jennifer used when she edited the time-lapse video. In short, use the Command-T function to chop the shots into pieces, and then select the pieces you like and put them in order. The difference here is that the order of shots is highly subjective. (The time-lapse material presumably has to appear in the order in which it was shot.)

How do you start? With a wide shot, to establish where the girls are?

Wide shot, back view

Or the close-up shot, showing some odd activity but not yet revealing who is there or where they are?

Close-up shot of hands and ceramics

Or the medium shot, clearly showing what the girls are doing, full of personality but in some ways ordinary?

Medium shot, side view

Your role as a director is to get the bits of coverage you need. But your role as the editor of this video is to make the hard decisions about how to tell the story.

We'll see how Christopher made his choices—but you should realize there are no right or wrong answers. The problems you face here have many solutions.

**1**    Select the wide shot and begin watching it in the Viewer.

The wide shot serves to establish where the scene is taking place, and has the benefit of creating a little mystery: Here's where they are, but what are they doing?

**2**    Use the Scrubber bar region and drag the playhead forward and backward until you see the moment you like.

When you come to a 3- or 4-second region where it seems the action is interesting and the camera is steady, back up and find a good place for the clip to start.

Christopher found a spot around 9 seconds into the clip. The actual count, in seconds and frames, is inscribed in the Scrubber bar near the playhead.

**3**  Use Command-T to break the clip, once you're stopped on the place you want your shot to start.

Notice what happens in the Clip pane when you use Command-T before you've added the shot to your workspace: The original clip is split into two pieces, and both remain in the Clip pane (and are highlighted in blue). The first segment has the original name; the second has the original name with an appended *1*: Wideshot/1.

**4**  Keep playing the Wideshot clip until you find a good ending point.

With both shots still selected, they play together in the Viewer as if they weren't chopped up, although you can see the split point if you look carefully. Use your best judgment as to where to end the clip, but the completed shot should be only a few seconds long. Christopher's is about 4 seconds.

**5**  Use Command-T to break the Wideshot clip again.

The first part, then, is the trimmed-off bit at the head end. The second part (Wideshot/1) is the "good" bit. And the third part (Wideshot/2) is the trimming at the tail. You don't want to delete these pieces yet, since you might need them later.

**NOTE ►** Be careful when you drag clips from the Clip pane to the workspace—particularly after you've chopped them up with Command-T. All the bits are still selected (highlighted in blue), and when you click and drag one, you may be inadvertently dragging them all. One of the greatest challenges when starting out in iMovie is keeping an eye on what shots are selected—both in the Clip pane and in the workspace—as you play, delete, and rearrange.

If one clip is highlighted in the workspace and you click Play, only that clip will play. If you want to play an entire sequence, you need to select either all the clips or none of them.

**TIP ►** Wide shots generally need to be onscreen a little longer than close-up shots in order for the audience to have time to "read" the image. There's a lot of detail in a wide shot, and it takes a few moments to look the frame over and satiate that need to know where you are, who is here, what is happening. A length of 4 or 5 seconds is usually better than one to three seconds.

**6**  Now that you've diced up the wide shot into a good piece and some trim-mings, drag the good piece into your workspace.

This will be the first shot in your sequence.

It doesn't matter if your workspace is set to Clip view or Timeline view; you'll see the clip there (highlighted in blue). For now, set the workspace to Clip view.

**7**  Perform the same technique on the MS Side clip, finding a good few seconds in the middle—where you like the action and the camera work feels solid.

**8**  And finally, do it again with the CU Cutaway clip.

There's lots of visually interesting images of hands and activity in this 45-second shot. Find a nice 3 seconds and place it after the MS Side clip by dragging it from the Clip pane to the workspace.

In Clip view, the three shots look like this. Watch them in the Viewer.

Sometimes it's easier to watch clips and orient yourself in a video by switching to Timeline view and dragging the playhead around to watch a video. You can immediately cue to the first frame of your sequence by clicking the Cue to Head button before you click Play. You can also choose to watch your video full-screen (rather than in the Viewer) by clicking the Play Fullscreen button (to the right of Play).

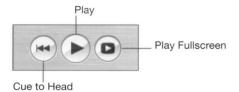

In a way, you're done. You've taken your three shots, found the best moments, and assembled them. If you wanted to, you could click and drag the shots around in Clip view to see if you could improve their order—perhaps starting with the close-up shot, then going to the medium shot, and finally ending with the wide shot. iMovie makes it very simple to shuffle shots in this way. But as you now know, this isn't really the heart of editing. To edit, you must listen to your gut, and Christopher's gut is saying, "The event I witnessed was much more than this 11 seconds reveals. The event I was shooting was sillier, stranger, longer…"

To accomplish this, you must go back to the raw material—the trimmed-off bits that you didn't use at first, and find more interesting moments.

9   Go back to the Clip pane, and start watching the MS Side/2 clip.

It has lots of interesting interactions between the girls. Christopher found another moment he likes around 5 seconds in.

10  Using Command-T again, chop out this bit (iMovie creates more new
    bits—MS Side/3 and MS Side/4; MS Side/3 is the one you want) and move
    it to the workspace.

    Similarly, there were other good moments in the CU Cutaway shot.

11  Review the pair of trims in the Clip pane, find a few more seconds of nice
    material, and, using Command-T, chop up the piece you like and drag the
    "moment" to the workspace after the last shot.

So now the sequence is about 17 seconds long. It begins wide, to establish
where the girls are, then has a typical Hollywood A-B-A-B back-and-forth
rhythm, which comes up often in editing. (You'll explore this in detail in
Lesson 11.) But it needs an ending. This A-B-A-B thing could go on all
day, or at least until you run out of material.

A good way to end a short scene like this is with another wide shot, to let
the audience back away from the action and take it all in. But after watching this sequence a few times, Christopher decides that the opening is
weak. Preferring to keep the viewer in suspense a little bit, he decides to
move the first shot to the end.

**12** Drag the first shot to the end of the sequence of shots.

Notice that when you move it, all the other shots slide around to accommodate the change.

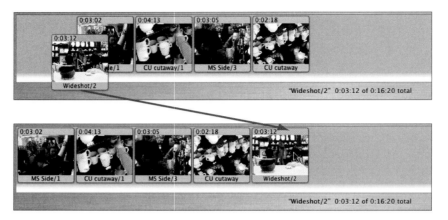

This is better, but Christopher experiments with some other arrangements of these shots, as should you. Opening, for instance, with the close-up (that is, moving the fourth shot to the beginning) is another interesting way to organize it. Truly there is no right answer.

What becomes apparent is that the opening shot must be much longer than the others. Whether close-up or wide or medium, it needs to play long enough for the viewers to settle in, get some kind of orientation for themselves, and be able to look around at what is happening. A few seconds (even three) isn't enough for this. Five seconds is more appropriate.

## Modifying Shots in Your Timeline

For much of your editing work, you will alternate between the Clip view and the Timeline view of your sequence. Moving shots around is easy in both the Clip view and the Timeline view; seeing relative lengths and playing from some spot in the middle of the sequence is easier in Timeline view. You can modify shots only from within Timeline view. When you're in this view, your pointer turns into a special (and powerful) trimming tool that allows you to adjust where shots begin and end, even after they're in the timeline. The Trim tool lets you not only shorten shots, but also lengthen them.

In the present configuration of shots (medium, close-up, medium, close-up, wide) Christopher wants to make the first shot—the medium shot—longer. The Clip view says it's 3 seconds, 2 frames long. The timeline shows it to be roughly the same length as the others. The timeline isn't as pretty a view of your work, but it's exceptionally functional.

> **TIP** ▶ If you want to see your whole sequence but can't, don't forget that you can use the Zoom slider to change the scale of the timeline. When it's all the way to the left, you will see your entire sequence, regardless of how long it is or how many clips you have. If you need to zoom in closer in order to work, use the scroll bar along the bottom of the timeline.

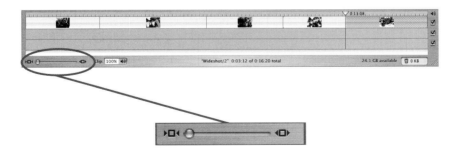

NOTE ▶ You might be interested to learn that the Timeline view is the only view that professionals use when working in Final Cut Pro and Final Cut Express (more on why in Lesson 11).

1    Select the first shot.

It will be highlighted in blue.

2    Move your pointer to the end of the first shot.

It will turn into a bar with arrows on both sides—this is the Trim tool.

3    Click and drag to the right.

This will extend the selected shot until you let go. The new duration of the shot is displayed in the ruler portion of the timeline.

Watch the frames you are adding in the Viewer above. Use the Viewer to help identify the frame on which you want to end this shot.

**NOTE** ▶ If you look closely, you may notice that in the timeline, shots that cannot be lengthened (because they are pieces that include either the beginning or ending of the original shot) have rounded corners.

No more can be added to the end of this shot.

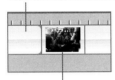

More material can be added to the beginning of this shot.

Using the Trim tool, you can extend or shorten any shot in your sequence. It is just the tool for tweaking those extra few frames from a piece that is too long, or clipping out a blip of something you don't want to see.

**NOTE** ▶ In the language of editors, this is called *nondestructive editing*. It means that when you cut up material and move the bits around, you aren't really cutting up or throwing out anything—you're only looking at a select piece of a larger whole, as if you were viewing the original video clip through a small window. Because of this, iMovie gives you instant access to the material you didn't use in your clips without having to go "get" it from somewhere else. It's always magically hanging around the edges of your clips in the timeline.

Without switching back to the Clip view, Christopher easily rearranges some of the shots to experiment with making the short video more dramatic.

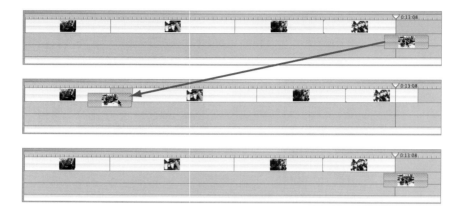

Christopher's sequence is about 20 seconds long. He added a 1-second fade in at the start and a 1-second fade out at the end, and is ready to move on to more challenging scenes with more complicated kinds of coverage. You can watch a QuickTime movie of Christopher's short sketch called **Finished_QuickVideo.mov** in the Lesson08 folder.

## What You've Learned

▶ Shooting and editing are interwoven, and they work together to make videos.

▶ Connect your camcorder to your Mac with a 4-pin-to-6-pin FireWire cable.

▶ Use the camera/scissors toggle switch to move from controlling a camcorder—for importing or just playing—to manipulating shots within iMovie.

► When your camcorder is in playback mode, you can control it from inside iMovie—playing, rewinding, and reviewing using the shuttle controls.

► When you want to move video from a tape in the camcorder into iMovie, click Import. The resulting clip or clips will end up in the Clip pane.

► You need to shoot at least two different angles on any action you are videotaping if you intend to edit it. This material is called *coverage*.

► The two angles should have a special relationship to each other—close-up/far off, in front/behind, someone looking at something/the object they are looking at.

► With even a minimum of coverage, you can use basic editing techniques to build a small story in iMovie.

► Command-T chops up bits of raw material in the Clip pane.

► Drag clips to the workspace to arrange them in the order you want.

► Use the Trim tool to extend or shorten shots in the timeline.

# 9

## Lesson Files
Lessons > Lesson09 > Start_Birthday_Project9

## Tools
iMovie, camcorder (optional)

## Time
Approximately 90 minutes

## Goals
Use your camcorder as a microphone to record audio interviews

Think of a finished video as having two distinct elements—pictures and sound—that can be managed independently

Separate the sound portion from the picture of a video clip in iMovie, and work with sound on a separate track

Use the Mac's built-in microphone to record narration while you're editing your iMovie

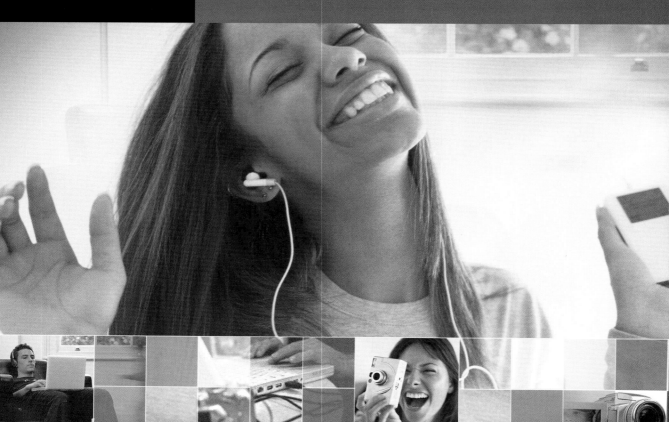

# Adding Narration to Your Dynamic Slide Show

Part of what makes projects interesting is using sound creatively. This might mean adding music to a slide show in iPhoto or sound effects and narration to a video in iMovie. There are many kinds of sounds (often categorized by professionals as dialogue, music, and effects) that combine to make a finished sound track. Like photography, sound is a specialty unto itself.

Unfortunately, sound can be really difficult to manage on your camcorder if you try to do it while you're shooting video. The built-in microphone is *omnidirectional,* which means it picks up sounds from everywhere around you while you record, resulting in a lot of unwanted noises. Also, because you shoot from a number of different positions—moving close to and far away from your subjects, starting and stopping the camera between shots—getting a consistent stream of audio is almost impossible.

If these challenges weren't bad enough, the results of poor audio make for really poor videos. For some psychophysical reason, bad-quality video looks better with good sound, and, amazingly, good-quality video looks worse with bad sound. Many factors go into what constitutes good sound: clear voices that are distinct from background noises; proper relative volume of speech and other elements of the picture; a rich tapestry of sounds to add texture and emotion to the video.

Because it's so hard to get good-quality sound from the camera's microphone while you shoot video, the fastest way to get good sound in your finished projects is to ignore most of the audio from your shoot and instead use music from a professionally created CD. Your video will benefit from the great production value of someone else's work. But if you want *production sound*—that is, the sound that's going on while you're shooting the video—it takes more effort. You need to use additional microphones and have someone carefully monitor how everything sounds while it's being recorded. For people like Charlie, Jennifer, and Christopher, this adds too much complexity, demands too much equipment, and probably requires too much work.

There are alternatives. You can use your camcorder not only as a digital video recorder but also as a digital audio recorder. And your Mac itself has a built-in microphone. With these handy audio tools and a little basic information, you can add professional-quality sound (and thus professional-quality production values) to your dynamic slide shows and, ultimately, your videos.

In this lesson, you'll revisit Christopher's dynamic slide show from the birthday party. Adding music as you originally did was an excellent option to create a sound track. Now you will take interviews Christopher recorded during the party and make a narration track with them. Later you'll check in with Charlie and see other narration alternatives that iMovie provides for his simple school report.

## Using Your Camcorder as a Microphone

Put the lens cap on your digital video camcorder. For the moment, forget that this small gadget shoots video. Instead, look around the body of the device and find the microphone. Every camcorder has one. While it may be hard to find, it should look something like the classic microphones you've seen before; maybe it's got a black or silver mesh over a little area toward the top or front of the camcorder. If you can't find it, check your manual.

Now, instead of shooting video, hold the camera in such a way that you can press the Record button while holding the microphone a few inches from the sound or person you want to record.

**TIP** ▶ If you're having difficulty knowing whether you're recording, you can keep the LCD flip screen open so you can see the red dot indicating that recording is under way.

Recording audio while you're shooting video can be extremely challenging for at least a couple of reasons. One is that every time you move to get a different shot, your distance to the source of sound changes significantly. When you record audio while shooting video, the microphone tends to take a backseat to the lens. The problem isn't the technology; it's just the nature of shooting video. Move away for a wide shot, and the microphone can't pick up any talking. Move close for a detail shot, and the voices boom. Using this sound is exceptionally difficult for technical reasons.

Another reason that it's quite challenging to record sound and video at the same time is because it's no small feat to record interesting conversation. When you really listen to it dispassionately, even enjoyable conversations are unbearably dull. You might have expected to record a fun bit of conversation, but it goes on and on, with no beginning and no end, and only a long stream of sound. Our brain fools us into thinking conversations are discrete and finite—when in truth they are very slow, very repetitive, and often missing key words or using half thoughts. Even with great tools and lots of practice, when you try to record one, you still end up missing parts; it's hard to capture the entire thing.

To circumvent the challenges of recording a conversation in video and audio at the same time, shoot video for the picture part first, and later record audio. That way you can focus specifically on the goal of getting good sound, and you have a better chance of getting the raw materials required to make high-quality product.

Christopher wants to record some of the endearing things his daughter and her friends are talking about at her 12th birthday party. But instead of shooting video and concentrating on the sound at the same time, Christopher concentrates solely on getting the images he needs to edit. Then, at some later point in the event, he makes a mental shift—using the camcorder only as a microphone to interview the girls, asking questions, eavesdropping a little, intently listening to the sounds of the event.

Using the camcorder as a microphone has many advantages, in addition to those just described. In the first place, there is something far less invasive about a microphone than a camcorder. People act differently when a lens is pointed at them. While they still might be a little uptight with you holding out a microphone (even one shaped like a camera!), they do tend to relax once you're making eye contact and standing closer—both possible now that the camera isn't in front of your face.

> **TIP** Keeping the lens cap on the camera tends to help disarm your subjects, for some reason. Anything you can do to help your subject relax will result in a better recording (audio as well as video).

Christopher holds the microphone about an inch or two from the mouth of whoever is speaking. This guarantees the voice will be very clear and much louder than any of the background sounds in the room. While it's always challenging to record people (as luck would have it, people always seem to be their funniest when you're talking to someone else, and the microphone is so far away you can barely hear them), holding a camcorder like a microphone is a direct and easy way to get live sound.

## Using Audio in iMovie

Once Christopher has recorded a few minutes of interviews, he could go back to shooting video or consider himself done. But Christopher isn't going to be making a video at all; instead, he wants to use the camcorder to get a few minutes of audio to add to his dynamic slide show.

**1**   Open the **Birthday Party** file in the Lesson09 > Start_Birthday_Project09 folder.

You may recognize this as the finished state of the dynamic slide show Christopher created in Lesson 6. In that project, it was easy to add music from a CD to give the video a finished feeling. But that outcome is very different from the result he gets by using the sound from the real event.

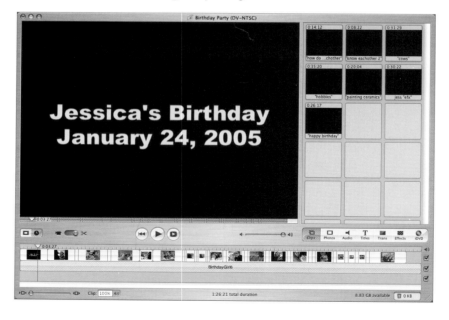

**NOTE** ▶ With interviews instead of music, a product changes from a "music video" into a "documentary."

**2**   Delete the music in the audio track by selecting it and pressing Delete on your keyboard.

The sound was fine before, but it's not required now.

**NOTE ▶** You could just mute the music track by unselecting the audio box on the far right of the timeline. But visualizing the work you'll be doing here is a little easier if the music is gone. So, the lesson will proceed with the music deleted even if you decide you'd like to keep it and mix it at the end.

Look at the Clip pane. In the pane are seven audio segments. Christopher imported the video from his camcorder precisely as he did with video and audio in Lesson 8. The screen is black, but this does not mean there is no video. The video is black. (It's the back of the lens cap, actually.)

**NOTE ▶** When there is no video image to help identify the clips, adding labels to each is more important. These clips are labeled, but you could adjust them to your liking by double clicking a clip and typing a new name.

And although these clips may not look like much, each contains a snippet of conversation on a given topic. They can be chopped up with Command-T to find small gems of dialogue, but for now we're going to treat them as good interview clips in their entirety.

### Separating Picture from Sound

Before you can work with sound alone, you must be comfortable splitting the sound from the video you shot. Imported clips in the Clip pane consist of merged picture and sound, even when the picture is black. Your first task, then, is learning to separate each shot into its components.

1    Set the workspace to present the Clip view and scroll down to the end of the sequence.

2    Go back to the Clip pane and, in the order the shots appear in the Clip pane (starting at the top left and moving through them as if you were reading), drag them to the end of the clips in the workspace.

> **NOTE** ▶ Or if you want to be fancy, shift-click the first clip and then each clip in the pane, and drag them to the workspace in one move. Check the order to make sure it's the same as the original order.

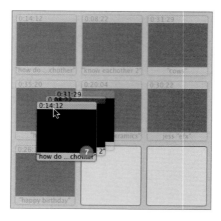

In this case, video clips already appear in the workspace (albeit clips with pictures and no sound!), but disregard them for a moment. You're going to be working in the space *following* the video made in Lesson 6.

You may need to readjust the slider to the right after each clip is added, to reveal the last clip, before you add the next.

3   Once all seven clips are in, change the view to Timeline.

Remember to slide the Zoom slider all the way to the left so that you can see the entire sequence.

Notice the dynamic slide show (which was built back in Lesson 6) at the beginning of the timeline, to the left, and the big (black) audio clips at the tail, to the right. Also notice that there are two empty tracks underneath the pictures. You'll explore these in a moment.

4   Choose the first interview clip.

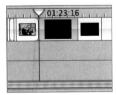

**5**    Choose Extract Audio from the Advanced pull-down menu at the top of the screen.

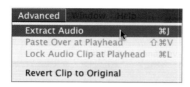

This will split the clip from the union of picture and sound into two tracks: the picture in one track (above) pinned to its sound in a second track (below).

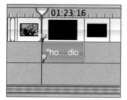

There's no discernible difference when you play it now compared with before, except that now you can manipulate the sound independently of its picture. The picture in this case is just black, but the Extract Audio function works with any video source clip.

**6**    Go ahead and extract audio from all the interview clips.

You can do one at a time or select multiple clips. It takes a moment for each clip to be "extracted."

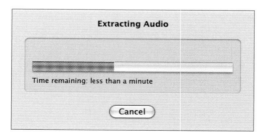

iMovie splits the picture from the sound and places the sound alone in the track below the picture.

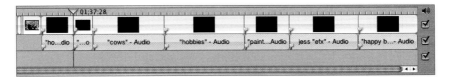

**NOTE ▶** While the distinction may be a subtle one, it may help to know that in iMovie, extracting audio doesn't really split the audio from the video and move the audio to the new track. In truth, it copies the audio to a new track and mutes the playing of the audio in the main (top) track.

Pause for a moment to examine the timeline. There are three tracks running together. The top one holds the video clips, picture, and sound together, as imported from your camcorder. The next two are for solo audio—music from iTunes, narration (which we'll create later in this lesson), or extracted audio clips. iMovie places audio clips where there is room. If you want to mute a particular track, uncheck the box on the far right of the timeline. Unchecking the box for the top track, for instance, plays your video without the production sound.

iMovie recognizes these audio clips as having a relationship with the video clips they accompanied when they arrived. That's what those yellow pins represent. While the picture and sound are now separated, you need to take it one step further—you need to unlock their relationship.

**7** Select all the interview sound clips by Shift-clicking each one.

**8**   Choose Advanced > Unlock Audio Clip.

The pins go away, and the sounds are set free from the (useless) black images.

**9**   Select all the black picture clips and press Delete on your keyboard.

### Developing an Independent Audio Track

Now you have what you need: free-floating clips of audio alone. You're ready to start integrating them with the video (alone) at the beginning of this timeline.

**NOTE** ▶ If you happen to look at your workspace in Clip view, you might be surprised that none of these interview clips are shown. The clip view presents only clips with video; music, narration, and other sound-only clips are effectively invisible. One more reason to stay in the Timeline view while working on sound.

Just by glancing at the timeline, you should clearly see that the aggregate length of audio interview material is longer than that of the video. Some of your work, then, is going to be to get the two tracks more in line: by shortening the sound part or lengthening the picture part. You can do this through a combination of making some of the dynamic slides longer and deleting some audio—either whole clips (using Delete) or parts of clips (using Command-T, then Delete).

Although much of the interview material is fun, it's best to stay focused on the goal of creating a dynamic and rich slide show.

1    Listen to all seven audio clips in the timeline again.

What material is superfluous? It cannot be said enough: As an editor, your job is not only to remove bad stuff, but to remove good stuff when it's just too much.

2    Delete audio clips 4, 5, and 6 (counting from the left; 4 should be "hobbies," 5 should be "painting," and 6 should be "jess efx").

Christopher felt that the most applicable and interesting interview material is the "cows" dialogue and the "Happy Birthday" audio segment. Using this material alone would make the audio too short. Consequently, Christopher chose to keep the interview answers about how the girls know each other. It's actually a pretty good introduction.

Unlike with video clips, when you delete these audio clips, the later clips don't automatically slide down to fill the gaps you create. You get to move each clip to the position you want it. (In fact, you could even overlap them as you work and move them around. It wouldn't hurt anything.)

NOTE ▶ If the clips don't snap to the edges easily, check the iMovie preferences. There you will find a setting called "Snap to items in Timeline"; make sure it is checked. (You may also want it to play sound effects when snapping, if you like that sort of thing.)

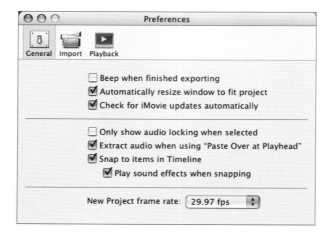

The snap and the sound effects cue you to a boundary between two clips. It's helpful to know when you're correctly positioned at the head of a clip.

**3**  Drag the remaining four audio clips to begin at the far left, under the dynamic slides, one after another.

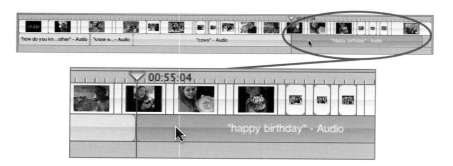

iMovie resizes the timeline to present the entire sequence, effectively stretching everything out to be larger and clearer in the space provided.

**4**  Play the entire sequence in this rough state to get a feeling for the audio and the video.

Always ask yourself questions: Where do they work together well? What misses?

One good way to keep an audio track moving along is to clear out the extraneous pauses in the interview; there are moments of stalling while people are thinking. To an audience, these are uncomfortable and often sound like mistakes. Christopher wants to remove them to improve the flow. He does this with Command-T and Delete.

**5**    Zoom in on the section you plan to edit, select the first audio clip, and then choose View > Zoom to Selection.

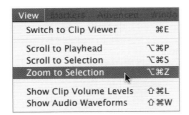

To make the audio clearer visually, you can turn on a display format for sound, called *waveform*, when necessary.

**6**    Choose View > Show Audio Waveforms.

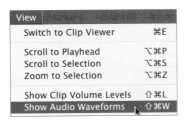

This adds a graphical representation of your sound's volume to the track.

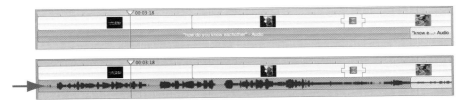

Now it's much easier to see where lines of audio start and stop, which in turn improves your accuracy while editing out bits you don't like.

There is one more technique that takes audio editing to the professional level: *scrubbing*.

When you grab the playhead and slide it back and forth over some part of your timeline, iMovie mutes the sound. Instead, let's make the sound play.

7   Press and hold the Option key on the keyboard *first* and then drag the playhead around.

You hear the sound, playing forward and backward at nonplay speeds. It sounds like an old record. It may be unusual, but this is the best way, along with the waveform, to locate precisely where to make cuts so as not to clip someone saying a word or making a sound that would otherwise make your track jarring to hear.

Now you have the required tools to do fine audio editing.

8   Find the pause at the end of the first audio clip.

The last words the girl says before the pause are "and now we go to school together."

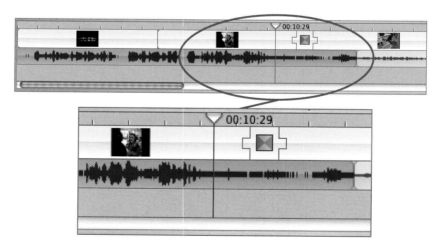

**9**  You could chop the clip here (Command T; Split Clip at Playhead) and delete the trimming. But instead, for a variation, use the Trim tool to pull the end of the clip to the place where the playhead is parked.

iMovie snaps the end of the clip into the spot where the playhead is parked—with that distinctive "snapping" sound—which makes this trimming easy to do and remarkably satisfying because of the crisp precision.

How to deal with the gap? You could slide the first clip down to fill it in, or you could pull all the following clips up. It's good to work on just one part of the video at a time, solve the problems you find there, and move on. In this case, Christopher doesn't want the interview to start right at the beginning,

**10**  Slide the first clip down to fill the gap—it solves two problems at once.

**11** Do the same thing for the second audio clip.

There's a bit of dead air at the end of the answer. Make the clip end after "like, three years."

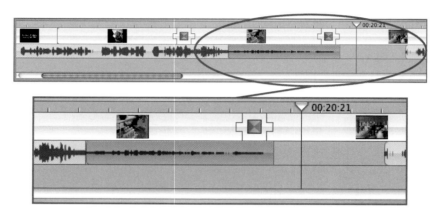

You'll learn a lot about sound and the acoustics of language when you focus on conversations at this level. Sometimes it's hard to know exactly when a word ends. You may make an edit and feel like you've clipped a word. But when you add a frame to the shot, it sounds like the next word is already starting. You just have to trust your ears and make the best edits you can without spending all day messing with frames.

**12** Slide the "cows" shot to fill the gap.

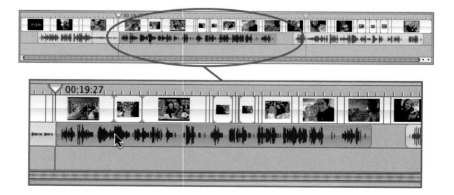

**NOTE ▶** It's possible to drag shots from one track to another if you have a creative need to overlap sounds or a functional need to set something aside while you work on an audio issue.

And now Christopher comes to a creative snag. The "cows" interview ends, there's a gap, and then the "birthday" interview begins. But he wants the birthday material exclusively to accompany the images of the birthday cake and candle ceremony, and conclude with the end of the last shot. Just from glancing at the timeline, he can see that the birthday audio material is far longer than the image sequence that includes the cake.

Sliding the birthday audio clip earlier to fill the gap only makes the problem worse. He could slide it down to end where he wants it to end, but that will only reveal the problem, not solve it.

**13** Drag the birthday clip so that it finishes at the end of the last shot.

The gap between the two audio clips isn't the only problem; the birthday audio clip is too long. (Or, conversely, the accompanying images run too short.) The solution lies in adjusting the picture track. By pushing and pulling images (and deleting some if required), it's possible to align the two tracks to synchronize a little better, with the goal of not having any blank spots in the audio track.

Before you resolve the problems by changing the pictures, some uncomfortable pauses in the "Happy Birthday" clip still need to be removed. After the first "Happy birthday, Jessica" is a long pause.

**14**  Use Command-T to chop up the clip and remove the silence.

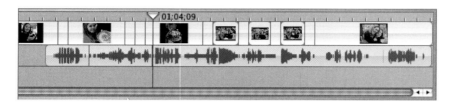

**15**  Slide the first part down to fill the gap that was created.

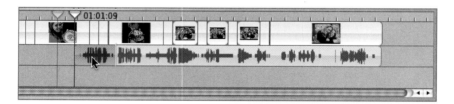

**16**  Slide the entire (new) "birthday" clip pair down to start where they need to—right under the birthday cake shot.

Technically speaking, the birthday cake shot begins at the start of the fade-in at its head, so position the playhead between the fade-out and fade-in, and then slide the pair of audio clips to begin here. (Shift-click both audio clips so they are both selected, then slide them until the first one coincides with the cake shot.)

### Adjusting the Picture Track

The audio clips extend past the end of the video track because they're too long. The solution is to lengthen the picture track.

**1**  Select the last photo in the sequence, Jessica getting a birthday hug from her friend Rachel.

You can't use the Trim tool to make this shot longer, because this isn't video; it's a still photo that has the Ken Burns Effect applied to it. The way to adjust it is through the Photos pane.

**2**  Click the Photos button.

**3**  Select the shot (again) to load it into the Ken Burns Effect workspace.

4    Adjust the duration of the shot from 8:03 to 10:00.

You could guess, but it's faster to use the playhead in the timeline to get an approximation of how much material needs to be added. The picture track ends at 1:23:16, and the audio track ends at approximately 1:25:10. About 2 seconds will get the shots in the ballpark.

5    Click Update.

The old shot will be replaced by this new, longer shot.

**NOTE ▶** Whenever you update a shot that has an effect or transition on it (in this case, a cross-dissolve transition), iMovie will ask if you want it to automatically re-create the effect after it has replaced the shot—a good idea in most cases.

6    Drop a 1-second fade-out transition on the end of the last shot.

Preview this part of the timeline. This last segment now works better, but you still must address the too-long stretch in the middle.

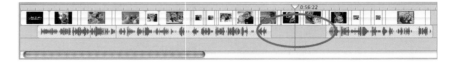

The easiest method is to remove shots to shorten the picture track. Using your judgment, you can visually recognize the size of the hole and estimate how many images you need to remove to approach that length of time.

**7**   Switch to Clip view for a moment.

**8**   Delete the shot of the girls from behind the paint display tiles (DSCN0106) and the one after it, too (DSCN0111).

The transition associated with the first clip will necessarily have to be deleted too (iMovie will ask you; say "yes").

**9**   Switch back to Timeline view.

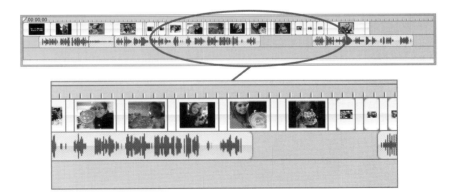

The birthday audio clip didn't slide when you removed pictures because it is not attached to anything. You don't need to adjust it yet, because you're about to do a little more moving. Since you can see the end of the "cows" audio and the beginning of the birthday video clip, you can see there's a little more of the picture track to be shortened before these line up. By measuring again with the playhead, you can see that about three more seconds need to be removed.

Rather than take little bits off lots of shots, or deleting any more shots, Christopher decides to shorten the long push in on Jessica and Rachel at the early part of the video.

**10** Click the Photo button, then click the third shot after the opening title.

**11** Change the length from 6:16 to 3:16 and click Update.

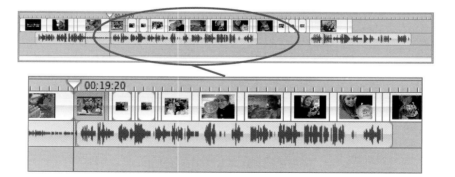

From glancing at the timeline, you can see that the end of the "cows" audio clip nearly aligns with the beginning of the cake video. Perhaps the fastest way to conclude this work is to slide the birthday audio back to fill the gap. (Or, if you prefer, line it up precisely by placing the audio in the second audio track—that way it can overlap slightly without requiring further work.)

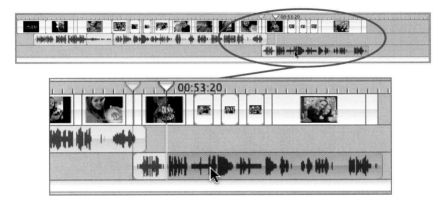

What you've accomplished is quite complex and is precisely the kind of work professional sound editors do. A QuickTime movie of Christopher's final version of this video is in the Lesson09 folder (**Finished_BirthdayCD.mov**).

## Adding Narration While You're Working in iMovie

Recording audio with your camcorder is not the only way to get an audio-only track for iMovie. If you're willing to use the microphone built into your Mac, you have a quick and easy way to add narration directly into iMovie while you're editing.

**1**   Create a new iMovie project.

**2**   Name the project *Ceramic Process*.

You're going to revisit Charlie's still photos to help him with his dynamic slide show.

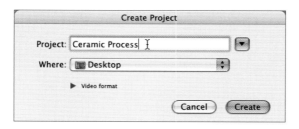

**3** Open up the text document called **CeramicProcess_script.txt** located in your Lesson09 folder.

Charlie originally used this material for the captions he printed out for his poster in Lesson 5. The narration tool in iMovie provides another option.

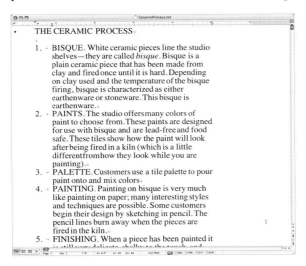

**4** Click the Audio button in iMovie.

The last time you used this part of the screen, you were importing music from your iTunes Library. Beneath the lists of songs is an innocuous set of items on your screen. Notice the word *Microphone.*

As you speak—or make any noise, really—the microphone on your Mac is picking up the sound. The series of small rectangles stretching from the word *Microphone* to the red dot represents the volume of the sound the microphone is picking up.

5   Say something and watch the green lights expand to the right and then disappear.

This means your microphone is on, working, and ready to record anything you say. In audio circles, this loudness scale is called a *VU meter*.

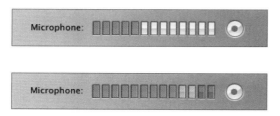

If a sound is too loud, the bar of lights will reach the yellow and then red zone. You want the sound to be loud enough, but not too loud. For most speech it's safest to stay in the middle of the green zone, with an occasional peak in the yellow or even red, as long as it's kept to a minimum.

You're ready to record.

6   Rehearse reading the first step in Charlie's report on the ceramic process. When you feel like you've got the words right, record it.

7   Click the red button to the right of the loudness meter and start reading the caption for the first photo in Charlie's album. When you reach the end of the first caption, click the red button again to stop recording.

It should take about 16 seconds to read the first bit. iMovie places the sound you've recorded directly into the timeline as a clip. Particularly for narration of this kind, where each caption is specifically for one photo, stop recording after each one to give yourself a moment to prepare and to make each caption its own discrete clip.

**8**    Read and record the next two captions, and make two more audio clips.

iMovie will place these after the first one in the timeline. If you make a mistake, stop the recording, delete the clip, and try again.

**9**    Click the Photos button, leaving this narration tool for a moment.

**10**    Open the Ceramic Process album from iPhoto to view Charlie's still photos.

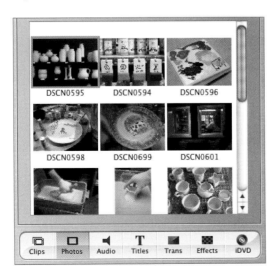

**11** Click the first audio clip in the timeline: the caption for the first photo.

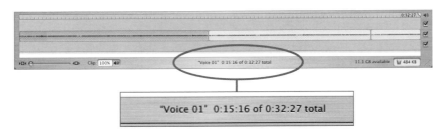

When you click a shot, the duration of the selection appears in the format of timecode in the top center part of the timeline. This clip's length is 15:16 (15 seconds and 16 frames). You're going to use this value to establish the duration of the Ken Burns Effect.

**12** Click the first photo in the album—the one of white bisque.

The caption should accompany this image.

**13** Set the duration of the shot to 15:16.

The colon between the units is important. It's not a decimal.

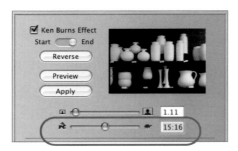

**14** Set up the start and finish points for your Ken Burns Effect.

**15** Click Apply. The shot will be added to the timeline, above the first audio clip.

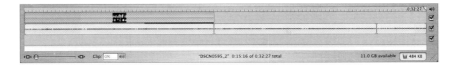

When the rendering of the effect is done, you can play the sequence.

**16** Continue this process for the second and third shots.

This is a streamlined method to add narration to photos in iMovie. Rather than trying to make the sound fit the picture, you'll often find it easier to make the pictures fit the sound. Of course, all the tools you've used in the first part of this lesson apply here as well—if you needed to trim sound or picture, to rearrange clips, to cut out mistakes and adjust the results, and so on. It's not always possible to add sound while you're working, but many kinds of projects (like Charlie's) can benefit from the narration tools built into iMovie.

## What You've Learned

▶   Sound is not ancillary to picture. In many cases, sound is more important than picture in giving the audience a feeling of completion and quality.

▶   You use the advanced feature Extract Audio to separate video material into its component picture and sound elements.

▶   You can unlock picture and sound elements before moving them around by using Unlock Audio Clip.

▶   Drag sound clips to any track. If you want to hear different sounds simultaneously, they need to be in different tracks.

▶   Use the microphone in iMovie's Audio pane to record narration right into the timeline.

# 10

Lesson Files    No files for this lesson

Tools           iMovie (optional), camcorder (optional)

Time            Approximately 45 minutes

Goals           Learn what kinds of events you can shoot for the best effect

                Get the best coverage in any shooting scenario

                Prepare for the most efficient and productive editing session
                following your shoot

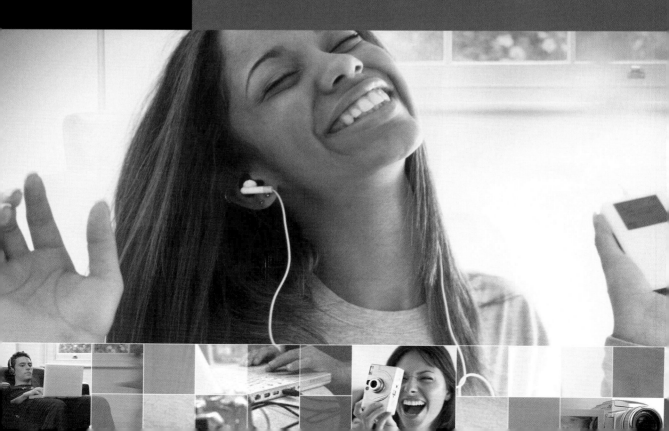

# Shooting with Hollywood-Style Techniques for Better Videos

Once you see how shooting and editing are related, you can see why you'll want to add different kinds of shots to round out your videos. There are also some shooting tricks you might try that facilitate your creating particularly cool results in iMovie. Not special effects, mind you—just simple concepts for gathering the right footage in order to give your videos a rather sophisticated style.

This lesson is really only half a lesson and must be approached with Lesson 11 in tandem: Shooting techniques can't stand alone and are realized only when it comes to editing with the shots they produce. In fact, even though there are no lesson files for this chapter, the illustrations that you'll see in this chapter come from the lesson files for Lesson 11.

Christopher gave you a quick taste of how shooting and editing work together in Lesson 8. At that time, you were introduced to the concept of *coverage*—that is, getting the material required to edit a scene. Now you will delve into more detail about coverage and how to get the best kind.

You don't need to prepare for a video shoot in advance, and you don't need to bring a lot of equipment to an event. But you do need to keep certain ideas in mind—primarily, you must know what pieces of video you need for editing and remember to get them during the event itself.

Now you will see how Christopher approaches shooting the birthday party in order to get the shots he thinks he might use. Getting the right shots now will make the time he spends editing much faster and more enjoyable.

## How to Approach Shooting a Video

In many ways, shooting with a camcorder is the same as shooting with a still camera. All the rules of exposure and lighting apply (keep light behind you, not behind your subject), as do the rules of composition (don't always center your subject; remember the rule of thirds). It's important to hold the camcorder steady (two hands, always) and frame any shot before pressing the Record button.

But a camcorder has the added feature of motion. It takes 30 pictures every second, and consequently it can do lots of things that a still camera cannot. You can move the camera. You can zoom the lens. The camera records all of this. So in addition to basic photography skills, you need to learn some rules about moving pictures and good video.

### Guidelines on Moving and Not Moving Your Camcorder

Before you get to move your camcorder, you have to come to grips with why you shouldn't. It's almost impossible to get good video when you're moving, and the material you do get is hard to watch and harder to edit.

Your camcorder is small. It's light. It fits in your hand. It seems natural to walk around with the thing recording, shooting up and down, left and right, following people around and so on. *Stop doing this immediately.*

In Hollywood, the camera certainly moves a lot, but it's not a trivial matter. Professional filmmakers get to move their cameras because of four important factors: (1) they use special equipment—like dollies and Steadicams—designed to move slowly and smoothly; (2) they have many people working together every time they set out to move the camera; (3) they get to rehearse the moves until they get them right; and (4) they are working in a controlled environment, so even if someone makes a mistake after rehearsing, they can do it again.

This isn't you. You're trying to make a good-looking, enjoyable video, and you've got just yourself and your camcorder. Once you've broken the habit of wandering around while recording and have seen the impressive results of this simple change, it's possible to add a little bit of movement to your projects to good effect.

### ▶ The Lingo of Motion

Before you start moving your camcorder around, familiarize yourself with the relevant vocabulary.

**Pan**  A move from side to side, along an imaginary horizon.

**Tilt**  Similar to a pan but up and down, like scanning a tall building.

**Dolly shot**  A shot from a camera that has been placed on a moving cart of some kind, to increase the stability of the camera and the smoothness of the move. A dolly is a cart designed specifically for doing this move, but you can create a cheap version by sitting on a swivel chair or in a shopping cart and having someone push it.

**Tracking**  Moving the camera to keep a moving subject "steady" in the middle of the frame. If you pan on a car as it drives by, it's a tracking shot.

**Steadicam**  A brand name of equipment that straps a camera to a camera operator in such a way that he or she can walk around while the device holds the camera steady. It uses gyroscopes and other mechanical means to keep the image from bouncing too much. These are prohibitively expensive for consumers, but mini versions (costing in the hundreds of dollars) are pretty good for amateurs.

### Your Pans and Tilts

The best way to move the camera, of course, is to use some equipment of your own: a tripod. A regular tripod is designed to hold a camera steady or still, but in the video and film world, tripods often include a *fluid head,* a rather pricey feature that provides smooth and controlled movement.

A fluid-head tripod enables you to make beautiful, smooth pans and tilts. But even then, the camera motion must be very slow and deliberate. There is a natural tendency to pan for a long time—along a coastline, perhaps—but if you look closely at pans in movies, they are actually quite short: just little moves from here to over there a tiny bit. Not 180 degrees, but rather more like 10 degrees. If you don't have a tripod, it's almost impossible to make a pan or tilt look smooth and professional. They are fun to do, but when it comes time to edit, you'll often end up skipping past them and opting for steady shots because moving shots look so bad.

Most of the time, you won't be using a tripod anyway (let alone one with a fluid head), and you must improvise. Creating a moving shot without extra equipment falls in the danger zone, and the responsibility is on you to restrain your use of pans and tilts, and to be controlled when you do try them.

If you don't have a tripod and you feel compelled to pan or tilt, hold your body very stiff, hold the camera close with your elbows tight to your body, and then move the camera just a nudge between two relatively close points. If the move is short enough, sometimes the pan will be slick and usable.

### Tracking

Pans and tilts are troublesome partly because you are just sort of looking around with the camera, leaving the audience searching everywhere in the frame for something to focus on. Tracking works a little better, however, because you follow an object and (generally speaking) keep it in the middle of the frame. The audience knows what it is watching in a tracking shot, and consequently the technique can be very interesting and effective. It takes some skill to follow a moving target, so practice as much as possible before you actually record the shot.

Think of moving the camera as a special effect—fun to do, cool looking, but something done only once in awhile, for good use at just the right moment.

### When to Use—and Ignore—Zoom

Everything just stated about moving goes for zooming as well. When shooting, don't zoom. It's really, really tempting, and it feels slick while you're doing it, but the resulting video is less than ideal.

Of course, the zoom control is critical to your videos. It's front and center—under your index finger—and second only to the Record button itself in importance. If you don't get to zoom, why is it there?

Instead of regarding this as a zoom, think of it as a big ol' bag of interchangeable lenses. What's great about the zoom lens on your camcorder is that it's equal to a bunch of lenses in one. Zoomed out, you see the big picture with a wide-angle lens. Zoom in a little or all the way, and you've got a telephoto lens, up close and personal.

Use the zoom to help you frame your shot, using your rules of composition and thinking about the coverage you want for editing. Once you've set the zoom, you can then record—without touching it. After you stop recording, you can adjust the zoom and record again.

**TIP** ▶ Once you're comfortable with the way shooting and editing are interrelated, you may find yourself leaving the camcorder on record while you zoom—from wide shot to close-up, for instance. The difference is that you're doing so only to get from one shot to another quickly, and you know you will be cutting out the zoom part when you're editing.

A camcorder won't let you zoom carefully or slowly enough to produce good zoom shots. But you can create the same effect by shooting two or three unmoving, unzooming shots of an object with your camera set to wide, then closer, then as close as you can. Cut these shots together, and you get a professional looking "push in."

Christopher began recording his video from the far corner of the studio. He wanted to get a nice, basic shot of the event from this initial position, but while he was there, he chose to cover himself by getting a couple of additional shots. Here's what he did:

1    With the camera zoomed out as wide as possible, he recorded the room for about 15 seconds, holding the camera above his head and using both hands to steady the shot.

Wide shot (also written as "WS" or "Wide")

This is a *wide shot,* which is defined as any shot in which the subject is fully inside the frame—a person seen from head to toe, for instance. The wider a shot and the more details present in the frame, the longer the piece of video needs to be so that the audience can get oriented and see what's going on. Because the party group is so tiny in the frame, this shot is actually an extreme wide shot (EWS).

**2**   After Christopher stopped recording the wide shot, he zoomed in a little bit—about midway between the widest and the closest settings—and, once he framed this shot, he recorded again for about 10 seconds.

Medium shot ("MS" or "Med")

This is a *medium shot,* in which you can see a person from head to waist. Medium shots should make up the bulk of your video material. They look good on TV and achieve a nice balance between being close enough to show what's going on and far enough to provide some perspective.

**3**   Finally, Christopher zooms in all the way to get a close-up shot.

Close-up shot ("CU" or "Close")

*Close-up shots* are nice and often look more attractive than other shots because the subject is so clear. A close-up comprises just a person's head, and traditionally you crop off the top of the head to get a little closer. It's the eyes where the expression is communicated, and the top of the head is considered superfluous.

An extreme close-up (ECU) is common too—just the eyes, or the eyes and nose.

**TIP** ▶ When working with a camcorder, it's easy to shoot everything too close. The LCD is often so small that it makes your subject look boring unless you get really close. Fight this urge, and trust that when you see the video on your TV set, the close-ups will freak you out with their intensity. The medium shot is the main kind of image you are looking for. Close-ups are powerful and a little scary, and they should be used more sparingly than it may seem.

These naming conventions aren't rules so much as guidelines designed to help you distinguish the shots you are recording and to help you keep your shots distinct.

**TIP** ▶ A wide shot will often answer the question "Where are we?" A medium shot will answer the question "Who is here?" A close-up will answer the question "What is going on?"

Why the need? Because when you edit, you cannot juxtapose two shots that are too similar. It ends up looking jarring, like a mistake. So although it's easy to cut from a wide shot to a close-up, cutting from a medium shot of a person to something only a tad different—say, to just their head and shoulders—likely wouldn't work. By recognizing the difference between shots and making sure they are appropriately distinct, you get material you know can be edited.

When you shoot scenes, you don't always need all three shots of each moment, but you should record at least two. That way, even if you get no other coverage, you have some way to edit the material into a video with impact.

**NOTE** ▶ You can shoot a close-up with your camcorder even when the zoom setting is wide-angle (just stand really close to your subject) or telephoto (stand farther away). So, there isn't a direct relationship between the zoom—in photo jargon, the focal length—and the size of your subject. In the end, when you work in iMovie, you won't care about wide angle or telephoto, but you will care about the distinct look of close-ups and medium shots.

### Determining What to Shoot

The central element of the subjects you shoot needs to be relatively repetitive. And it should be something that is ongoing—like girls painting and talking, people eating dinner, kids building with blocks in the living room, or athletes playing soccer. While it seems like these activities consist of very random actions, all involve a certain repetitive motion (painting, eating, running), and this is what allows you to get Hollywood-style coverage of the event without having to interrupt the action and ask everyone to do it again.

Unlike still photography, your videos should have a *scene* at their core. For professional filmmakers, a scene is a scripted event that takes place between a set of characters in a fixed location. For you, the moments you shoot with video probably are not planned events. You're just minding your own business and wham! Something cool (cute, amazing, unbelievable, funny, dramatic) starts to happen. You think, "Man, I wish I had a video of that," and then you run off, get your camera, and run back. The event that started this is the core of your scene.

At the birthday party, there are in fact lots of little scenes. There's the scene you worked on in Lesson 8, where the girls are at the shelf of bisque selecting what they want to paint. It's small, it's fast, but it's a scene. In the current lesson (and Lesson 11), the girls are sitting and painting, and this is a scene, too.

Christopher wanted some video of the girls painting, so, in order to be as non-invasive as possible, he began shooting video from a distance across the room. This is a good strategy. In many videos, you will want to start discreetly from far away—zoomed in, if necessary—and then work your way closer, remembering not to shoot as you move but rather to move, frame, and then shoot.

Your first task is keeping in mind the core (repetitive) activity you are shooting and getting the coverage that you need to edit.

## Getting Coverage in Your Scene

We touched on the relationships between shots in Lesson 8. There, you learned that each shot needs to have at least one other corresponding shot with which it has a natural dynamic. This section will outline the most important (and easiest to get) shots that create this dynamic.

Christopher is not doing a documentary on ceramics or even on his daughter; he's just making a sketch of a moment in her life. The still photos were far better for getting bits and pieces of the whole event (arriving, painting, chatting, and eating cake). The video is intended to preserve a moment and make it interesting. The moment he chooses is the painting.

Earlier in this lesson, you saw Christopher start the shoot by going to the edge of the room and shooting both a wide shot and a close-up from there. This is the first guideline for shooting: Get multiple shots from each position.

## Multiple Shots from Each Position

You don't want to move around too much with your camera. You want to get the coverage you need from just a couple of fixed locations—maybe two or three. If you're good, maybe four. But not 10. A common mistake is to shoot a little bit from here, wander around, shoot some more from over there, stop for a while, and then shoot from some new location. All of this will be more challenging to put together into a cohesive video.

From whatever position you make your first shot, you want to get two shots. When Christopher made his first wide shot of the girls painting, he recorded for about 10 seconds and then stopped. Then he did the important thing: He zoomed in for a closer shot and recorded again, for 10 more seconds. If he was not in a hurry, he might have shot three shots from this location (a wide, a medium, and a close-up), but at least two are critical. Make two shots, then move to the next location.

## Shots and Reverse Shots

Once Christopher got to his first position and recorded a couple of different shots from there, a question arises: Where to go next? The answer is easy. Once you've shot everything you can see from the first vantage point, move to the other side of your subject and shoot back toward where you were standing. In very general terms, you're moving about 180 degrees from where you started. The name for this is the *reverse shot*.

**NOTE** ▶ Technically speaking, you're not going to move exactly 180 degrees opposite your original position. It's going to be closer to 120 degrees, but it's a detail that you can refine once you're in the habit of getting a reverse shot.

When you are done shooting from the reverse position, you'll have two sets of shots (called, of course, shots and reverse shots), and those have a very specific dynamic between them. As long as the action is similar from both positions, these shot/reverse combinations can be cut together to give a remarkable experience to the viewers—as if they were in two places at the same time.

The shot/reverse dyad works wonderfully if a pair of people are talking or directly interacting. Focus on one of the two people for the first shot and on the second person for the reverse shot. Christopher's job was challenging because instead of two girls talking and painting, there were five. Still, by concentrating on two of them at a time, he was able to get the coverage he needed.

Interaction between two people is almost always a compelling core to your videos. Everything else is just setting and ambience. The back-and-forth of human interplay is, in many ways, the precise reason you are using video and not still photography. Consequently, the shot/reverse shot is often the main element of your projects.

You don't have to load up your camcorder and follow along with Christopher for this lesson—primarily because what he's doing won't precisely match what you're going to do in any given shooting situation. Hopefully, seeing his process will still be of value to you when you shoot your own projects.

If you want to try these basic shooting guidelines, and you are encouraged to do so, set up a very basic scene. Two people sitting in chairs facing each other and playing a game—tic-tac-toe, perhaps, or chess, or cards. Let the two "actors" play a real game, ignoring you—and you shouldn't bother them. Shooting and getting this coverage will be straightforward and, while you won't use it for editing in Lesson 11, once you've finished that exercise, you could edit the material you just shot.

**1**  Find your subject, frame it as a medium shot, and start recording.

This first shot should go on for a minimum of 10 seconds, probably more like 15. There are no rules; just hold still and let the person do whatever it is she is doing.

**2**  Before leaving the first position, don't forget to get a second shot (either zoomed closer or farther).

Getting two shots is not required, but it will give you a little flexibility later when it's time to edit. You'll be glad you have them.

**3**  As soon as you stop recording, move to a position opposite where you were with the first shot.

The easiest way to do this is to imagine a line between the subject and the person your subject is interacting with. With luck (and for easier shooting), these two people should be facing each other, sitting on opposite sides of a table or something. Walk from position 1 to position 2 and, framing the subject in a medium shot similar to before, shoot for another 10 to 15 seconds.

**4**   As before, it's usually a good idea to get a second shot (probably a close-up) from this same position.

When you've finished shooting from these two positions, you have the core of your video coverage. With a shot and a reverse shot, you can build a compelling moment easily in iMovie.

> **TIP** ▶ Another specific shot used often in Hollywood is the over-the-shoulder (OS) shot. Instead of having a single shot of a person alone in the frame, keep the edge of the other person's back in the frame. This shows the physical relationship between them—how close they are to each other—and reminds the audience that two people are there, not just one. In conversations on film, particularly for medium shots, they are the standard.

## The Cutaway Shot

Shots and reverse shots may make up the core of your video, but it's almost impossible to watch these two shots all day. What you need is something else to look at, a break. Behold the *cutaway shot*. It is a close-up of something other than the people in your video. It doesn't include anyone's mouth moving. Its sole purpose is to show you details and texture of what is going on.

Any number of subjects can constitute a good cutaway shot. You'll probably find a half-dozen or more. You almost can't have too many, they're so useful. In some ways a good cutaway is almost a still photo: You frame some odd detail as a kind of still life. It doesn't have to be an image from the action (like hands painting) but instead could be anything that provides details within the environment (other people in the studio, odd bisque items on the shelves, the slide show running on the big display at the bar, and so on).

Don't shoot your cutaway shots until you're satisfied with your shot/reverse coverage. You can cheat the cutaways a little bit; they don't have to fit precisely with the shot/reverse and can often be shot very late in the event. You don't know how (or even if) you will use these shots while editing, but when you need one, you won't believe how important it is to have it. You'll end up picking one or two—whatever fits best with the video you're making. But those decisions will come later. For now, your job is to get all the coverage you might need.

Here are some of Christopher's cutaway shots that he might use with the shot/reverse combinations you saw previously.

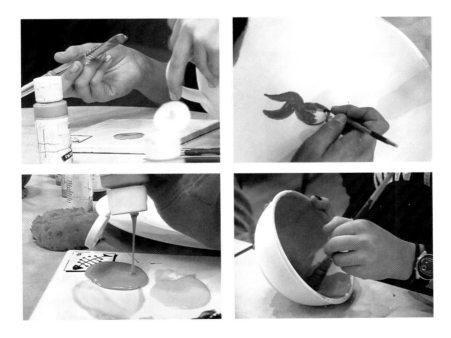

Unlike the more standard shot/reverse combinations, cutaways beg for creativity. From any position (wide from across the room, from the side getting the shot/reverse), you've always got the opportunity to point the camera in a slightly different direction, zoom in, and get a cutaway shot. Remember that fewer shooting positions is generally better. Still, in some of the shots Christopher took, he set the camera down on the table or shot from high above his head, pointing the lens down at the table.

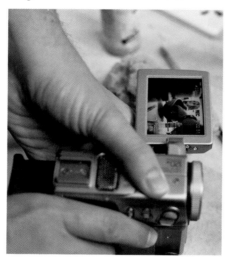 

### The Establishing Shot

Finally, you'll always need at least one *establishing shot,* which shows where this event is taking place—a wide shot that depicts not only your main characters but also where they are situated. Sometimes this is the first shot you get; remember how Christopher started wide and far away before getting close for the shot/reverse? But don't be limited by a wide shot or a shot that includes the girls. The outside of the studio is perhaps a better establishing shot.

Sometimes it's natural to get the establishing shot at the end, after the cut-aways. Since the participation of the birthday girls isn't required, it's good to focus on them first and get the extra material afterward. It doesn't matter when you take the shot; just remember that establishing shots, particularly if they are wide, often need to play onscreen for a little longer than normal. Hold still (don't pan—it isn't necessary). If the venue or vista is too large for a single shot, stay in your position and point in a few different directions, changing from wide to closer as necessary. All these bits can be combined into a short establishing shot sequence.

**TIP** ▶ Establishing shots can be exceptionally creative too. Don't just wander far away and shoot a big wide shot. Think about shooting from up high, over your head. Shoot through a window—reflections and all. Look for signage around that might help place you ("Welcome to Petroglyph Ceramic Lounge" or "Hot, Hot, Hot. Careful around kilns!"). The signs are good for establishing your location, but they don't need to be full frame, dead center—just an edge of a sign or a snippet of a logo is often enough.

## Looking for Story Structure

The final aspect of coverage is that of story structure—that is, finding shots that in some way represent what might be a "beginning" of your video as well as an "ending." Your video isn't just a random sequence of shots, but a short story. While you can build a sequence that is visually dynamic using shot/reverse combinations with the occasional cutaway, your videos will be better if they have a natural beginning, some climax or punch line, and then a natural ending. Only the best videos nail these story elements—you can't script them, and they don't always happen when you shoot. At best, you can be looking for them so that you can record them when the moment arrives. Shooting video is a little like trick-or-treating on Halloween: You get what you can, go home, dump the bits on the kitchen table, and see how you did. No matter how hard you try, sometimes you just don't get all the coverage you hoped to get. You can try to edit anyway, but it will be that much harder to make a great video.

A few tricks can facilitate good beginnings and endings. In the first place, since you now know not to move the camera, you can achieve the excellent effect of letting your characters move into and out of the frame. If you know where something is going to happen—say, the girls just arrived at the studio and are about to start looking for ceramics at the shelf of bisque—then you could point your camera there, start shooting, and hold still. In no time, the girls will wander into the frame. Presto: a beginning shot. Similarly, if you know they've found their pieces and are about to go sit down, frame them and hold still. They'll exit the frame, and you'll be left looking at a shelf of ceramics—a nice ending.

Many natural events make good endings. People walking off into the sunset is a classic (even clichéd) finale. Somebody pulling up in a car, opening a door to enter a house, or walking into a room are all natural introductions. Shooting these moments isn't required for a video, of course. If you don't get this kind of coverage, you'll force the editor (again, you) to improvise. A simple fade-in or fade-out is the fallback position.

## What You've Learned

▶ You need sufficient coverage to edit a video. With just a few simple bits, you will have enough to make interesting videos when it's time to edit.

▶ Shoot from a finite set of positions to get your video—at least two, and probably three or four. More than that will likely produce too much coverage, the majority of it not useful.

▶ Always shoot a wide shot and a medium shot from a given position. If you have time, shoot a close-up too. The medium shot is your primary shot. Make sure you have enough material from each shot.

▶ Wide shots need to be longer than close-ups. Think of recording your wide shots and establishing shots for around 15 seconds each. Medium shots and close-ups can be closer to 10 seconds.

▶ Look for shot dyads—a shot/reverse shot, a shot/cutaway shot, a shot/establishing shot. These make editing a snap and give your projects a sophisticated look.

# 11

**Lesson Files**    Lessons > Lesson11 > Start_Project11

**Tools**    iMovie

**Time**    Approximately 90 minutes

**Goals**    Handle the coverage you shot when editing

Use basic editing skills to create dynamic scenes

Recognize how to use interactions between characters to guide your editing

Create a high-quality archive copy of your finished video

## Lesson 11
# Editing and Finishing a Professional-Looking Movie

In Lesson 10, Christopher shot coverage of the birthday party at the ceramics studio. The party's over now; the cake is eaten, the brushes are washed, and the girls have gone home. Now it's quiet time, and Christopher has an hour or two to see if he can make an interesting video from the material he shot.

The techniques you've learned over the last ten lessons all come together when you're developing a video: incorporating music from iTunes (Lesson 1), adding moving still photos with titles and transition effects (Lesson 6), and taking advantage of the fundamental editing tools (Lesson 7). There is no way around it—making a video incorporates all the tools, tricks, and capabilities of iLife. With basic coverage (from Lesson 10) and familiarity with the editing tools in iMovie (which starts right here), you can whip out a video in no time.

Getting to your Mac with your video material and starting to work in iMovie can be a little emotionally challenging. If your photographic skills are competent, most of the material you shot is good. Even so, most of the material will not end up in your project.

Keep one thing in mind (you might even want to print this out and hang it above your Mac): *Editing is not about throwing out bad material. Editing is about building something interesting and watchable.* Sometimes you toss bad bits of video, but mostly you have to get rid of many good parts to make the remaining parts even better.

If it makes you feel better, you're not really throwing anything away. It's all on the videotape you shot. That original tape is an archive. When you finish this lesson, you'll also learn how to archive your final project in high-quality digital videotape for any future uses that may arise.

## Editing Material from the Camcorder

The material Christopher shot is in iMovie for you already. If this were your own material, and you were going to make a log sheet for your videotape (described in Lesson 8), a good time to do it would be while you imported material into iMovie.

Once you've imported the video, you can turn your attention to the kinds of coverage that you'll be editing.

### Setting up the Basic Structure

In this case, we'll look at Christopher's footage, which focuses on four of the girls at the party—our "characters." Since you'll be watching their individual coverage as well as their interactions, it's practical to refer to each of them by name.

Here are our characters:

Jessica          Chloe          Rachel          Alison

**1**   Open the **Start_Project11** project from the Start_Project11 iMovie folder
(in the Lesson11 folder).

By now you're familiar with iMovie and will notice there is one clip in the
Clip pane.

Why only one clip? Didn't Christopher get a lot of shots? Yes—but as you
learned in Lesson 8, iMovie gives you the option to break up material
into discrete clips in the Clip pane based on the camera's starting and
stopping points. In prior lessons, you saw the clips already broken into
shots in the pane. But you also have the option of not breaking up material in that way; it isn't always helpful (as with the time-lapse video in
Lesson 7)—and it may be misleading.

As your skills increase, you won't need to rely on stopping and starting the
camera to distinguish between shots. For instance, if you zoom from a
wide shot to a close-up and then quickly move the camera to get a cutaway shot, all without stopping the camera, iMovie will see these continuously recorded but discrete shots as a single clip. If it gave you only one
clip in the pane for these shots, you might inadvertently miss part of the
coverage.

Consequently, before he imported this video, Christopher disabled the preference (iMovie > Preferences > Import) that tells iMovie to separate clips while it places them in the Clip pane:

In this lesson, you'll approach the video the way it is on the videotape—and move through the "single" clip, getting the pieces you need (to start with).

**NOTE ▶**  This clip is only 3½ minutes long and is pulled from the 10 minutes or so that Christopher actually shot at the party—a necessary practicality. This makes the video easier to work with in this lesson, but it deprives you of all the coverage Christopher gathered for himself and slightly limits what you can build from this material.

2   Begin by watching the entire clip: Click the clip in the Clip pane and watch it in the Viewer, making mental notes about the coverage and which shots have a relationship to other shots.

One of the most important ways to get the best cut of something through editing is by being exceptionally familiar with the material you're using. Moments as short as 1 second are sometimes remarkably valuable when it comes time to solve a problem during editing. Fast-forward through your raw videotapes, and you'll often miss important shots. The only way you'll be able to use these is if you notice them, so it's a good idea to watch the raw material at least twice before you make any cuts.

The sound of the girls talking (the "production sound") is really hard to hear, and consequently it's practically useless, as you might expect. When you watch the video, it's good to notice when you see people speaking, but don't be concerned with what they're saying. In a video like this, instead of dialogue you'll end up using background music (making a kind of music video) or a narration track (as you did in Lesson 9), which parallels but does not synchronize with the video. Either way, the actual words spoken are relatively unimportant.

Time to make your first cut—but where to start? Since you can add shots anywhere to the sequence at any time, there's no need at this point to focus on what you think might be the "first" shot. Instead, just start working with shots as they show up on the tape, in the order things were shot. You can decide on the order in which to place them as you build your sequence.

The first shot on the tape is of Alison—it starts as a medium shot and then zooms quickly to a close-up.

**3**  Cut 3 or 4 seconds of the medium shot and the close-up, and put them in the workspace.

Your goal is to find moments where the camera is steady and there is no zooming.

If you can't remember how to chop up these bits using Command-T and then dragging them to the timeline, review those skills in Lesson 7 or Lesson 8.

**4**  Continue working through the material of each girl, adding a medium shot (MS) and then a close-up (CU), until you have a series of shots of each of the four girls painting.

Your sequence workspace will look something like this:

You've created a little mess in the Clip pane—mostly trimmed bits you don't need, and one large piece that is still untouched. That's okay; it's a different kind of workspace. You may move shots back and forth from the Clip pane to the timeline in Clip view and sometimes back to the Clip pane. In the same way that you can rearrange shots in the timeline, you can pull out shots while you work.

It's a good time to change the names of the shots in your workspace. iMovie defaults to some pretty cryptic names. Finding material and working with shots is easier if the names are useful.

**5**    Click the first shot in your timeline (which highlights the shot), click the name of the shot, and change it. Use the naming methods you learned in Lesson 10.

This first shot is a medium shot of Alison.

**6**    Proceed through all the shots in the timeline and rename them as follows:

This is a good start, but remember that the order in which you shoot has little to do with the order in which you will place the shots. Feel free to play through the sequence. The current organization of shots is a little dull.

**7** Try rearranging these shots by dragging the clips to new positions in the timeline.

Without adding any new material, this same bunch of video can become something like this:

After this quick adjustment, the editing is beginning to create some feelings in the audience as they pick up on dynamics between the girls. The sequence begins with a medium shot of Jessica (the birthday girl), and in the same frame we can see that Rachel, on the right edge, is speaking to Chloe, who is off camera. Jessica is keeping an eye on their discussion. In the next shot, we see Rachel painting and speaking to Chloe, whom we can't see. Next the audience needs to see Chloe, who up to this point has been participating but hasn't appeared in the frame. And thus, we then cut to the MS Chloe shot.

The characters' eyes drive the direction of the edits. (An audience tends to want to see the things the characters are looking at.) Since this is a dynamic conversation—we can't really hear what they're talking about, but we can tell they're interacting—let's go back to Jessica, this time for something closer, more personal, more intense. It might have been too much to start with that intensity, but now that we've looked around, it's okay.

Again, Jessica is watching Rachel and Chloe. So we move on to Rachel painting in close-up, and then Chloe returning the looks. If there is back and forth between characters, it's often good to keep the characters the same size in the frame in shots edited together (keeping close shots cutting to close, or medium cutting to medium); this provides a good visual and emotional balance for the viewer. When you "punch in" to a close-up, you want to do it for a good reason (and not just because you *have* a close-up shot).

But what about Alison? Through the whole dialogue, Alison is hard at work painting on her own and is not participating in the conversation. The medium shot of her depicts this. In truth, the close-up of Alison is superfluous.

**8**  Drag the last shot, CU Alison, back to the Clip pane.

You may want it later, but you don't need it now.

> **NOTE** ▶ When you want to play the sequence, it's generally easiest to pop back to Timeline view and drag the playhead to the point from which you want to start watching. Clip view is good for rearranging shots and seeing at a glance what material is present, but ultimately you will go back and forth in your workspace view while editing.

### Adding Other Types of Shots

Now the stage is set for moving on, digging further into the material on the "tape" (in the Clip pane). Don't worry yet about the length of these shots—they may be a tiny bit too short or too long, but they can be trimmed later. For now it's important to pay attention to the structure.

> **TIP** ▶ If the shots in the Clip pane get confusing, you can label the clips or delete the bits you are confident you don't need, or you can do some of both. Be sure to keep an eye on the "big" piece—most everything here is a few seconds long, but one clip is more than 2 minutes long. Get familiar with looking at the durations of the clips to help orient yourself as to what is what. Bits of video you delete go in the trash can in iMovie—as long as you don't empty the trash, it's possible to restore the deleted pieces.

**1**  Go back to the big hunk of video in the Clip pane that you haven't worked on yet.

The next shot you come to as you play it is a close-up of some hands. It's a cutaway shot.

**2**   Cut out about three seconds of this shot and use it in the sequence.

Once it's cut, the question is where to put it. It doesn't make sense to drop it at the end of the sequence. This is a close-up of Jessica painting; it could go between a shot of Jessica and one of another girl, or you could break one of the shots of Jessica in two and drop it between them. Based on watching what is going on in each of Jessica's shots, it makes good sense to place it between the close-up shots.

**3**   Drag the cutaway shot to after the CU Jessica shot.

It makes sense here, as Jessica looks down in the close-up shot right before we move to the cutaway. If she were already looking up at Rachel at the end of the close-up, it might not work as well. It also fits nicely because when the sequence cuts to Rachel, she's painting, too.

After the cutaway of Jessica painting is one of Rachel painting.

4   Clip out another few seconds of Rachel's cutaway shot and place it in the sequence after the medium shot of Rachel.

Placing the shot here not only makes logical sense (we just saw Rachel painting, and now we can see more detail of what she is doing), but it also helps the pacing. It now takes a moment longer before Chloe responds to Rachel, so you begin to feel that they aren't having just a conversation, but one punctuated by painting and watching each other paint.

There's one more nice cutaway—a top-down shot (a shot taken from overhead) of Chloe working on her cow picture. It begins with Chloe looking toward Rachel and ends with her looking down. The ideal now is to find a point that connects with these moments in the sequence you've built.

5   Play the sequence and look for a good place to put the cutaway of Chloe.

What you'll notice is that all the shots of Chloe begin with her looking up toward Rachel and end with her looking down at her plate. Consequently, the choice may be to place the cutaway after either the medium shot or the close-up of Chloe, and then trim the cutaway shot so that it begins after she looks down.

**6**   Insert Chloe's cutaway after the close-up.

**7**   Change to Timeline view and, using the Trim tool, shorten Chloe's cutaway shot to begin after she looks down.

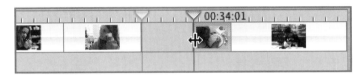

Before shortening the clip

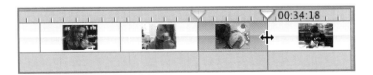

After shortening the clip

Now the cutaway is much too short.

**8**   Use the Trim tool again, this time on the tail end of the cutaway shot, to
add more time. Keep an eye on the shot in the Viewer window to make
sure you're adding the material you want to add.

This is pretty good. It's far more interesting to watch than the raw material, particularly now that the order has been changed. Remember that all the material for this short sequence was made from one shot of each girl, with a little zoom to create two bits of coverage per position. Add to that a tiny bit of cutaway detail, and the result is a rather compelling (and maybe emotionally realistic) 38-second scene.

9   For the sake of this lesson, spend a moment cleaning up the Clip pane. Selecting shots and pressing Delete on your keyboard, delete the trimmings that you aren't using, leaving only the CU Alison shot that we specifically placed here and the balance of the source material.

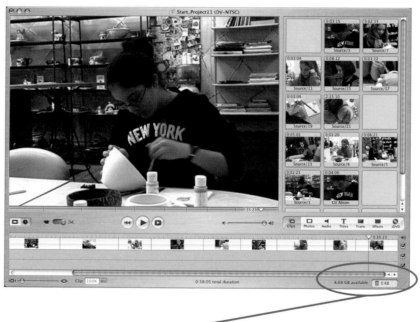

Before cleanup

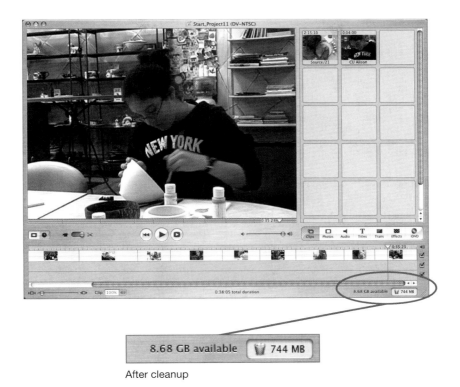

8.68 GB available     744 MB

After cleanup

**NOTE** ▶ When you delete shots, they go into the trash can at the bottom of the window—you'll notice that the number of megabytes (MB) grows as you throw out more material. iMovie will keep shots here until you empty the trash can. Unless you are out of space on your Mac, don't empty the trash can until you're done with your project, just in case you toss something you shouldn't.

More detailed trimming will be appropriate once you've completed a first pass of the whole scene. Then you can balance the length of the shots with each other and make the pacing feel inviting. But for now, the first part of this sequence is done, and it's time to move on to the next bit of coverage.

## Editing a Dialogue Scene

From here, the coverage moves into the shot/reverse shot material of Alison speaking with Jessica. Later, Rachel joins the conversation—which makes the editing a little more complicated but not beyond your control.

In this part of the scene, you'll use the basics of shot/reverse shots to build a dialogue (even if you can't make out what people are saying). You'll do this at its simplest form—but you can use the same coverage and simple techniques to build quite complex and sophisticated sequences.

1   Find a medium shot of Alison in which she is clearly speaking to Jessica. (It will be the material that begins the longest clip in your Clip pane—the bit you haven't done any cutting to yet). Clip it out, keeping it as long as you can—almost 9 seconds.

2   Drop it into the timeline.

Notice the difference between this shot of Alison and the one just before it in the sequence. They're both medium shots, but the second one has the edge of Jessica in the frame. It's an over-the-shoulder (OS) shot, which is important in dialogue scenes to help the audience maintain a connection to the interaction between two people. You'll notice that all the shots in the dialogue are OS shots.

**3**   You don't need both shots of Alison, so get rid of the first one (of her painting alone in the frame; called a "single" by filmmakers). Since you might want it later, drag it back to the Clip pane.

**4**   Find the reverse shot that matches this first shot in terms of the size of the characters in the frame.

It's a medium shot of Jessica, over Alison's shoulder. What you're looking for is a moment in this shot where Jessica is speaking. Ideally she'd look up to make the connection to Alison, but unfortunately, because everyone is painting while they talk, eye contact is infrequent.

**5**   When you find a moment where Jessica speaks, clip it out.

It may be short, but as long as it's more than a couple of seconds, it's okay. You also may need to be careful to clip out a shot that doesn't include a zoom.

**TIP** ► Use the arrow keys to move frame by frame forward or backward through shots in order to locate the exact frame to cut on—where there's no zooming or moving.

The place you want to insert Jessica's shot is not after Alison's shot but within it, right after Alison finishes speaking. (Watch for her to finish moving her lips, since you can't really hear her well.)

**6**   Change to Timeline view, and then stop the playhead right after she speaks.

**7**   Split this clip at the playhead (Command-T) to create two clips.

**8**   Drop the shot of Jessica between these two clips.

To insert shots into the timeline, you don't necessarily have to be in Clip view. Dragging clips from the Clip pane into the timeline works fine.

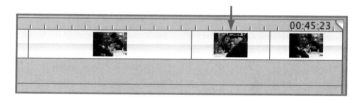

Now this scene is starting to have the flow of a dialogue: Alison speaks, Jessica listens and then speaks, and then we see Alison again.

**9**   Roll farther into the raw source material to find another medium shot of Jessica speaking, and clip some of it out.

Notice that in OS shots, you can often tell that the person with her back to the camera is speaking, even if you can't see her lips moving. This can be useful and effective for the dialogue.

**10**  Place this shot at the end of the sequence, after the medium shot of Alison.

**NOTE ▶** Notice how in both the shot and the reverse shot, Jessica is on the left side of the frame and Allison is on the right. This is good form. The effect is created because when Christopher shot the reverse, he was about 120 degrees from his first position, on the same side of an imaginary line he visualized between the girls.

Instead of continuing ahead in the raw source material, you may recall that all your medium and close shots of Alison were trimmed out earlier and still reside in a hunk of film you've set aside.

**11** Go back to the close-ups of Alison in the Clip pane and find a few seconds of her speaking, with her head up (as we can see she is doing in the OS shot).

Here's one:

**12** Cut out a few seconds from this angle and place it after the last shot.

In this case, the CU Alison shot ends when she looks away from Jessica and toward Rachel to bring her into the conversation. Using her line of sight as the cue, you are now free to explore the shot/reverse between Alison and Rachel.

**13** Find a short shot of Rachel speaking to Alison (a medium OS shot), cut out a few seconds, and add the piece to the end of the sequence.

**NOTE ▶** You can't trust the names iMovie automatically adds to clips as you chop up material in the Clip pane. It uses numbers that are available, and some numbers become available again and again as you use the pieces in your sequence. In the end, you may have multiple shots with names like Source/26. Again, if you're relying on names to guide you, rename shots in the Clip pane or timeline to help keep oriented.

Finally, end this dialogue with a shot of Jessica to give it some closure. You could continue indefinitely, cutting back and forth, medium to close, person to person. But your job as editor is to make the hard judgments and know when to stop.

**14** Find a CU Jessica shot from the trims.

**15** Cut out a few seconds and add the shot to the end of the sequence.

## Adding Finishing Touches to the Video

This video is getting closer to what we want in the finished product, but the beginning and end still need some sculpting.

As you roll through the end of your raw material—the final moments of video Christopher shot—you'll see a few more cutaways and finally a wider shot, an establishing shot, of the group painting.

The video doesn't need the cutaway shots (although you could experiment by dropping short bits into the scene), but it does need the wider shot. There is precious little material shot from a distance to give the audience any sense of where we are or the overall relationship between the girls sitting and painting.

1    Cut 5 seconds from the wide shot and add it to the sequence as the very first shot—ahead of the initial work you did in this lesson.

That really helps set up the coming scene. While there are other places it could go (and it can be a little clichéd to open *and end* with these wide shots), you can't go wrong structurally using the wide shot as a pair of bookends.

**2**   Add another segment of the wide shot to the end of the sequence.

**3**   Add a 1-second fade-in to the opening shot and a 1-second fade-out to the final shot.

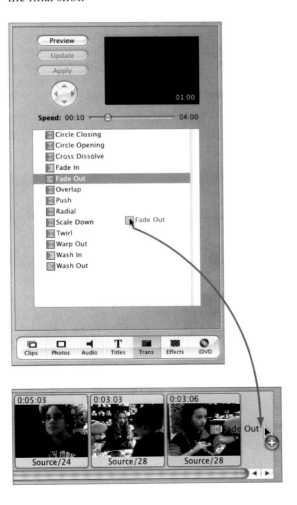

**TIP** ▶ Special effects are fun when you're playing around or when you want to impress friends with the power of your software, but in real videos they are not only unnecessary in most cases, but actually distracting. Skip special effects in your videos and use transition effects sparingly.

The sequence is done, unless after you watch it a few times you see places you could trim in or out by a few frames.

4   Use the Trim tool at the transition points to tweak edits.

In particular, watch out for blips in sound where you may have cut right in the middle of a word or sound.

5   Add (or delete) frames to soften any jarring edges.

## Adding Background Music

While this kind of video works pretty well with the simple ambient sound that goes with the images, sometimes it's better to drop in a more professional soundtrack.

1   Click the Audio button and access your iTunes playlists.

2   Position the playhead in your timeline at a point where you want the music to start.

In this case, starting at the beginning is logical, but on some videos—those with titles, for instance—you might want to start the music midway into the title display, or after the title appears but before the video images start. Regardless of where you drop the music, you can easily slide it around afterward if you don't like the location.

3   Select a track to add to the video.

**4**   Click Place at Playhead, or just drag the name of your song to your timeline.

iMovie will import the clip, and a purple bar will appear on one of your audio tracks.

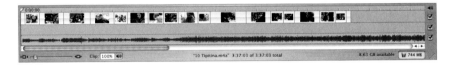

**5**   If the song is longer than the video track, cut it off after about 1 second following the end of the picture, using Command-T, and delete the tail.

> **NOTE** ▶ If you're using GarageBand to generate a background track (Lesson 12), use the duration of the project in iMovie to guide your music creation. In this case, the video project is 1 minute, 15 seconds, 24 frames long. Round it to 1 minute, 16 seconds, and use that as your guide in GarageBand.

The most important aspect of background music is the *mix*—that is, the balance between the loudness of the music and the loudness of the audio track of the video.

**6**   Click the volume percentage menu at the bottom of the iMovie window.

This lets you change the volume of the entire track by using a pop-up slider (or typing in a percentage) or change the volume at precise locations in the song by manipulating points on a line. For now, just change the volume of the entire track to 35 percent, which is in the appropriate range for a background track, although it truly depends on the music.

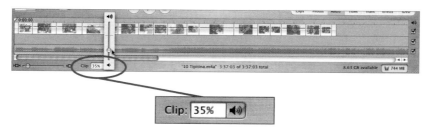

**TIP** To change the volume at specific points within the track, click the line superimposed over the audio track. Big yellow dots will appear on the line. You can then raise or lower the volume at one of these dots without changing the entire track's volume. By choosing these dot locations carefully, you can achieve an impressive sound mix. More on your sound mix in Lesson 12.

## Saving Your Video

Once a video is finished (a finished version is in the project folder; Finished_Project11.mov), it can be distributed for the enjoyment of others and the deep satisfaction of the creator. iMovie provides a number of avenues of distribution, but before turning your attention to sharing, you should explore the most important output option available—creating an archive.

Unlike music, video is remarkably large relative to typical hard-disk storage capacity. At 5 minutes of video per gigabyte, finished video in even a small collection can overwhelm a typical Mac. Consequently, archiving video is imperative. While it's great to be able to burn DVDs and CD-ROMs, put videos on the Internet, and even email them, all of these methods are for distribution—they take the high quality of your digital video and squeeze it

**7**  When you're done checking the tape, recue it to a spot in the black material that follows the recording.

By always starting to record over these black pieces of "leader," you guarantee that timecode will count continuously. This also gives you a moment to make sure you're not going to record over something you didn't mean to.

> **TIP** If you are serious about your video work, it is often a good idea to save an additional copy of your video without music. Delete the music track, and make a recording to your DV tape. Then you can undo the music deletion and save your project with it there. The point of having a version without music is simply that once the music and the rest of the video are merged together on tape, they are harder to separate should you ever want to reedit the video (making it shorter, for instance, or combining parts with other videos to make longer movies), or if one day you decide the music is wrong for the project. For many reasons, it can be a good practice for advanced users.

Now that a copy of your video is in DV format and is safely back on tape, you can output other formats of your video for distribution. Eventually, you can delete the project and media from your computer, knowing that if you need to you can bring the project back into your Mac for new output options or a little reediting.

## Uploading Your Video to the Web

Once you're done archiving, it's a fine moment to share your video with the world (or, maybe just your friends). In the same way you created the archive, you can place the movie on your .Mac account.

**1**    Choose File > Share, click HomePage, and either rename the movie or leave the name as it is.

**2**    Click Share.

The movie is compressed and copied to your iDisk. It takes a few moments for iMovie to perform these functions.

**3**    Once the file is uploaded, you're coached through the process of selecting a theme for the Web page and then publishing the movie.

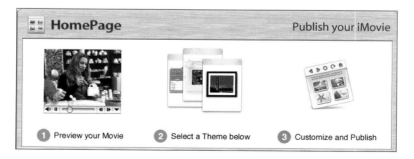

**4**    Choose a theme.

Christopher picked a movie projector theme and then went on to customize the page.

**5**   Click Publish.

The page is loaded into the .Mac Web site, and you are given the Web address for viewing the movie.

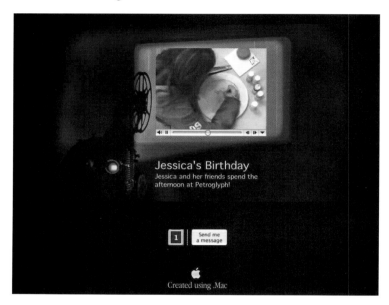

## What You've Learned

▶ Roll through your material in the order you shot it, in search of bits to use.

▶ Use Command-T to chop up your raw material into usable bits.

▶ Click shots in the Clip pane or the timeline to change labels to readily identifiable names.

▶ Alternate views of your workspace from Clip view to Timeline view while working: moving shots around, dragging shots out, playing, and trimming.

▶ Build structure first. Use cutaways after you've set up the structure.

▶ Don't use every shot. In a first pass through your material, it might be okay to start by including everything you shot in your sequence, but you'll want to quickly become discerning and remove unnecessary angles as well as material that runs long.

▶ In general, the sound recorded with the video is difficult to hear. Don't try to use it or follow the conversations too closely. It's good ambient sound, but it's less useful as the driving force of the video.

▶ There's no need for special effects. The strength of the video is in the action and dynamics onscreen. There's no need for transition effects either, except in the opening and closing moments.

▶ Add background music from iTunes to match the duration of the video.

▶ Use the volume controller at the bottom of the window to adjust the mix of the music track to the sound recorded with the pictures.

▶ Use Share to create a high-quality digital archive of your video back to your camcorder. If you have a .Mac account, you can also quickly share your video to the Web.

# 12

| | |
|---|---|
| Lesson Files | Lessons > Lesson12 > Finished_Timelapse_Project7 alias |
| Tools | GarageBand |
| Time | Approximately 90 minutes |
| Goals | Learn how to build an original music track from prebuilt instrument loops |
| | Adjust the length of loops |
| | Adjust the relative volume of tracks for a balanced mix |
| | Export custom music to iTunes and place it in your videos |

# Creating Unique Music for Your Projects

Creating new music is a great deal more challenging (and can be more rewarding) than loading your CDs into iTunes and listening to them on your iPod. GarageBand, an application in the iLife suite, addresses the fun and complexities of music creation. It's an obvious coup for musicians, wannabe musicians, and those with hidden musical talents and dormant dreams. The world of copyrights and permissions may lead even less-musical types to explore creating their own acoustic content rather than ripping other people's tunes. In the case of, say, music that's played with movies and slide shows in the public arena, even a musically challenged business owner can quickly make some original music with no fear of recrimination.

Some people may want to avoid GarageBand. It isn't as simple or intuitive as the other iLife products. Whereas all the rest (iTunes, iPhoto, iMovie, and iDVD) take in existing digital content, manage it, organize it, and prepare it for output, GarageBand synthesizes content from a virtually blank slate. If you don't have the time or inclination to make your own music, there's nothing wrong with settling into your great CD collection with iTunes and skipping the rock star bit altogether.

That said, you should at least try it. This lesson is designed to provide a short and safe look around. Who knows? You may discover a deep, lurking talent for making your own music. It's powerful, exciting, and (dare I say it?) narcotic. You may not be able to stop once you lay down your first tracks. Even without a guitar or keyboard, you will be on your way to making original music with GarageBand after this lesson.

## Creating New Music

Jennifer likes taking pictures and enjoys the process of making videos (as long as it's quick). But she really doesn't have any musical aspirations or, frankly, skills. Still, as a business owner she has an obligation not to accompany videos and slide shows in her retail studio with the copyrighted music she listens to on her iPod. Charlie shouldn't either—playing his music in presentations he makes at school is technically improper, but since he's a kid and the use is non-commercial (and probably one-time), he can get away with it. Charlie's interest in GarageBand is far more extensive than making background music—he's a great guitar player, and he uses GarageBand to help him practice and record his professional-sounding tracks without needing to coordinate with a group when he feels like jamming. Christopher is allowed to use copyrighted music from CDs in his personal home projects, but he's attracted to GarageBand because he wants music in his videos that sounds hip but without lyrics—since they might compete for the attention of the audience. Jennifer needs music, however, and she has a limited budget.

It's always an option to buy the rights to some music, or find some royalty-free tunes. (There are many sources online.) Apple provides a large online assortment of short musical riffs if you have a .Mac account. Called Freeplay music, it's on your iDisk in the software folder for .Mac members.

But even with that viable option, the Freeplay songs—like virtually all prepared music—have preset lengths (10 seconds, 30 seconds, 1 minute) that may not meet your project's specific needs. And ultimately, they are publicly available tunes (although you cannot use them commercially), and you may want something a little more customized. For a small business, the cornerstone of a successful operation is often being unique. For Jennifer, her brand and business are all about creativity. Confronting her fears, Jennifer launches into GarageBand to make some very simple, quick background music for her in-studio presentations.

### Setting Up for Your Song

**1**    Open GarageBand.

Launching the application takes you to the start-up window from which you can open either a new project or an existing one.

**2**    Click the Create a New Project button.

The New Project window opens, in which you'll establish some basic parameters for the song you'll create.

**3** Give your song a name, but leave the rest of the defaults set as they are, and then click Create.

This will open the main window for music creation. The project is saved in the GarageBand folder, which resides in the Music folder in your Home directory.

4   Move your pointer to the Grand Piano keyboard and click some ivories on the instrument sitting in the middle of your window.

You should hear the sounds of a grand piano. (You're making music!)

If you had an electronic keyboard with the appropriate USB connector, you could connect it and play that Grand Piano interface using your full-size keyboard. But Jennifer doesn't have a keyboard sitting around, so she's going to get rid of this onscreen diversion altogether.

**NOTE ▶** If you did plug in a USB keyboard, you'd need to connect it to your Mac prior to launching GarageBand in order for it to be enabled.

5   Click the red button in the top-left corner of the Grand Piano interface.

The keyboard disappears, although the green Grand Piano track it was related to remains onscreen. It is okay to leave this track here, but you won't be using it. (More about tracks in a moment.)

Now that the window for music creation is mostly empty and ready to go, how to start? Since Jennifer has no intention of playing any instrument or singing into a microphone, she needs to find some music.

6   Click the Browse button (with the eye icon) on the bottom left of the window.

This opens the Loop Browser: the place where you'll search for, listen to, and ultimately select the appropriate instrumental loop to add to your song.

### Adding Loops

A *loop* is a small segment of music that can be played over and over, popping from the end back to the beginning to sound like a smooth, continuous musical track. It's short, lasting perhaps only 1 to 4 seconds, and can repeat indefinitely. A typical real-world loop might be the drumbeat in a rock song—it may be basically the same rhythm, keeping time for the length of the song. One-person bands often use machines to generate repeating loops of sound to play along with. The Loop Browser provides access to hundreds of loops that come built into GarageBand.

The menu side of the Loop Browser

Although there is certainly no single way—and no wrong way—to build a musical track for your videos and slide shows, Jennifer is going to follow an easy way.

**1**  In the Loop Browser, select All Drums.

This reduces the number of options to only the drum loops. The remaining categories are grayed out.

Just to the left of the Volume slider, you can see that there are 281 loops that can be classified as drums. Jennifer needs one. On the far right side of the Loop Browser are all 281 search results that meet the conditions specified on the left.

| | Name ▲ | Tempo | Key | Beats | Fav |
|---|---|---|---|---|---|
| ♪ | 70s Ballad Drums 01 | 80 | C | 8 | ☐ |
| ♪ | 80s Pop Beat 07 | 110 | – | 8 | ☐ |
| ♪ | 80s Pop Beat 08 | 110 | – | 16 | ☐ |
| ♪ | 80s Pop Beat 09 | 110 | – | 16 | ☐ |
| ◀» | 80s Pop Beat 10 | 110 | – | 16 | ■ |
| ♪ | Ambient Beat 01 | 100 | – | 16 | ☐ |
| ⩕ | Blip Synth 01 | 90 | – | 2 | ☐ |
| ♪ | Classic Rock Beat 01 | 140 | – | 16 | ☐ |

The six columns have some interesting information. The leftmost column shows an icon, either a green music note or a blue waveform. The green note indicates the loop is MIDI—that is, a computer-generated sound. A MIDI loop is not a recording so much as a mathematical instruction for playing music. It has properties that make it attractive to the beginner. Most important to know is that when you merge MIDI loops, the computer can work for you to make them sound good together.

The blue waveform represents an audio file, not unlike the files in iTunes. This is an actual recording of sound. The Mac cannot augment this sound to make it fit with other sounds the way it can with the MIDI loops. Audio files are less malleable as raw material for beginners and are a little harder to make sound good. For that reason, don't use them for this lesson. Focus on the items with green notes, the MIDI loops.

Besides the name of the loop and the icon, you can ignore the rest of the columns. But if you're curious, what you've got is the loop's *tempo* (a measurement of how fast a song will be played), its *key* (not relevant to drums, but a reference to a song's position on the musical scale), and its *beats* (the number of beats per measure, the unit of a song). Fav (favorites) is a convenience for you to mark loops you like so you can find them quickly later on.

When you use loops in GarageBand, the software automatically adjusts their listed values to fit together. So you don't need to limit yourself to selecting loops that have matching tempo, key, or beats.

**2** Single-click an item and it will start to play; explore different loops in this way.

Feel free to make notes about the ones you like, or click the Fav check box to easily search for the loop later. Click a playing loop and it stops.

**3** Scroll down through the list of drum loops to Straight Up Beat 02.

**4** Click and drag Straight Up Beat 02 to the space under the Grand Piano track.

If you drop it in the Tracks column, GarageBand creates a new track for the loop and places the music at the beginning of the timeline area to the right of the Tracks and Mixer columns. This region is the musical workspace.

You have now created a new track for the drum loop and added the loop to the numbered timeline on the right, starting at the 1.

The little dark bars and dots in the green loop represent the notes. The vertical red line at the head of this loop is GarageBand's playhead. From the numbers in the timeline ruler, you can see that this loop is two measures long.

**NOTE** ▶ Unlike movies and the timeline in iMovie, music is built in measures, which are counted along the ruler. A measure is a musical unit but not a fixed span of time, so it varies depending on the song. Notice the number 1 at the beginning of the timeline, rather than a 0 as you'd find if this were a time scale. The 1 denotes the beginning of the first measure. A loop that extends from the 1 to the 2 is one measure long. Similarly, a loop that extends to the 7 results in a piece of music six measures long.

5    Click the Play button in the shuttle controls at the bottom of the window.

The music will play, continuing forward right past the end of the loop and into silence.

Did you hear it? It was short.

6    Move the pointer to the edge of the green loop in the timeline.

The great thing about loops is that you can repeat (or loop) them.

When the pointer approaches the edge of the loop, it changes into one of two tools. If you point at the middle-to-lower edge of the loop, you'll see a Trim tool, which extends or shortens the loop segment itself. When the pointer moves up to the top edge of the loop, it turns into the Loop tool, which lets you grab and drag the loop forward in time, rolling out more and more loops (or parts of loops) as you go.

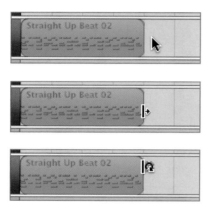

**7**    Use the Loop tool to click and drag the loop to extend to the end of the sixth measure (and thus to the 7 on the scale).

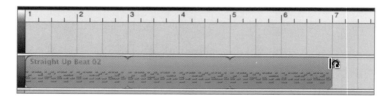

**8**  Now go back to the Loop Browser and click Reset (in the top-left corner of the browser).

This brings you back to the top level of the Browser so you can find your next piece of music.

**9**  Click Bass.

A reliable method of building a bit of music is to start with the drums, add bass, and then end with something more melodic like a guitar or piano.

Instead of scrolling down the column of the 183 bass loops that GarageBand found, you can further refine your options by selecting one of the attributes on the right side of the Loop Browser.

**10**  Click Cheerful.

The number of options is reduced to 58

**11**  From the resulting bass selections, look around until you find Funky Pop
Bass 01. (It should be on top.) Click and drag it up to the empty track
region beneath the Drum Kit track.

**12**  Drag the playhead back to the beginning of the timeline (the left side of
the tracks) by clicking in the ruler portion of the timeline and then dragging left. (Alternately, you can click the Cue to Start button in the shuttle
controls—the backwards arrow against a vertical line—to pop to the
beginning of your song.)

**13** When the timeline is positioned at the start of the tracks, click the Play button (or press the spacebar on your keyboard).

> **NOTE ▶** The entire loop in the Electric Bass track is four measures long—meaning it repeats itself half as much as Straight Up Beat 02. This tends to make it less repetitive sounding. You can see how long the original loops are by the small indentations in the edge of the loop as it repeats in a track. In general (but certainly not always), it sounds better when you add loops in these full units—notch to notch.

Sounds good—pretty cool, pretty easy. Let's get one more track, one more instrument.

**14** Go back to the Loop Browser, reset the options, and then find Piano > Classic Rock Piano 02. Drag it to the track space under the Electric Bass track.

GarageBand does its best to make these disparate instruments sound good together. If the tracks are in different keys (Classic Rock Piano 02 is in the key of D; Bass is in C), GarageBand transposes one to match. If the tempos are different, GarageBand slows them down (or speeds them up) to synchronize them with the tempo you chose when you opened the project. (The default is 120 beats per minute.) But even after this clever work, many tracks will sound really lousy together. If you're not really musical, your best option is to experiment a lot and work hard to keep it simple.

**TIP** ▶ In the world of background music, very simple arrangements work well. It's not a cop-out. One or two tracks—sometimes just a drum, other times just a clean piano with a shaker—often are all you need to enrich your videos, particularly those with dialogue. You don't want the music to compete. You want it only to enhance the texture and mood.

## Making Adjustments to Loops

The three tracks in your workspace may be all you need for the background of a video. If you dragged the loops so that they all extend to the same length, you might consider yourself done. But Jennifer is not satisfied with the Classic Rock Piano 02 loop. The piano is nice, but it's too busy for her taste.

1   Select the Classic Rock Piano 02 loop and press Delete on your keyboard.

    The piano track remains, but the loop of music is gone.

2   Grab the Funky Pop Bass 01 loop from its position in the Electric Bass track and drag it down to the Piano track. Now play it.

Notice that? The notes that the bass was playing are now being played by a piano. This is because the loop is a MIDI loop. It means that you can instruct the Mac to play it as if it were any instrument, depending on the track you place it in.

**NOTE ►** If you want to hear something truly odd, drag the drum loop down into the bass track. That percussive music is quite unusual when "played" by an electric bass. Drag it back to its starting point when you're done—too avant-garde for the ceramic studio.

3    Instead of dragging the Funky Pop Bass 01 loop back to its rightful spot, Option-click and drag it back.

This will copy the loop, leaving one in the Piano track and placing a duplicate in the Electric Bass track. Now you have the same music, the same notes being played simultaneously by different instruments.

Doubling up makes the notes a little richer and is a great effect to apply when you're looking to add some musical sophistication with little risk of it sounding bad.

4    Drag the loop in the piano track to delay it by two beats (in this case, half a measure).

This offsets it from the Bass track playing the same tune—another interesting musical touch that works for short periods without becoming grating.

**5** Use the Trim tool at the tail of the piano loop to shorten the music to end when the bass ends.

**TIP** ▶ A razor blade is really the only tool you need to edit—whether it's video or audio or music. GarageBand provides a chopping tool identical to the one in iMovie. Command-T breaks a selected track at the playhead (called Split in the GarageBand Edit menu). Using Command-T with the Move and Copy functions you've already used will let you build far more interesting combinations of loops (or parts of loops).

GarageBand is all about loops, and you've been working with a series of musical loops. Now it's time to loop your tracks.

**6** Click the Loop button.

This button (a pair of curved arrows) is in the shuttle controls. It lets your music repeat over and over.

When you select Loop, a yellow bar pops into the ruler area of the time-line. This yellow region determines what section of your creation will be looped.

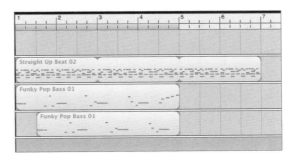

By clicking the end of the yellow bar, you can drag the loop duration in or out to be shorter or longer, whatever you prefer for evaluating the music you've created.

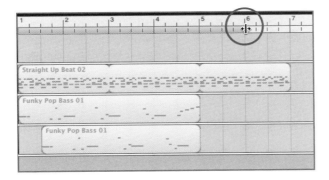

**7**  If your loop region is not aligned with the 5 in the ruler, drag the end of the yellow bar so that it is.

**8**  Click the Play button.

No matter where your playhead is parked, it will always pop to the beginning of the yellow bar to start playing. When it reaches the end of the bar, it will pop back to the beginning and continue, no matter how far your music extends. Now you're looping.

## Mixing Your Music

You put three tracks together in GarageBand, and it placed them where you wanted with the instruments you selected. But you may want to make more fundamental adjustments to the music before you decide you're done. The art of determining the relative volume of each track, as well as whether you hear music from the left speaker or the right, is critical to the musical experience. Setting up these parameters is called *mixing*.

Between the Tracks column and the workspace you've been using is the Mixer.

The Mixer provides some volume and pan controls for each track (known as a slice) of your creation. These settings are not variable within the track but remain fixed for the entire track. The pair of bars above the volume control are *peak meters,* which alert you to sound that is loud enough to result in distortion when played in most audio equipment. It's okay if the red lights on the right edge flash a little during a loud piece of music, but for the most part the lines need to be in the middle of the bar and mostly in the green. A small vertical bar appears in each meter to indicate the peak level reached as the music volume pulses.

Move the Volume slider around to get the sound volume of one track to balance with the others. Use the Pan knob to move the sound from one speaker to the other—or balance it between the two. Sometimes when you have lots of instruments, you want them to appear to occupy different locations in space, and you can do this by selecting how much you hear with each ear. For the music we're working with, there is little need to mess with the balance.

If you want the volume of a track to vary during the playing of the track itself—known in the business as using a *dynamic fader*—you must leave the Mixer and look in the Tracks column. You'll see three buttons there; the one on the right is a small triangle, which reveals your work for adjusting volume variably.

Clicking the triangle will reveal a new track below the one you're working on.

With this special volume track revealed, you will be able to move a line to increase or decrease the volume. You also can click the line to add points at which you can change the volume—very much in the way you can dynamically adjust the volume in iMovie.

This process is a little more complicated than Jennifer wants. Uncheck the Track Volume check box to mute your volume work and close this dynamic volume control by clicking the triangle that opened it. Far more useful at this point are some of the other buttons in the Tracks column.

### Listening Only to the Tracks You Want

Two buttons give you two great track-auditioning capabilities in GarageBand. The first, the Mute button, is represented by a little speaker. Click it and it turns blue, indicating the track is silent.

Muting a given track lets you get rid of it (temporarily) as you develop the mix of your song.

The opposite of muting a track is soloing it. The Solo button is indicated by a headphones icon. Clicking it lets you hear *only* the track selected.

You can use the Mute and Solo buttons at any time during the editing and mixing of your music.

## Adjusting Your Time Scale and Working with Real Time

All of this musical notation—keys and measures and tempos—are great for the musically inclined, but Jennifer has had no musical training. All she wants is a loop that will run as long as her video. She knows her time-lapse video (from Lesson 7) is 1 minute long. How does that translate into measures?

Luckily, no math is required. At the bottom of the workspace is a digital counter.

The music note to the left of the numbers indicates that the counter is displaying musical measurement. For more practical applications of your music, change the counter to display time measurement by clicking the note.

The note becomes a clock, and the display changes to show hours, minutes, seconds, and thousandths of a second—perhaps more accuracy than you need. Now, by positioning the playhead in your music, you can see how long your music is running—or where you are within a piece of music.

> **NOTE** ▶ When you loop a bit of your music, the counter restarts at zero—the beginning of the loop—no matter how many times the loop repeats.

The ruler across the top of the workspace is always expressed in measures. And measures do not consistently relate to elapsed time in different pieces of music. But as you build your music, and the length of your song increases, you may need to see more duration of your tracks at a glance.

The Zoom control for the workspace is (somewhat cryptically) nestled at the bottom of the Tracks column.

Click and drag the knob to increase (or decrease) the time span represented on the right side of the workspace. Whenever there is more to see than what is shown in the window, the familiar Mac scroll bar is available along the bottom of the workspace.

The measurement of time is the ideal way to find events in your video and make them correspond to moments in your music.

**1**   Open Lesson12 > **Finished_Timelapse_Project07 alias.**

This is the finished version of Jennifer's illustration of the Italian brush-stroke technique. With the titles and fade-out, the video is precisely 1 minute, 0 seconds, and 7 frames long. The music for this should probably be relatively subdued. The only musical cue—that is, the only instance in the picture where she might want to have a corresponding change in the music—is when the video goes from the medium shot to the closer shot.

**2**   Move the timeline to the point where the video cuts close.

The counter at the playhead indicates this is 37 seconds, 8 frames from the start. This will be our cue point.

**3**   Go back to GarageBand.

With the counter set to display time measurement, you now have three factors to keep in mind as you develop your music: The song starts at 0, something happens at 37:08, and the song ends by 1:00:07.

As you continue to work on your tracks, these cue points will be central to the creation of the structure you build in your song.

## Combining Loops to Vary Your Songs

Keeping the music simple is often the key to building a successful track of background music. But you can use a number of simple strategies to make your music slightly less repetitive. One is to combine loops from within one family of instruments.

**1**   Start from the song we've been building. Click the Loop button in the shuttle controls to turn off that feature, as it won't be necessary for the time being.

**2**   Delete the Grand Piano track on top by selecting the track on the left and then choosing Track > Delete Track.

**3**   Delete the Drum Kit track also—the whole track, not just the loop of music placed there.

You're going to continue reshaping your song until it feels appropriate for the time-lapse video.

It's also good to know that in the process of sculpting a song, you may create many tracks, add more to them, and either mute or totally delete parts as you go. In this case, ignore the Bass and Piano tracks and explore some different sounds.

4    Mute the Electric Bass and Piano tracks.

5    Click Reset in the Loop Browser and find the guitar loop called Southern Rock Guitar 01.

6    Listen to all the tracks in the Southern Rock Guitar family (01 through 05), noticing the similarities and differences.

Some of the loops lend themselves to long stretches of video, and some sound more like emotional transitions.

7    Click and drag Southern Rock Guitar 02 to the track under the Piano track.

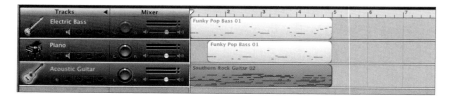

This has a nice sound to it. The loop comprises four measures, which— according to the counter—is 8 seconds long. This is pretty long by loop standards. It means the sounds in it repeat only every 8 seconds, which is good for a loop that will play over and over a few times without getting too repetitive.

8    Drag the guitar loop out for 12 measures (to the number 13).

That's about as much as Jennifer can take before she wants to hear something else. Change your scale using the Zoom slider on the left to see more of the ruler. (Thirty measures is about 1 minute—the length of the time-lapse video this song will be for, so make sure you can see at least that far.)

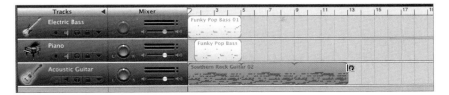

9    Click and drag Southern Rock Guitar 01 to the same Acoustic Guitar track, following the first loop.

It is also a pretty long loop, and it sounds similar enough to Southern Rock Guitar 02 that they form a nice duo—an almost imperceptible variation, but enough difference to eliminate some of that repetitive feeling.

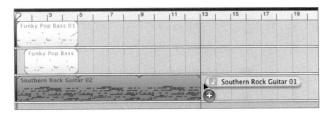

10    Drag the Southern Rock Guitar 01 loop out by one more full loop—another four measures—and play some (or all) of the resulting music.

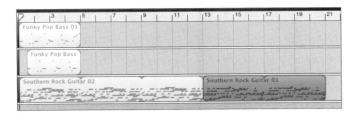

### Making the Music Match the Video

As you're playing the music that you've got so far, watch the time counter. Somewhere in the middle of the added area, the counter says you're at 37 seconds. According to your notes, that's where the video cuts from the wider shot to the closer shot, and you want a transition in the music here. The transition could be a different instrument, maybe a new track, or just a musical interlude of some kind.

1   Park the playhead on the measure closest to 37 seconds.

    GarageBand snaps the playhead to the measure boundaries; the closest is at 36 seconds.

    There is a nice musical transition in the Southern Rock Guitar family, loop 05.

2   Click and drag Southern Rock Guitar 05 to the Acoustic Guitar track, and drop it over the end of loop 01, aligned with the playhead.

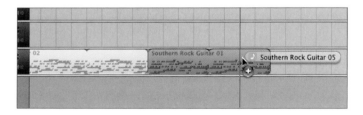

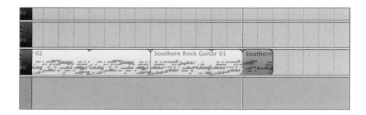

Play the track. The transition works, but loop 05 is short; it feels like you need more of it to be satisfying.

**3**   Drag loop 05 out by another full repetition, to the measure 23 line.

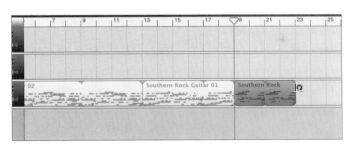

**4**   Click and drag loop 01 onto the track to follow loop 05.

This should bring the sound back to a familiar verse. After playing one loop, the song's overall duration is only 52 seconds; the song needs to be longer to fit with the video.

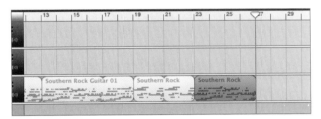

**5**   Drag loop 01 out until the song is 1 minute long—30 measures.

You could end it here, but it would sound better to make it slightly longer and fade out the music after the video ends. Editing the song is best done here, from within GarageBand. The actual musical fade-out could be done (earlier in this lesson, you learned about the Track Volume check box), but it is sometimes better to do that fine-tuning with the video while in iMovie after the song is imported.

**6**   Either way, drag out loop 01 a couple of beats further, a couple of seconds more than 1 minute.

## Adding Texture to the Song

This is a nice, simple track of acoustic guitar that, even without drums and bass, seems to feel light and dynamic enough for the video. To give the guitar just a touch of texture, a small amount of percussion would probably help. A drum is too much, but let's try a shaker.

1   Reset the Loop Browser. Select Shaker and find Shaker 16.

    Nothing fancy, just a little salt for the stew.

2   Click and drag the Shaker loop to the track underneath the Acoustic Guitar track.

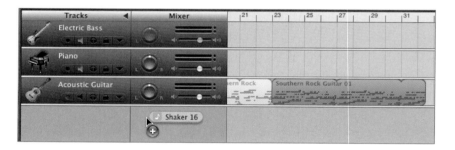

    This starts the shaker immediately at the beginning of the song. Sometimes it helps to break up the repetition of a long track by staggering the intro-duction of other instruments.

3   Slide the Shaker loop to begin after the Guitar loop completes its first cycle.

    Look for the notch in the Guitar loop if you want to see the unit of the actual music loop before repeating.

**4**  Drag out the Shaker 16 loop all the way to the end of the Guitar loops.

**5**  Play the tracks.

The shaker is a little loud; it needs to fall into the background more.

**6**  Reduce the volume of the Shaker track using the slider in the Mixer until the sound is audible but not noisy.

**TIP**  Songs tend to have familiar structures—sometimes as simple as verses and chorus. Verses have one kind of sound, and the chorus has a different but compatible sound. If you call the verses A and the chorus B, a song's structure is often something like A-B-A-B or A-A-B-A.

## Getting Your Music into iTunes

Getting music from GarageBand into iTunes is a necessary first step to being able to use the music in your other iLife applications (iPhoto, iMovie, iDVD), and it's incredibly easy.

When you're done making a piece of music (or even before then—you can make interim versions to your heart's content), you can export the music directly into iTunes.

Before exporting for the first time, you may want to verify the settings for precisely where GarageBand will place this music in iTunes and how it will label it. (Remember, you can change the labels in iTunes if you're so inclined, but it might be better to make sure it's set up properly here first.)

**1**   Choose GarageBand > Preferences.

**2**   Click the Export tab, which lets you can confirm (or set up) how the music will go into iTunes.

If these settings are good, close the window (with the red button). Now
you are ready to export, and you know where the music will end up
when you do.

**3**   Choose File > Export to iTunes.

This will mix your entire sequence of music (not just the part indicated
by the yellow loop bar) down to a single track. This is referred to as a
*mixdown*.

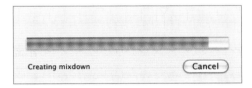

**NOTE** ▶ A mixdown is the musical equivalent of the rendering of special
effects that's done in iMovie. The program takes a bunch of discrete elements and—through some computer processing—combines them into a
single element. If you make a change to some part of the original parts,
the computer has to do it again to keep the combination current. Faster
computers—with more MHz in the CPU—perform these kinds of tasks
quickly.

The process takes a few moments, but when it's done, the song is placed in a special playlist in iTunes.

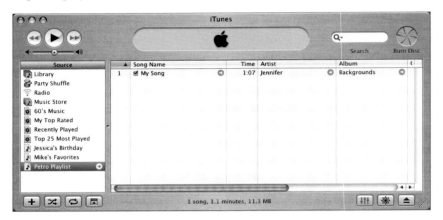

After exporting, your Mac will automatically open iTunes (presumably so you can play it there). If you want to see the song you've created, browse in iTunes and go to the designated playlist. Your music is waiting for you there. And of course, it is now also accessible from the other iLife applications for use in your slideshows, DVDs, or movies.

**NOTE ▶** You can export to iTunes at any time while you are working, to create interim versions of tracks. But remember that if you change the music in GarageBand, it's not automatically reflected in the song in iTunes. You need to export again to get the current version.

**4**    Open iMovie, if it's not already open.

**5**    Open Lesson12 > **Finished_Timelapse_Project07 alias**, and park the playhead at the beginning, for good measure.

This is where you want the song to begin, during the opening titles.

**6**    Click the Audio button to access the iTunes playlists.

**7**   Open the playlist to which you exported your music.

For Jennifer, it was the Petro Playlist.

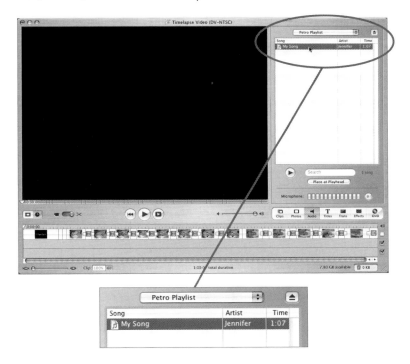

**8**   Select the song.

**9**   Click the Place at Playhead button.

The song is immediately imported and dropped into an empty audio track aligned with the playhead (which should be at the start of the video).

**10**   Play it and see how the song syncs with the picture.

The only thing left to do is fade out the music after the video ends.

**11** Choose View > Show Clip Volume Levels.

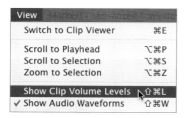

This adds a volume control line to the audio tracks that you can modify.

**NOTE ▶** This method is comparable to performing the same kind of work in GarageBand using the Track Volume check box.

**12** Click the line in the music track at a place where you want the song to fade out.

A yellow dot will appear here, and a smaller, purple dot will also appear to its left. These two points control the beginning and end of the fade-out, with a curve of steadily decreasing volume spanning between them.

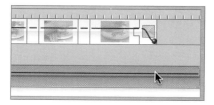

**13** Drag the yellow dot to the position at which the fade-out should be completed, and pull it down to a volume of zero—the lowest you can drag it.

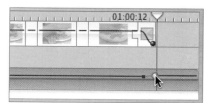

**14** Drag the purple dot back to the position you want the fade-out to begin—probably in the middle of the video fade-out, but the precise location is pretty subjective.

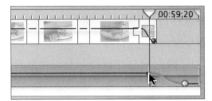

When you like the relationship of the video fade-out and the music fade-out, you're done.

Play the entire video now, with the song mixed in. The two should fit together pretty well, and the fade-out at the end should get softer as the picture disappears, but should end a moment after the video is gone. That's a nice conclusion and typical in professional videos. Good job.

## What You've Learned

▶   Click the Browse button with the eye icon to use the Loop Browser.

▶   To find the instrument you want using the Loop Browser, select instruments on the left, add more criteria on the right, and view the results in the scroll window on the far right.

▶   Drag a loop to the Tracks column to add the music in its instrument track.

▶   Click the trailing edge of a loop to edit it or repeatedly loop it out; click the trailing lower edge for the Edit tool and the trailing upper edge for the Loop tool.

▶   Use the Volume slider in the Mixer to adjust the relative volumes of tracks for a balanced mix.

▶   Solo or mute tracks using the buttons in the Tracks column.

▶   Toggle the counter from musical notation to elapsed time by clicking the music note in the counter window.

▶   Use Preferences > Export to set up the location in iTunes where exported music is placed.

# 13

| | |
|---|---|
| Lesson Files | Lessons > Lesson13 > Start_BizOwnerVideo13 |
| Tools | iMovie, iPhoto, .Mac account |
| Time | Approximately 40 minutes |
| Goals | Grab still images from videotape |
| | Move folders of images into iPhoto |
| | Show off your iPhoto slide shows on the Internet with Apple's .Mac service |

# Putting Your Slide Show on the Internet

DVDs are great for small distribution, and digital video cassettes make good archives and are often fine for watching videos at home. But sometimes it's important to get your material out to a wider audience— on the Internet. At the end of Lesson 11, you saw how quickly you can upload a finished movie directly from iMovie to a Web page at Apple's .Mac Internet service. Now you're going to see the corresponding simplicity of uploading a slide show to the Web.

Throughout the lessons in this book, you've been learning to improvise. Not everyone has a digital camera and a camcorder, and even if you did, you don't always use them both in every situation. In Lesson 6, you learned to make a movie with photographs from a camera. Now you're going to learn to make a slide show with video from a camcorder.

The studio owner, Jennifer, doesn't use her still camera very often; she is more comfortable with her video camcorder. She sees iMovie as a tool that helps her find just the right frames of video, grab them, and turn them into photographs that she can then manage easily in iPhoto.

iPhoto makes it easy to organize the stills into albums and upload them to the Web for presentation. While the image quality of video frames is far inferior to that of dedicated still cameras, the Web demands that images be compressed, and therefore degraded from the high resolution you get in prints. The lower resolution of a camcorder makes it a perfectly suitable *camera* for shooting photographs for the Web. Jennifer keeps a gallery of shots from around her studio online and updates it often. It's easy because she pulls the still shots from the videotapes she shoots and uploads them to her company Web site with iPhoto.

All of this is contingent, of course, upon having an account with .Mac, Apple's suite of Internet services, including Web hosting. As a sophisticated Macintosh user for many years, Jennifer initially imagined a user-friendly Internet account like .Mac to be unnecessary. Her company maintains a Web site on a local hosting service, and she has been very happy with it. Still, the .Mac account is more than an ordinary Web host; it's one that's highly tuned to work with the iLife applications. In the same way that music effortlessly moves from iTunes to iMovie and iPhoto, .Mac interacts with iLife to make Web pages, slide shows, and movies easy to build, update, and share. After years of conspicuous avoidance, Jennifer got a .Mac account to streamline all her iLife work—and she even found a way to integrate it with her existing Web site for maximum effect. (For more information on .Mac accounts, see the Getting Started chapter.)

This lesson has two distinct parts, both of them simple and both of them important. The first happens in iMovie—the process of grabbing a bunch of still images. The second happens in iPhoto—building a slide show and putting it on the Internet through a .Mac account.

## Getting Still Photos from Your Video

At some point, you'll face the choice of grabbing either your still camera or your video camcorder. You can't always shoot with both. You saw in Lesson 6 how to turn still photos into a dynamic slide show. Now you will see how to turn video into acceptable-quality still photos. It begins in iMovie.

1    Create a new folder (choose File > New Folder) on your Desktop called Petroglyph Stills, where you will store all the photos you'll get from your video.

   This isn't required, of course, but it streamlines the process of moving the images into iPhoto.

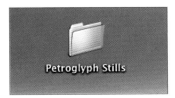

**2**   Open Lesson13 > Start_BizOwnerVideo13 > **BizOwnerVideo**.

Only one clip is here; the truth is, you don't need to do any editing. Right now you're using iMovie for its capability to grab still images from video.

**3**   Click the single clip and shuttle through it in the Viewer until you find a frame to grab. Pick any shot that appeals to you.

Since a camcorder records 30 frames every second, there are many to choose from.

**4**   When you find a good shot, use the arrow keys on the keyboard to move forward and backward a little until you identify just the right frame.

**5**   Choose File > Save Frame.

**6**  Name the image and select a location on your Mac for storing it.

In this case, select the folder you created on the Desktop to keep your frame grabs from this (de facto) roll.

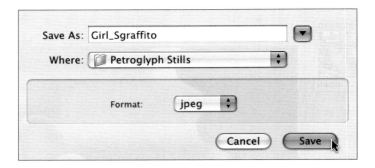

The default format for the image is JPEG. This is a good fit with iPhoto, so don't change it.

**TIP** ▶ If it's a challenge to navigate your computer by way of the Where pull-down menu, you can always deposit images on your Desktop and organize them in a folder later.

And that's it; the still is created and placed in the folder you selected.

**7**  Continue through this process until you have made a still from each unique shot on the videotape—around 15 of them—and placed them in the Petroglyph Stills folder.

That's all you need from iMovie. Close the project (no need to save anything, since you didn't do any editing). Now you're going to move back to iPhoto.

## Putting Digital Files into iPhoto

Just as you did in Lesson 3, you're going to bring photos into iPhoto. And as you did there, you'll add folders of photos as if they were rolls. (Before, however, you were simulating importing rolls from a digital camera.)

**1** Open iPhoto.

**2** Drag and drop the Petroglyph Stills folder of photos from the Desktop onto iPhoto's Source column.

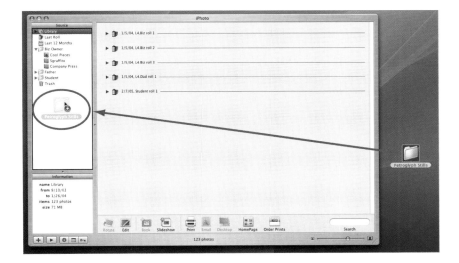

You can import a folder by dropping it in the main window, but you might as well take it right to Sources—this simultaneously creates an album for you, with the name of the folder (Petroglyph Stills), and loads all the photos into it (as well as into the Library).

Now all the stills from the video are in iPhoto, in an album and ready for you to organize.

**3** Open the Petroglyph Stills folder.

**4** Rearrange the photos to your liking.

As with editing video, they don't need to be in the order you shot them—and in fact, they probably shouldn't be.

**5** Drag and drop the photos into a new order.

**6**    When you're ready to put your slides on the Internet, click HomePage.

This will let you access your .Mac account and open the album in a preset template.

**NOTE** ▶ If you don't see the column on the right of Themes, click the Show Themes button at the lower left of the window. There are a number of Web page themes to choose from.

The names under the images come from the filenames of the photographs. The style of the page is set according to your choice from the themes, presented along the right side of the window. Try a few different themes to see what they look like, but ultimately come back here, to the Aquarium theme.

**7**    Change the text on the page. You can change the title at the top of the page, the small block of text under the title, and of course the captions. Write a pithy description in the text block by first clicking the title. Click the photo names to change them into captions.

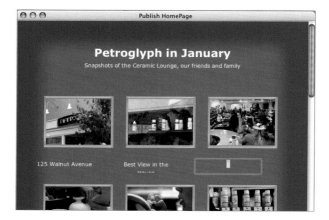

At any point in your creative process, you can change the theme.

**8**    Click the Pushpin theme.

When you've got the page the way you'd like it to be seen online, you're ready to publish it.

**9**   Click Publish.

Immediately, iPhoto makes a connection to your .Mac account—in particular, your allocated iDisk space—and uploads the photos from your computer to the .Mac server. (You must be connected to the Internet for this to work.)

In a few moments, the transfer is complete, your page is published, and a window pops up to alert you. You can visit the page directly, go back and edit the page if you'd like, or just click OK (and the window goes away).

Your .Mac account will email you (or the person listed on the account as the contact) with information about your new page—including the URL— as well as some other tips. So, although you may have the urge to write down this long Web address, you'll have other opportunities to save the page as a bookmark or email the URL to friends and family or a mailing list of customers.

**10** Click Visit Page Now.

Your default Web browser will go to your new Web page. It will look pretty much the same as it did while you were building it, with the addition of one particularly interesting option. There's a button near the top that turns this Web page into a slide show. It's not an automatic show as in iPhoto; instead, viewers can manually move from slide to slide at their own pace.

**11** Click Start Slideshow.

The slide show opens in its own window, and you can navigate it with the arrows in the bottom-right corner.

**12** Peruse the slides you uploaded to the Web.

Of course, this method for uploading images from iPhoto to the Web works regardless of where the photos came from—video camera, still camera, scans, and elsewhere. As long as images are in iPhoto, they can be shared by way of your .Mac account this easily.

## What You've Learned

▶   You can use videotape as a quick source for still images that will be printed small, emailed, or posted on the Internet.

▶   Use the Save Frame feature in iMovie to create still frames from video.

▶   Drag folders of still images to iPhoto to create the equivalent of rolls of these images.

▶   Use HomePage to build Web pages of your stills and to generate user-controlled slide shows.

# 14

**Lesson Files**

**Tools**    iDVD, SuperDrive

**Time**    Approximately 90 minutes

**Goals**    Learn how to make DVDs that include movies and slide shows

Learn how to customize DVD themes and menus

# Burning DVDs of Your Videos and Slide Shows

It's great to be able to flip open your iBook laptop and present a slide show live, but there are times when you want to leave the slide show with someone, such as your sister, to watch at her own convenience. Similarly, once your videos are archived onto digital tape, it's likely that you will want to distribute them. A DVD is a remarkably convenient way to distribute digital content, and burning a DVD has never been easier.

Christopher can't wait to make a DVD to send to Jessica's grandparents. They live in another town and are hungry for photos and videos from her life. Charlie's parents just got a SuperDrive to burn DVDs, and he archives his video journals onto the discs and removes them from the family Mac to conserve hard disk space (and maintain a little extra privacy). The ceramics studio has a large flat-panel display that customers often watch. Studio owner Jennifer cycles through a few DVDs each day—presenting slide shows of finished pieces (to give customers ideas for their own projects), quick techniques to try (like the sgraffito step-by-step), and other creative touchstones (the time-lapse videos are always crowd-pleasers, both instructive and entertaining).

In the same way that all the iLife applications integrate so effortlessly—adding music to slide shows or adding still photos to videos—burning a DVD in iDVD is just as painless with its direct connection to your music, your photos, and your movies.

## Getting to Know a DVD

DVDs are for more than playing movies. A DVD can play all kinds of media— from videos to slide shows to music—but it's also a big storage device. A DVD holds 4.7 GB of data—actually more like 4.3 GB (the discrepancy is partly because of the way computers measure the capacity). There are primarily two types of DVDs. One kind holds movies (a regular DVD), and the other holds software and files (sometimes referred to as a DVD-ROM).

iDVD has the great capability to combine these attributes. You can play movies from your disc, and you can also store files in folders that recipients access by popping the disc into a ComboDrive or SuperDrive (or any other DVD player hooked to your Mac). In the latter case, the DVD would be just like a giant CD-ROM.

**NOTE ▶** At first, there were only CD players in Macs. Then there were drives that would both play and record CDs. Then came DVD players. Since the DVD format is backward-compatible, as they say, a DVD player can also play a CD. Next was a drive that could play the DVD, but both play and record a CD. This is a great set of features, and Apple sells this as a ComboDrive. Finally, there is the DVD player and recorder, which also plays and records CDs. This is a SuperDrive.

The video and other media content on a DVD must be encoded in order to play on your DVD player and TV. The files are squeezed to fit on the disc *(compressed)*, which decreases their quality slightly but makes them considerably smaller. The digital video files you work with in iMovie are large (1 GB per 5 minutes of video, as you may recall), but after iMovie prepares them for the DVD, the same gigabyte can hold between 15 and 30 minutes of video (depending on some of your preferences in iDVD, but don't worry about that now). Consequently, a DVD can hold up to 2 hours of your videos.

**NOTE ▶** This compression is one reason you can't go backward, moving videos from DVDs into iMovie, without a lot of work.

**TIP ▶** Because of the way iDVD squeezes video to fit on the disc, recording less material to the disc (say, an hour or less) will yield slightly better quality than putting on more. For the best quality, keep the length of your DVD material under an hour.

When you use a DVD for data storage (as a DVD-ROM), you don't want to compress files at all—you want to leave them exactly as they are. iDVD has the capability to manage all of this, which is one of the excellent features of the product.

**TIP ▶** There are many, often confusing, DVD formats, which you may have come across once you got a SuperDrive. There's DVD-R, DVD-RW, DVD+RW, and more. While most are generally interchangeable and play in a ComboDrive as well as typical consumer DVD players, some won't. Never mind the subtleties between formats; the blank discs available from Apple tend to record easily in SuperDrives and play without problems on most players.

## Getting an iMovie Movie Ready to Burn

Once you finish making a video in iMovie, there's not a lot you have to do to put it into iDVD, but there are a few things you might *want* to do. The most fun of all the options is to add *chapters* to your movie. (Chapters are midpoints in your video that can be directly accessed from the opening DVD menu.) This way, for longer videos, you can choose between playing from the start or popping to specific locations within the movie, which saves you from having to fast-forward every time you want to watch a certain part of the video.

None of Jennifer's videos is long enough to really merit chapters, but since adding them is easy enough, it's worth seeing how it's done.

**1**   Open the Lesson14 > **Timelapse Video alias**.

This is linked to the project you worked on in Lessons 7 and 12.

**2**   Place the playhead at the edit between the wide shot and the close-up.

(If you have trouble finding it, the running time at the playhead is 37 seconds and 8 frames.) It's the only change in camera position in the entire video, so it's a plausible choice for this demonstration of chapters.

**3**   Click the iDVD button from the array of buttons beneath the Clip pane.

This changes the pane into the iDVD Chapter Markers workspace.

**4** Click the Add Chapter button when the playhead is positioned at the location in the video where you want to add a chapter.

This does two things: It places a little yellow mark in the timeline to denote the chapter mark, and it adds details about the chapter mark to a list that will grow in the iDVD Chapter Markers pane.

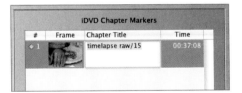

**5** Click the chapter title, and change the name from the default "timelapse raw/15" to the information you'd want to describe this chapter on your DVD.

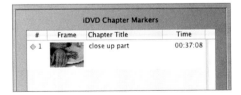

This information is saved as part of iMovie's data about your video. When iDVD examines an iMovie project in preparation for bringing it into your disc, it sees this chapter information and places these markers into the DVD menus it makes.

**6** Save and close your project.

All your file preparation is complete. You're done with iMovie for now and ready to work with iDVD.

## Building a DVD of Your Movies

In this lesson, you'll follow Jennifer as she builds a DVD for her studio, including much of the material you and she have been building throughout this book. Having just added chapters to your movie in the previous exercise, you could start from inside iMovie and access iDVD (which is what the Create iDVD Project button let's you do in iMovie's iDVD window). You can also launch iDVD directly and pull in content, which is what you'll do in the next exercise. Either way, iDVD lets you drop one or more movies onto a DVD, as well as more than one kind of project (such as a slide show).

iDVD gives you direct access to iTunes, iPhoto, and iMovie through its connection to the Music, Photos, and Movies folders in your Mac's Home folder. By default, music and photos reside in these folders when you use them in iLife, but movie projects often get saved all over a computer. Your iMovie projects should reside in the Movies folder. iDVD is designed to look into an iMovie project file and extract what it needs in order to make the DVD, both the edited video and the chapter information you create. This is a remarkable feature and makes your job of DVD creation much simpler.

If you create QuickTime movies of your completed iMovie projects (using the Share exporting option), save these to the Movies folder as well, particularly if you want to access them from iDVD. The movies you'll be using in this lesson came on the book's DVD and need to be positioned in your Home folder before we can work with them in iDVD.

**1**  Move the following finished project files from their position in the Lessons folder into the Movies folder in your Home folder:

▶  Lesson6 > **Sgraffito Technique.mov**

▶  Lesson12 > **Finished_Timelapse_music.mov**

**NOTE** ▶ If you want to access QuickTime movies from locations on your Mac besides the Movies folder, you can expand your options through the iDVD Preferences (under the Movies tab), although this won't work for entire iMovie projects. It's generally best to keep everything in the Movies folder.

When you load a DVD into a DVD player, usually the video doesn't begin playing right away. Instead, what you most often see is a menu that introduces you to the content on the disc. It might say what the disc is about, display what different videos it contains, and maybe give you options for accessing specific chapters within a video. The menu provides information and access, but it can also have personality.

Half the fun of iDVD is customizing these menus. While there are some practical considerations about what theme your DVD has, in general the choice is entirely personal, and any will do.

**2** Open iDVD.

There are a few ways to do this. One is through the Share option in iMovie, which includes an iDVD button. We won't use this method right now, but sometimes it's a great way to initiate the process, particularly when you want to burn a DVD of the movie you just completed in iMovie, but nothing else.

In many cases, your DVDs are compilations of different videos and photos. Consequently, let's not start from a particular iMovie project but rather from iDVD itself, pulling in content you want to have on the disc. To do this, you'll need to open iDVD from the Dock (or from the Applications folder).

This opens the iDVD 5 launch window.

**3**   Select Create a New Project.

**4**   Name the project (the name will end up being the name of the DVD you're going to make), and make sure it will be saved where you want it.

Jennifer is calling her disc PetroDVD.

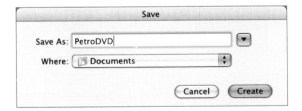

Your Mac defaults to placing projects in the Documents folder, which is fine, but you might change this to the Desktop (by using the pull-down menu) if that's the way you like to work. Jennifer is going to keep hers in the Documents folder.

**5**   Click Create.

This launches iDVD. When it's open, you'll see one of the DVD templates onscreen in the iDVD workspace. The odds are good this theme isn't the one you're looking for. You have many to choose from.

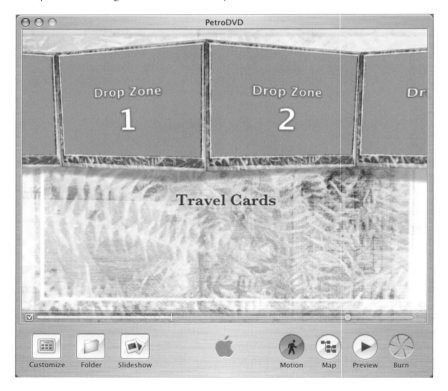

At the bottom of the window is a series of buttons that will help you build and customize your DVD.

**6**   Click Customize.

The Customize button opens (and closes) a sidebar that presents your DVD themes. The sidebar, which actually lets you access a few different workspaces via four buttons at the top, will appear on the left of the main window.

You'll notice that when you click a theme, you get to explore its details in the big window to the right.

**7**   Scroll through the options available, looking for one that feels appropriate for Jennifer's ceramics studio.

There are many themes to choose from, and more get added with each update of the software. Once you've reviewed the 5.0 Themes—the new ones released in 2005 with iLife '05—click the Themes pull-down to view themes from prior iDVD editions. In the 4.0 Themes, there is one Jennifer likes for Petroglyph: Pop Art.

**TIP** A template for a travel theme or a wedding theme doesn't necessarily have to be used for a travel or wedding project. Any theme might provide a good look for a disc about your child's first years, for instance. Don't be fooled by theme names. When you look at a theme template, you'll see it's just some stock elements and colors. Wedding Bronze One, for instance, shows a curtain rippling and provides space for you to add a photo—there's nothing inherently "wedding" about it. If you don't like following the crowd, one nice way to customize your disc is to augment prebuilt themes and use them in original ways, all of which you'll learn in this lesson.

8    Select the Pop Art theme.

Although each theme is slightly different, all work in the same way, so even if you experiment with only one theme, you can learn the basics of building discs and designing menus.

Like most theme templates, this one has a title on top—which you can change simply by clicking it and typing a different title. (The typeface and size are set, though you'll shortly learn how to modify them.) There's also a space labeled as a "Drop Zone." Drop zones are placeholders that may contain photos or movies.

Not every template provides a space that accommodates both photos and movies—some hold only one or the other.

The Drop Zone concept begs the question: Drop photos from where? From iPhoto, from the Desktop, from somewhere else? Of course, the answer is from everywhere.

Here is a photo being dragged from the iPhoto Library open in another window.

To make it easier to find photos, or movies if you're looking for them, iDVD provides inside access—much like what iPhoto and iMovie offer.

**9**   Locate the set of four buttons at the top of the Customize pane on the left side of the main window. You've been working in Themes. Click Media.

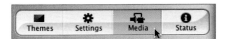

Under the row of buttons is a pull-down menu that connects you to the appropriate iLife application (or more specifically, to the corresponding folder in your Home folder: Music, Pictures, or Movies).

**10**   Choose Audio.

You will see your Library and playlists from iTunes.

**11** Choose Photos.

Here is another workspace that lets you add photos by dragging them into the main window when appropriate.

**12** Drag the photo of the petroglyph (DSCN0261) to the center of the template so that your menu looks like Jennifer's.

This photo is from Jennifer's L4.Biz roll 1, which you loaded in Lesson 4.

**13** Choose Movies.

The two QuickTime movies (with the .mov extension) are available here—earlier in this lesson, you dragged them into the Movies folder from the

DVD's Lessons folder. (Depending on what you've been doing on your Mac, there could be other movies here as well.)

These two short videos are key elements of the DVD Jennifer wants to create.

**NOTE ▶** The image quality of these videos is not comparable to finished projects in iMovie. iMovie is always working at the full quality of the video from your camcorder—probably DV video quality—and it's very good. The newest release of iMovie also can work in high definition (HD) quality. This is comparable to professional material, and while it is less likely you'll be using HD, iMovie will always keep your material at the highest possible resolution.

**NOTE ▶** These particular QuickTime videos were necessarily compressed to be small enough to fit on the enclosed DVD with all the rest of the content for this book, and consequently lost a fair amount of resolution. Keep in mind that your own projects and DVDs will have better-looking video than these examples.

**14** Click **Finished_Timelapse_music.mov** and drag it to the template. Drop it on the template anywhere but on that graphic in the middle of the screen—if you put it there, it will replace the photo already placed with the movie you're dragging.

These theme templates often contain some kind of graphical element that can present moving video—but don't mistake these for the places you drop your videos.

When you drop the movie onto the template in any of the white space around the graphic in the middle, a link will be created to the movie from here.

**15** Drag **Sgraffito Technique.mov** to the DVD template as well.

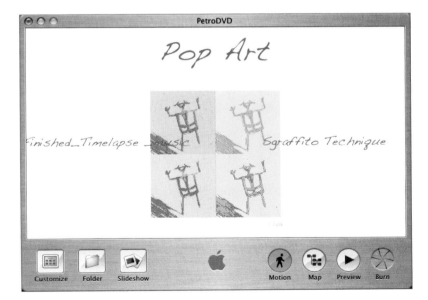

This particular template forces titles to alternating sides of the graphic in the middle. You'll find that different templates have their own idiosyncrasies as far as how they handle title placement, line breaks, and other minor issues.

Now that both movies are set up for the DVD, it's time for a little cosmetic work. Let's fix the titles.

**16**   Click **Finished_Timelapse_music.mov** and change the name to something more descriptive and user friendly, such as Italian Brushstroke. Change the second title as well.

Since both of these movies are essentially examples of techniques, Jennifer decides to save visual space by removing the word "Technique."

One of the minor irritations of this template is that the titles overlap the graphic image a little. This makes the word "Brushstroke" hard to read. Jennifer could force a line break between the words in that title, but she opts to finish the DVD structure first and then review legibility issues.

**NOTE ▶** You will learn how to customize these titles later in this lesson.

**17**   Finally, before moving on, change the DVD title from its default Pop Art to something appropriate.

The video will be shown in the studio, so its title should be something like the name of the business or perhaps something more specific like Spring 2005 Videos. Petroglyph is a simple title, so let's use that.

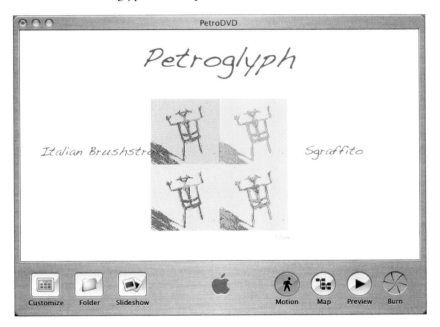

If the DVD were to contain only this pair of movies, you'd be done at this point. But Jennifer can do much more to make this disc useful and interesting.

## Adding Photos and Slide Shows from iPhoto

While you're in iDVD, you can access your photos and entire albums in iPhoto. But before you go digging through them, you need to make a place in iDVD where your photos will go.

**1** Click the Slideshow button at the bottom of the window.

This adds to your menu a link to a special type of slide show—which is different from what you'd get if you simply copied photos to the DVD like they were data files. (It's also different from using iPhoto to convert a slide show into a QuickTime movie of a slide show—something you didn't do in this book, but may have discovered at some point.) The slide show you place on this DVD will produce just as interactive an experience as you get with the Slideshow tool in iPhoto.

iDVD will add a link with the title My Slideshow (which, of course, you change when you're ready). Jennifer changes hers to Around Petroglyph.

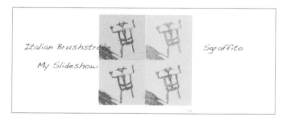

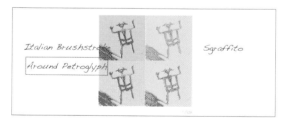

**2** Double-click the title of the new slide show.

This changes the main iDVD window into a slide show workspace. Displayed at the top is the title, along with how long (in minutes and seconds) the slide show will run, given the number of slides and each slide's duration. Time to add some slides.

**3**   Click the Media button in the Customize pane, and choose Photos. From the menu of folders and albums you've created while working on the projects in this book, select Biz Owner > Company Press.

You may recall this album from Lesson 5. Jennifer was going to make two different books—the first was an idea book, the second a linen-bound hardcover book. But because most customers won't see the book, a slide show of this material seems like suitable content for the DVD—she can show that in the studio.

You could drag one shot at a time to the large workspace on the right, but it's easier to grab an entire album and drag it there.

As soon as you drop the album, thumbnails begin to be created in the workspace.

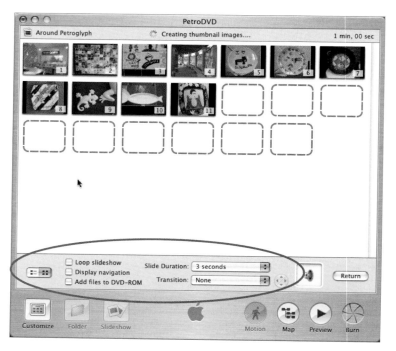

The controls at the bottom of the window let you specify whether you want this show to loop, how long each slide appears onscreen, and what kind of transition you want between slides.

**TIP ▶** You'll also find an Add files to DVD-ROM check box. This option lets you include a folder of the slide show images at their best quality possible. Christopher chooses this option when he wants to distribute photos to the grandparents. They can watch the slide show first and, if they want, make prints from iPhoto, using the original files on the DVD. Jennifer has no need for this feature for her DVD, but it's a great option.

Because this slide show is running unassisted and in a public space, Jennifer decides to let the show loop indefinitely and to present each slide for 5 seconds, a little longer than she might ordinarily. She also likes to use dissolves as a transition between shots.

From this set of tools, you can also add audio to your slide show.

4   From the Audio tab in the Media window, access your iTunes Library.

5   Click and drag a song or playlist to the Audio button (also called the audio well) beneath the workspace.

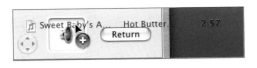

When you drop the music, the audio well changes to reflect the file types it "holds" (like MPEG4 or AAC) and to indicate that music will be played with this slide show.

If you decide you don't like the audio you've placed in the audio well, click and drag it from the well to the Desktop and watch it "vaporize."

### Changing and Modifying Themes

You've now established some content for this disc (two movies and one slide show) and chosen a background image for the template. But before you leave this part of iDVD, it's a good idea to investigate the other themes and how to customize them. Because every theme manages its template components a little differently, sometimes it's interesting to see the benefits (or problems) of each.

You've been working in the Pop Art theme. Without changing any other features of your DVD, select some different themes.

1   Click the Return button at the bottom of the slide show workspace.

This returns you to the previous workspace. It's not required, but it can help keep you oriented as you navigate iDVD.

2   Click the Customize button at the bottom of the screen.

This should put you in familiar territory.

3   Go back to the 5.0 Themes. Change the theme to Anime Pop, and take a look at how the template changes, but how the menu items remain.

There are more drop zones in this theme, so it could accommodate other photos or movies in the menu.

**4**   Change the theme to Portfolio.

This template also has drop zones for many photographs or movies. But in each case, you can still see the links that connect to the time-lapse and sgraffito movies, as well as the Around Petroglyph slide show. These links transfer regardless of theme.

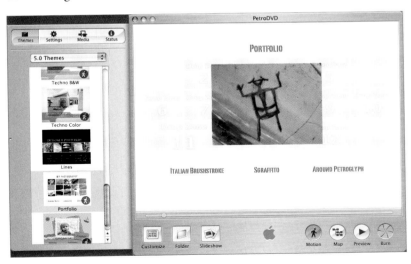

Notice that many of these themes have moving video in them already, some incorporate music, and others include ambient sounds. Templates that feature such built-in activity are designated by a Motion icon on the theme.

If the sound (or action or noise) bugs you, you can turn it off by clicking the Motion button at the bottom of the workspace.

Now the screen is probably calm enough to allow you to explore and experiment.

**NOTE ▶** With each revision of iDVD, the themes have become more dynamic and complex, with more drop zones and more kinds of moving elements. These take advantage not only of the greater CPU power of modern Macs, but also of the increasing sophistication of you, the customer. But Macs with less RAM or slightly slower CPUs can be taxed with the newest templates, and it is always possible to use 4.0 Themes or other Old Themes that might be more comfortable on your particular hardware configuration.

**5**    Switch to 4.0 Themes and change the theme to Montage.

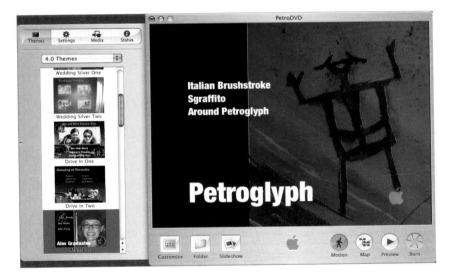

Up until this point in iDVD, you've worked with the Customize tools, alternating between Themes and Media. Now let's work with a set of more specific tools.

**6**    Click Settings.

This opens a set of tools for customizing the template you're looking at.

To customize the template, you can modify many of the preset attributes. When you're done, it will likely have little resemblance to the original Montage it began as. First of all, get rid of the music.

**7**    Click and drag the file in the audio well to your Desktop.

It will disappear from its position in this template, and the well will be empty.

You could add your own tune here, but leave it blank for now.

**8**    Change the button style.

Right now, the style of button comes from the template; it's just the text with the title of the button. That's why the Style field says From Theme.

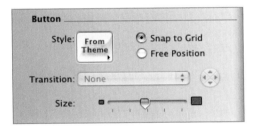

The disclosure triangle on the button indicates there's a pull-down menu of options for the button style. Click and hold it, and check out your options. Select the oblong square.

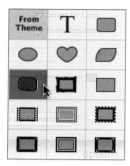

The buttons include windows with glimpses into each video or slide show. Unfortunately, these buttons are stacked too closely to see fully. It's because they are locked to a grid in the template.

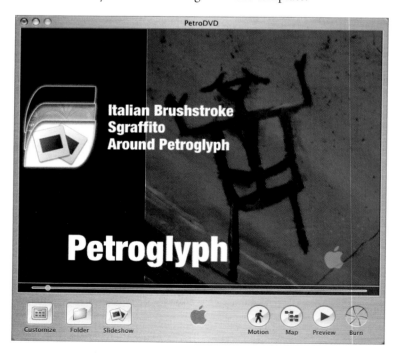

**9**   Click Free Position.

This lets you drag the buttons around onscreen to the location you choose.

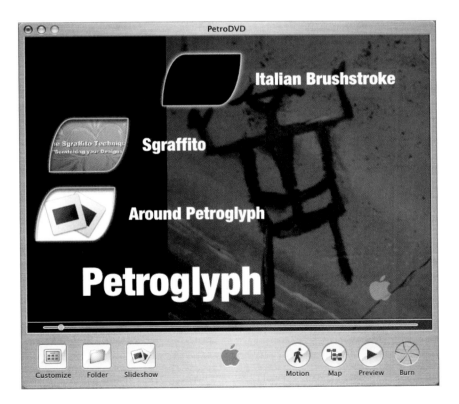

Most videos start with a fade-up from black, so in many cases these buttons will look black. Let's adjust those now.

**10** Click the Around Petroglyph button.

A slider appears over the clip allowing you to choose the image that is presented in the button.

**11** Move the slider around and find a different image.

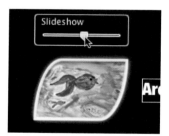

For buttons linked to video, you can choose whether you want the button to play the video or just show a single nonmoving frame.

**12** To play the video, select the check box above the Movie slider.

**TIP** ▶ Moving the video is a pretty neat feature, but if you have lots of little movies going on at the same time on your menu, it's actually distracting and somewhat irritating. An impressive demo, but consider using moving video in buttons sparingly.

Now that you've got the buttons looking the way you want, you can position them exactly as you'd like.

**13** Reposition the buttons creatively.

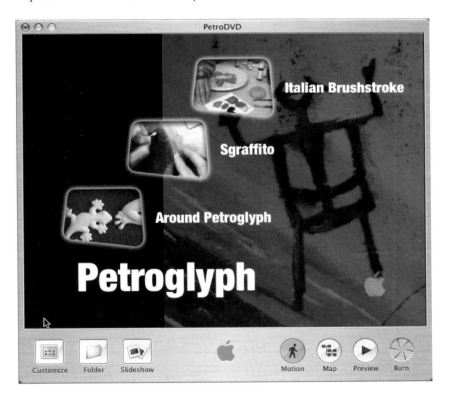

**NOTE** ▶ Other text attributes you can change include the size, the color, and, obviously, the font.

When you work with text onscreen, it becomes increasingly important to recognize the "safe" area of the screen. A computer monitor displays the entire frame of video from a videotape or DVD. But when you put that same material on a regular TV set, the edges are chopped off. Exactly how much depends on the set, but a video frame has a well-defined safe zone. Before you burn a DVD, you should always check to see that your most important material is within the safe area, particularly text.

**14** Choose Advanced > Show TV Safe Area to turn on that option.

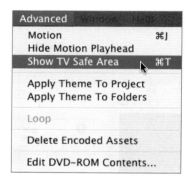

Some of the screen will be grayed out a bit; a red border separates the safe region from the risky.

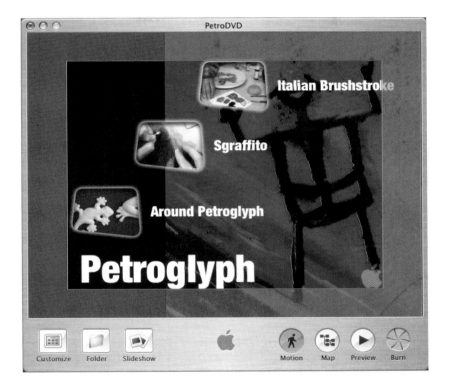

Adjust your DVD menu so that all the text is inside the safe area.

**15** Click Themes. Find the Pop Art template again and click it.

The screen will return to its familiar facade.

These are some of the many ways you can customize menu templates. Any template can be saved (using the Save as Favorite button at the bottom of the column) or discarded at will.

What you've seen is that regardless of what theme you select, the button names and videos remain unaltered. The themes are just cosmetic overlays of the same content and structure. The structure of the DVD—that is, the way it is organized hierarchically and the way its audience navigates its menus to find the videos and slide shows—remains the same across all of these themes.

To view the DVD's structure, which you may want to see if you're confused about how the user access and experience are built, for instance, click the Map button.

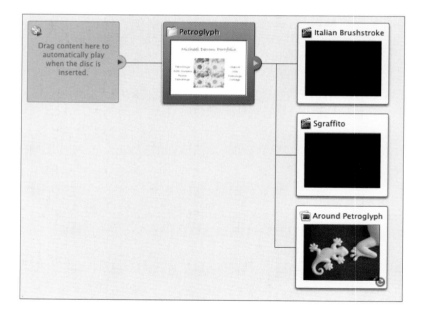

Now it should be clearer how your DVD is structured. The Map view is a good way to navigate your DVD while you're building it. It also gives you access to a unique option: You can set up an opening video (or slide show) that will play as soon as the DVD is inserted into a player—before the opening menu appears. The first square—called an *autoplay well*—is built into the structure of the disc, and is presented to the left and connected to the main menu—in this case, the Petroglyph Pop Art menu. The autoplay well is labeled PetroDVD. You can drag video or slide shows onto it to use as the opening sequence, which cycles endlessly until someone selects Play to see what's on the disc.

Jennifer will leave the autoplay feature alone for now, but it's an interesting option that she may use as she increases her library of videos from her studio.

### Adding Submenus to Menus

While Jennifer's DVD is probably too simple to warrant complex organization, you have the option of adding more levels of menus to your DVD. For instance, if you have more videos or slide shows than will fit on the first menu page (for many themes, the limit is six items), you'll need to create another menu—a *submenu*. To create a submenu, you must first create a new page.

**1**    Under Themes, return to the Montage theme.

Notice that some customizations you made earlier to the theme are lost as you circulate among different themes. Other attributes remain fixed.

**2**    Create a new page by clicking the Folder button at the bottom of the screen.

This adds a link to a submenu attached to your top menu.

The default name for the link is My Folder, but you can change this to whatever describes the new area.

**TIP**    If you show the buttons as images, the folder button onscreen will show a folder icon. You won't see a video or slide images when you click the folder and slide the slider. Still, the button is a well, and you can drag and drop an image from the photos in the Media Browser to this well to give it an image.

**3**    Double-click the folder.

This reveals a new place (a new menu) to add your videos and slides. There will always be an arrow on this page, pointing left, which allows you to return to the previous menu. (On some templates, it's harder to see than others.)

**4**    If you want to, experiment by adding videos and slides, following the same steps you did earlier in this lesson for customizing your first menu.

A submenu can have any theme, and doesn't need to match the theme of the top one. As you expand your DVD's structure, the Map view of the disc's contents becomes increasingly important. In the Map view, you can see which menus are submenus, what is linked to what, and any menu's theme.

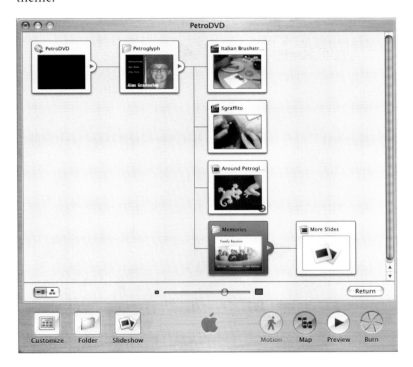

## Previewing Your DVD

All this work preparing the DVD is pretty easy, but it's important to be able to test out the user's experience. Since the disc doesn't really exist yet (the work you've done to create menus for videos and slide shows are not yet burned to disc), you can't try it out in a DVD player. The alternative is to preview the disc's content.

The Preview button at the bottom of the screen lets you do exactly that.

**1** Click the Preview button.

The tools go away, and now you can experience the disc exactly the way you will when it's burned.

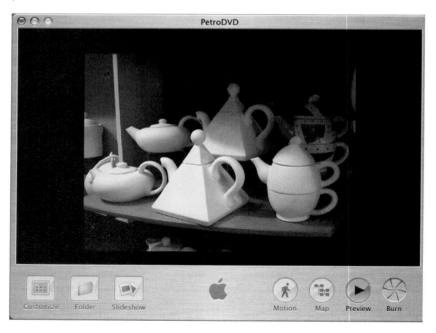

An onscreen DVD remote control pops up, which you can use to play, stop, and test the chapters and other attributes of your disc's navigation. Of course, you can also just watch the disc's videos.

2   To end the preview, click the Preview button again.

iDVD returns you to the Customize pane.

3   Continue this back and forth of building and previewing until the disc feels ready.

When you're happy with the look of the preview, it's time to burn your DVD.

## Burning a DVD

Burning a DVD is easy for you to arrange, but it's a lot of work for a computer. The compression required and the encoding into the DVD format is what scientists call *computationally complex,* meaning it requires a lot of math. Your Mac's processor (G4 is good, G5 is better) and clock speed (the megahertz or gigahertz number that is bantered about) are the important elements. The faster the clock speed and larger the processor, the more quickly your DVD will burn.

Just like burning a CD in iTunes, all you really need to do is click the Burn button. It will open up to reveal the "real" Burn button, with a warning symbol.

Click the Burn button, and iDVD will coach you through the rest of the process. Insert a blank DVD in your SuperDrive, and that's it.

How long iDVD takes to burn a disc is highly variable. A rule of thumb is twice the length of time required to play the disc—maybe an hour or two.

Some advanced settings can augment the speed and quality of the disc you burn, but the defaults are generally appropriate.

> **TIP** ▶ If you're going to make multiple copies of the disc, now is the time to do it (when iDVD prompts you). It'll take much less time to do it now than later.

When the recording is done, iDVD will eject the disc for you.

## What You've Learned

- ▶ Keep all your media in the appropriate folders (Movies, Music, and Photos) in your Home folder. This makes accessing content from the Media Browser in iDVD easy.

- ▶ Use the Customize button to reveal a selection of menu templates.

- ▶ Drag and drop menu elements as each template indicates. Drag and drop content from the Media Browser onto the blank portions of the template; that prepares the content to be added to the disc.

- ▶ Personalize templates using the Settings button—in particular, change DVD button styles and position, background music, and fonts.

- ▶ Use the Show TV Safe Area feature to make sure the DVD will look good on a TV set, and to make sure you don't cut off words on menus.

- ▶ Use Map view to review the structure of your disc, and, if you want, to add an opening movie to the autoplay well.

- ▶ Preview your DVD before burning to make sure the user's experience matches your expectations.

- ▶ Burn your DVD when you're ready; iDVD will coach you through recording the disc.

# Index